Churches of Minnesota

Churches of Minnesota

AN ILLUSTRATED GUIDE

Alan K. Lathrop

PHOTOGRAPHY BY BOB FIRTH

University of Minnesota Press

Minneapolis — London

The two photographs of the interior of the Cathedral of Saint Paul are printed here with permission of the Cathedral of Saint Paul, Saint Paul, Minnesota.

Frontispiece: St. Bernard's Catholic Church, St. Paul.

Copyright 2003 by the Regents of the University of Minnesota

Published by the University of Minnesota Press
111 Third Avenue South, Suite 290
Minneapolis, MN 55401-2520
http://www.upress.umn.edu

Library of Congress Cataloging-in-Publication Data

Lathrop, Alan K., 1940–
   Churches of Minnesota : an illustrated guide / Alan K. Lathrop ; photography by Bob Firth.
      p.   cm.
   ISBN 0-8166-2909-9 (pbk. : alk. paper)
   1. Church architecture—Minnesota—Guidebooks.   2. Church buildings—Minnesota—Guidebooks.
  3. Architects—Minnesota—Biography.   I. Title.
   NA5230.M5 L37 2003
   726.5'09776—dc21

                                                                              2003005693

Printed in the United States of America on acid-free paper

The University of Minnesota is an equal-opportunity educator and employer.

12 11 10 09 08 07 06 05 04 03   10 9 8 7 6 5 4 3 2 1

For the kids and grandkids,
for their love and for making life a joy,
and especially for Peggy,
for her love, faith, and support
through many hours of work
and waiting until it was all done.

CONTENTS

Acknowledgments   XIII

Glossary   XV

Introduction   XXI

CHURCHES OF MINNESOTA

Albert Lea
   Zion Lutheran Church   3

Annandale
   St. Mark's Episcopal Chapel   5

Arden Hills
   St. Katherine Ukrainian Orthodox Church and Cultural Center   7

Austin
   Church of St. Augustine   9

Blue Earth
   Church of the Good Shepherd Episcopal   11

Bramble
   Saints Peter and Paul Orthodox Church   13

Browerville
   Christ the King Catholic Church   15

Burnsville
   Prince of Peace Lutheran Church   17

Cannon Falls
   Church of the Redeemer   19

Center City
   Chisago Lake Evangelical Lutheran Church   21

Cold Spring
   Assumption Chapel   23

Collegeville
   St. John's Abbey Church, St. John's University   25

Danvers
    Church of the Visitation   29

De Graff
    Church of St. Bridget   31

Duluth
    First Presbyterian Church   33
    First Unitarian Church   34
    First United Methodist Church   37
    St. Paul's Episcopal Church   39

Eden Prairie
    Wooddale Church   41

Eitzen
    Portland Prairie Methodist Episcopal Church   45

Fairfax
    Fort Ridgely and Dale Evangelical Lutheran Church   47

Faribault
    Cathedral of Our Merciful Savior Episcopal   49
    Chapel of the Good Shepherd, Shattuck–St. Mary's School   51
    Fourth Avenue United Methodist Church   53

Freeport
    Church of the Sacred Heart   55

Frontenac
    Christ Episcopal Church   58

Garden City
    First Baptist Church   61

Hanska
    Nora Unitarian Church   62

Harmony
    Greenfield Lutheran Church   65

Hastings
    First Presbyterian Church   67

Hay Creek
    Immanuel Lutheran Church   69

Hazelwood
    Church of the Annunciation   71

Heron Lake
    Church of the Sacred Heart   73

Hibbing
    Our Savior's Lutheran Church Pilgrim's Chapel   77

Lake St. Croix Beach
    St. Francis of Assisi Catholic Church   79

Lenora
    Lenora United Methodist Pioneer Center   81

Little Falls
    Episcopal Church of Our Savior   83
    Our Lady of Lourdes Church   85

Mankato
    First Presbyterian Church   87

Melrose
    Church of St. Mary   89

Millville
    Swedish Evangelical Lutheran Church   90

Minneapolis
    Basilica of St. Mary   93
    Christ Church Lutheran   97
    Church of Saints Cyril and Methodius   101
    Hennepin Avenue United Methodist Church   102
    Lakewood Cemetery Chapel   105
    Plymouth Congregational Church   106
    Redeemer Missionary Baptist Church   108
    St. Constantine's Ukrainian Catholic Church   111
    St. Mary's Orthodox Cathedral   113
    Wesley United Methodist Church   114

Minneota
    St. Paul's Lutheran Church   117

Minnetonka Beach
    St. Martin's By-the-Lake   119

Monticello
    Community United Methodist Church   122

Morton
    Zion Evangelical Lutheran Church   125

Nerstrand
    Valley Grove   126

New Prague
    Church of St. Wenceslaus   129

New Trier
    Church of St. Mary   133

Northfield
    All Saints Episcopal Church   135
    Skinner Memorial Chapel, Carleton College   138

Owatonna
    First Baptist Church   141
    St. Paul's Episcopal Church   143

Pierz
    St. Joseph's Church   145

Pipestone
    Good Shepherd Lutheran Church   147

Rochester
    Calvary Episcopal Church   148

Rollingstone
    Holy Trinity Catholic Church   151

St. Charles
    Trinity Episcopal Church   153

St. Joseph
    Church of St. Joseph   155
    Sacred Heart Chapel, College of St. Benedict   157

St. Louis Park
    Beth El Synagogue   159
    Lutheran Church of the Reformation   161

St. Michael
    St. Michael's Catholic Church   163

St. Paul
      Cathedral of St. Paul   165
      Church of the Assumption   168
      Church of St. Columba   171
      First Baptist Church   172
      The Living Word Church   175
      Mount Zion Temple   176
      St. Agnes Church   179
      St. Bernard's Catholic Church   181
      St. Clement's Memorial Episcopal Church   183
      St. Louis Church   185
      Weyerhaeuser Memorial Chapel, Macalester College   186

St. Paul Park
      St. Thomas Aquinas Church   189

St. Peter
      Church of the Holy Communion   190
      Union Presbyterian Church   193

Simpson
      St. Bridget's Catholic Church   195

Sleepy Eye
      Church of St. Mary, Help of Christians   196

Stillwater
      St. Michael's Church   199

Taylors Falls
      First United Methodist Church   201

Thief River Falls
      United Methodist Church   203

Tyler
      Danebod Lutheran Church   205

Vasa
      Vasa Evangelical Lutheran Church   206

Veseli
      Church of the Holy Trinity   208

Vista
      Vista Lutheran Church   211

Wabasha
    Grace Memorial Episcopal Church   212

Warroad
    St. Mary's Church   215

Waverly
    Marysville Swedesburg Lutheran Church   217
    St. Mary's Catholic Church   218

Welch
    Cross of Christ Lutheran Church   221

Willmar
    Vinje Lutheran Church   222

Winona
    Central United Methodist Church   224
    First Baptist Church   227
    First Congregational Church   229
    St. Paul's Episcopal Church   231
    St. Stanislaus Polish Catholic Church   233

Wykoff
    St. Kilian's Catholic Church   237

Zumbrota
    First Congregational Church   238

Other Sites of Interest   240

Architect Biographies   278

Acknowledgments

A S ANYONE WHO HAS EXPERIENCED the arduous process of producing a book knows too well, there are always far too many people to thank individually, especially in a work such as this. So, first, profuse apologies to all those not mentioned by name; rest assured that your very kind assistance has been duly noted, and I hope you will find in this book something that you contributed and take pride in it. Thank you very much for your time, patience, skill, and diligence.

My deepest gratitude goes to the church secretaries, pastors, priests, and members of congregations who provided information that helped fill in the blanks in the histories of the churches included here. Without their willingness to dig through closets and filing cabinets of records in search of the answers I felt I could not do without, it is safe to say this work would not have been completed. Special thanks also to architects who provided biographical facts and who assisted in myriad other ways. And, of course, the resources of many historical societies and museums, large and small, in Minnesota and elsewhere, and their highly dedicated and competent employees and volunteers are duly recognized and deeply appreciated. These unsung heroes are owed an enormous debt of gratitude by any researcher, and no acknowledgment is ever sufficient.

Now to those who shall be named. First, it would have been impossible to have produced this book without the able assistance of the staff of the Minnesota Historical Society's State Historic Preservation Office, who permitted me unrestricted access to the voluminous survey and National Register files that are absolutely packed with valuable information. Susan Roth deserves special thanks for her generous help and time. Patricia Maus, curator of the Northeast Minnesota History Center at the University of Minnesota–Duluth, was extremely helpful in locating facts about buildings and architects in Duluth and the surrounding region. My longtime assistant, Barbara Bezat, contributed a great deal of time and patience in seeking information about buildings and architects from the collections of the Northwest Architectural Archives. And I will always be grateful for the guiding hand of my editor, Todd Orjala, through much of the process.

Above all, I wish to acknowledge the love, support, and assistance of my wife, Peggy. From the beginning, her invaluable organizational skills and advice got the project off to a good start and kept it rolling smoothly thereafter. If this book is successful, it is due in great measure to her confidence and devotion.

Glossary

BEFORE LOOKING AT RELIGIOUS ARCHITECTURE, one should become familiar with its specialized terminology and with the styles prevalent in Minnesota. This glossary identifies the most commonly used terms and characteristics; readers are also encouraged to consult dictionaries of architectural terms, widely available in bookstores and libraries.

ALTAR   worship table

ALTAR SCREEN   screen between chancel and nave; also called *rood screen* or *iconostasis*

AMBULATORY   passageway around the apse, or a covered walk of a cloister

AMBULATORY CHURCH   a structure with a domed center bay surrounded on three sides by aisles

APSE   area around the altar and reredos

ASHLAR   building stone that is squared off for joints, with a dressed face, either smooth or rough

BALDACHIN   canopy over altar, usually made of wood or stone

BAPTISTERY   room for baptisms

BARGEBOARD   a decorative board that hangs from the projecting end of a roof

BASILICA   an architectural plan in which a long nave ends in an apse, flanked by colonnaded side aisles that are identified on the exterior by shed roofs projecting from the nave walls

BAY   the division of walls into compartments or sections by vertical elements, such as pilasters or columns; also, projecting windows

BEAUX ARTS   an artistic and architectural style popular in the United States from the 1880s to the 1940s, used especially for government, educational, and commercial buildings; named for the École des Beaux-Arts in Paris, whose design tenets followed strict rules and favored classical Greek and Roman forms

BELFRY   portion of the tower in which bells are hung

BELVEDERE   in churches, the uppermost portion of a tower, open on one or more sides

BOARD AND BATTEN   closely spaced boards applied vertically to the sides of a building; covering joints with narrow wood strips (battens)

CAMPANILE   bell tower, especially one detached from the main religious structure

CANOPY   decorative hood over pulpit or choir stalls

CARPENTER GOTHIC   a style in which Gothic motifs are applied in wood construction by artisan carpenters

CHAMFER   angled or oblique edge or end of a corner

CHANCEL   area reserved for clergy and choir between the altar and altar rail; also called *sanctuary*

CHOIR   area where choir is seated and organ may be located

CLAPBOARD   lap siding

CLERESTORY   uppermost row of windows in the nave

COLUMBARIUM   a room or hall constructed with a series of niches to receive human remains, especially ashes after cremation

COMMUNION RAIL   rail that divides the nave and chancel; also called *altar rail*

CORBELING   brickwork that projects steplike from the side of a building, growing progressively wider as it rises to support or create a cornice

CORNER TOWER   short tower at the corner of a main tower base or at the end of a roof ridge

CRAFTSMAN   a style prominent in the late nineteenth and early twentieth centuries featuring exposed structural members such as roof beams, low-pitched roofs and low profiles, and generally boxlike shapes, especially associated with the Prairie School style in the Midwest

CRENELLATION   pattern of repeated indentations in brickwork

CROSS AISLE   row between pews

CROSS GABLE   gable set parallel to the ridge of the roof

CRUCIFORM PLAN   plan in the shape of a cross

CUPOLA   a structure often set on the ridge of a roof; having a domical roof on a square or circular base

DENTIL   a toothlike block, commonly of brick or wood, in cornices

DOME   a roof formed of rounded vaults or arches on a round base

DRUM   the round base for a dome

EASTLAKE   a style derived from the works of Charles Eastlake, an English architect, that featured rich, somewhat delicate ornamentation and heavy bracketing and served as a forerunner of the Stick style

ENGAGED BUTTRESS   a support buttress attached to the building throughout its length

ENGAGED COLUMN   nonsupporting column built as part of the wall; also called a *pilaster*

ENGLISH GOTHIC/ENGLISH RURAL GOTHIC   a style based on Gothic motifs for smaller churches but lightened in nature, usually employing wood and stone but with much more rusticity than is seen in the more finished, larger buildings erected in the Gothic Revival style

GAMBREL ROOF   roof constructed of two slopes, with the slope of the lower portion steeper than the upper portion

GOTHIC REVIVAL   an architectural style that originated in medieval Europe and is characterized by pointed arches over windows and doorways and an emphasis on verticality

GREEK CROSS PLAN   a plan in the shape of a cross with the arms equal length

GREEK REVIVAL   an architectural style prevalent in the United States from 1815 to about 1860, characterized by its strong resemblance to buildings of Greek antiquity

HAMMER BEAM   a short horizontal beam attached to the foot of a principal roof rafter or truss in place of a tie beam

ICONOSTASIS   *see* altar screen

LANCET WINDOW   a narrow, sharply arched window usually open and lacking tracery

LANTERN   windowed superstructure crowning a roof or dome

LATIN CROSS PLAN   a plan in the shape of a cross, with the lower arm longer than the other three

LECTERN   desk or stand from which part of the Scriptures is read during services

LYCH GATE   covered gateway into a churchyard

MASSING   the exterior form and bulk of a structure

MODILLION   block of wood or stone carved into the form of an ornamental bracket, used under a projecting cornice

NARTHEX   entry area just inside main entrance of church; also called *vestibule* or *porch*

NAVE   central area of church where congregation is seated; also, central aisle of this area

PARSONAGE   residence for clergy

PEDIMENT   triangular portion of the facade formed by the roof gable ends and the cornice above an entrance

PILASTER   nonsupporting engaged column, often built as part of the wall

PULPIT   raised platform from which the clergy preaches

QUARRY-FACED   stone straight from being cut at the quarry with an unfinished face, only squared off for joints

QUEEN ANNE   a revival style popular in England and the United States in the late nineteenth century blending several elements, notably Colonial, Tudor Gothic, and English Renaissance; its forms were often irregular with such features as turrets, dormers, high chimneys, and a variety of surface coverings, including wood shingles, clapboard, and stone or brick

RECTORY   residence of clergy, especially in Episcopal churches

REREDOS   sculptured screen behind altar, usually made of wood; it may be part of the altar

RETICULATION   crisscross network pattern, often used in brickwork

ROMANESQUE REVIVAL   an architectural style based on Roman architecture; frequently called *Richardsonian Romanesque* in the United States after H. H. Richardson, a Boston architect who designed buildings of stone with a heavy, massive appearance, often with rounded arches over window and door openings

ROSE WINDOW   circular window with mullions radiating from a center axis, like spokes of a wheel; also called *wheel window*

RUSTICATED   cut stone with strongly emphasized recessed joints and dressed faces, either smooth or rough

SACRISTY   room adjacent to chancel where sacred vessels and vestments are kept and where clergy prepare for services

SCAGLIOLA   imitation marble or granite, made of a mixture of gypsum and glue, and colored and polished to resemble stone

SHINGLE   a blend of several styles in which the predominant exterior wall covering was unpainted wood shingles

SIDE AISLE   aisle alongside nave, sometimes under a roof projecting from walls of the nave

SPIRE   tower that tapers to a point; also called *steeple*

STATIONS OF THE CROSS   fourteen points for the devotion and contemplation of the Passion of Christ on the way to his crucifixion, usually located along side aisles in Roman Catholic churches. The stations are as follows: condemnation by Pontius Pilate; reception of the cross; the first fall; meeting with Mary; Simon of Cyrene; St. Veronica; the second fall; meeting with women of Jerusalem; the third fall; Christ stripped of his garments; nailed to the cross; dying on the cross; Mary receives the body of Christ (the pietà); the body of Christ laid in the tomb.

STEEPLE   top of a tower that tapers to a point; also called *spire*

STICK   an eclectic style in which the exterior treatment is so designed as to express exposed frame construction

TIE BEAM   horizontal beam that connects or ties roof trusses or rafters

TOWER   structure on or beside a church that usually contains the bells and may be capped by a steeple

TUDOR REVIVAL   nineteenth-century style that revived the architecture of the reigns of Henry VII and VIII, characterized by half-timbering (wood strips expressing exposed frame construction) punctuating stucco walls

VESTRY   dressing area for clergy and storage area for vessels and robes for the service; also called *sacristy*

Introduction

THERE QUITE POSSIBLY IS NO STRUCTURE in North America that is so readily recognizable to so many people as a church. When one approaches a town, the most prominent features on the landscape are usually church spires soaring above all else except modern high-rises, grain elevators, and transmission towers. Religious buildings exist in every town and in every rural area, and they play a significant role in many people's lives at one time or another. Even buildings wrapped in new styles that seem to have strayed from the traditional, Eurocentric types are readily recognizable as places of worship.

In a world that seems to care little for the past, religious structures are the one unchanging element, the part of the built environment that rejects change and destruction. It is likely that there are more eighteenth- and nineteenth-century church buildings in existence than any other type of structure, with the exception of residences. It is also true that more attention is given to the design of religious buildings, more loving detail lavished on them, than any other architectural creation. They are, understandably, a source of pride to those who create them and worship in them.

It is difficult to say exactly how many buildings in the United States are devoted to religious functions, but there are between 300,000 and 500,000 congregations, many of which have their own buildings. In Minnesota alone, there are more than 5,000 such structures, some 2,200 of which are in rural areas. The relatively flat terrain of Minnesota makes it possible to spot churches from miles away, especially on the prairies, where lofty spires rise far above their surroundings, intended as beacons for the people and to indicate, as did the medieval cathedrals of Europe, that they are reaching toward heaven.

The various ethnic groups (almost exclusively European in origin) who settled in Minnesota in the nineteenth century customarily built their churches in familiar, traditional styles that reflected those prevalent in their native countries or regions. Settlers who came from the eastern United States also brought styles common to them, and all merged and blended in the landscape, creating a rich panorama of architectural heritage. German Catholics, for example, tended to erect buildings that were Romanesque or baroque in appearance. English Protestants leaned toward Gothic or, in earlier decades of the nineteenth century, Greek Revival.

This tendency was strengthened as professional architects moved into the state. Their designs either conformed to the ethnic cultural traditions of the individual congregations or reflected their own backgrounds. Architects were often employed by congregations of their own religious persuasion and infrequently crossed religious lines; some concentrated almost solely on certain denominations of which they were members. For example, virtually all of the churches designed by Hermann Kretz of St. Paul (a German Catholic) were for German Catholic congregations, whereas Augustus Gauger of the same city (and a German Protestant) worked mainly among Protestant congregations, especially Lutherans.

The first church structures built in Minnesota were often as raw as the frontier itself. Few were intended to be more than temporary places of worship. Many were erected quickly of logs, serving only to enclose a space in which services could be held. Others were less crude, built of stone or wood frame covered with shingles or clapboard siding. The early frame buildings were customarily erected by their own congregations, relying on the carpentry skills of the members. They were usually built as soon as a congregation was organized, followed by construction of a parsonage for the first resident pastor.

Because of rapid population growth on the frontier, congregations expanded quickly, forcing the replacement of the first religious structures within a few years of their construction. Frequent fires helped the process along. The next generation of churches was constructed of more durable and prestigious materials such as stone or brick. They were larger and more decorative, reflecting the increased wealth of the congregations and engendering a greater sense of pride, and they embraced a wider variety of functions in addition to worship. In numerous instances, these second-generation buildings were built with tall spires, intended to call attention to themselves and to act as magnets for the community. There was a good deal of competition among congregations in some towns to see who could build the tallest steeple. Because they were loftier than anything else around them, they unfortunately attracted lightning during thunderstorms and were destroyed, along with the rest of the church, by the subsequent fires. This resulted in third-generation churches that were even larger and grander than their predecessors. Many of the oldest religious structures existing in Minnesota are second- or third-generation churches.

These later generations of churches were frequently architect-designed. This is because the congregations demanded larger, more complex buildings requiring architectural and engineering skills that were simply beyond the talents of the local labor force. Professional contractors were hired to erect these buildings, and together with the more elaborate furnishings and equipment that went into them, they almost always cost significantly more than the structures they replaced. Yet, owing to the pride and the dedication of the congregations, the huge expense of these churches could be easily raised and the construction costs paid off within a few years.

When architects entered the church-building field by the early 1870s, the style of the structures became much more sophisticated as well. The simple Gothic or Greek Revival buildings that constituted many of the first- and second-generation churches were replaced by edifices reflecting styles in vogue at the time of construction. Whereas Greek Revival had died out in Minnesota by the 1870s, Gothic Revival remained popular among both Catholic and Protestant congregations long afterward. In the mid-1880s it was joined by Romanesque Revival, thanks in large measure to Henry Hobson Richardson of Boston, one of America's most influential architects, who popularized the Romanesque. Other prevalent styles were Renaissance Revival, beaux arts, and highly manneristic forms of Queen Anne and Italianate. After 1900 styles such as the Prairie School, art nouveau, Craftsman, and even art deco and moderne were called upon by architects to satisfy both their and their clients' requirements. Some churches were elaborate blends of two or more styles, as if their designers were trying to cram as much into the building as possible.

The typical floor plan in the early frontier churches was a rectangular open space that accommodated an altar or platform at the front for the conduct of services and seating for the congregation in the main body of the church. Some of the more "finished" structures had a basement where there might be a classroom or hall for meetings and social functions and, in rare cases, a furnace. Most of the first churches were heated by a stove placed in the center of the sanctuary. The next generation of churches were built on rectangular, Latin cross, and Greek cross plans, or occasionally a basilica plan. The basilica plan consisted of a central sanctuary or nave flanked by side aisles. The exterior form reflected the plan by having a high-roofed center portion with a sloping shed roof projecting outward from about halfway up its lateral sides to cover and identify the side aisles. This form originated in the Middle East or Europe in late antiquity.

As time progressed, church plans became more complex. Today, architects have almost entirely discarded the traditional forms in favor of innovative approaches to accommodating modern liturgies and functions. These contemporary designs are highly individualized, and while they may still draw upon deep-rooted traditions, especially in some ethnic congregations, they are endowed with new twists on old styles. The interiors, in particular, have been adapted to new demands caused by revolutionary changes in liturgies as well as new functions. Not incidentally, materials including glass, architectural metals, and concrete or prefabricated masonry products have been used by architects and contractors in highly creative and inventive ways.

One might argue that the churches of seventy-five to one hundred years ago are much more attractive architecturally speaking than contemporary ones. While this may be true to some extent, one must be wary of overgeneralizing. Many modern religious structures seem somewhat plain or lackluster, even though there is a greater variety of forms than one would have seen at the turn of the century. The new buildings are not nearly so decorative or ornate, reflecting a general deemphasis on such detail among modern congregations, the exorbitant cost of unnecessary frills, and changes in liturgies. Many contemporary churches manage to be extremely attractive through the use of rich and complementary textures created in wood, stone, tile, glass, and concrete. Yet newer buildings often appear uncomfortable in their surroundings. Granted, one might wonder how the older churches could be said to fit their environments, but an astonishing number seem to do so, and maybe this is because they were intended to be recognizable. They were so extraordinarily different from anything around them that, almost by virtue of their distinctiveness, they became part of the environment. If they were deliberately planned to be monumental in scale, it was to impress and inspire awe in the communities, not solely to be "different." Put simply, older churches seem to be more "picturesque."

It is a pity, then, that so many of the older churches in our state have had their distinctiveness and picturesqueness harmed by unsympathetic additions or alterations. Some of the work is so poorly designed that one can only shed a melancholy tear for the loss of the oftentimes elegant original structure that was dealt such a cruel blow. Regrettably, the two most damaging factors seem to be education and the importance of providing access for the handicapped. A great many fine buildings were omitted from this book because they have either had narthexes tacked onto their front facades to accommodate handicapped entrances, or unattractive education/office wings attached to their sides that detract seriously from the original beauty and symmetry. Only infrequently does one find instances in which thought and care were given to planning and constructing additions and ramps for handicapped access. When done sensitively, they can be so unobtrusive as to be almost invisible, and there are several included here from this category. One wishes this happened more often.

The buildings chosen for this book represent the rich ecclesiastical heritage in Minnesota. The selection of religious structures has been difficult at best and admittedly a subjective process. This is not a "top 100" list of churches, and there are many that could have been included, but space limitations prevented it. Some of these are listed in the Other Sites of Interest section.

An attempt has been made to provide at least one example of every architectural style known to be present in the state and to be as inclusive as possible of all time periods. All of the structures are in active use, even if "active" means only for special occasions. No abandoned buildings or churches that have been converted to other uses are included, aside from a few listed in the Other Sites of Interest section that are on the National Register of Historic Places. Finally, an effort has also been made to include at least one example from every major faith tradition. Regrettably, some are not represented because architecturally significant examples do not yet exist in Minnesota.

The reader may notice that many of the sites selected for inclusion are on the National

Register of Historic Places. The National Register is maintained by the National Park Service of the U.S. Department of the Interior in Washington, D.C. It serves as a mechanism for recognizing the architectural and historical importance of buildings of all types throughout the nation. Most such structures are privately owned, and designation may cover interiors as well as exteriors. Listing on the National Register carries no legal authority; owners may modify their buildings to suit themselves, even tear them down, if they feel like it and do so at their expense. Public buildings and projects are excepted; in those cases, a hearing must be held before any work on the building can be carried out. Fortunately, most people who have buildings on the National Register are proud of the recognition and strive to maintain them in as authentic condition as possible.

This book is intended to be an introduction to existing religious buildings in Minnesota and to increase readers' appreciation of the state's religious architectural heritage. Most of the selections were based on external appearance rather than interior distinctiveness alone. Many people will probably see these structures only from the outside, and the author felt that this consideration should be the main criterion for inclusion.

The buildings represented here were chosen solely for their visual appeal, architectural significance, structural integrity, and historical importance. It is worth noting that people worship in a wide variety of structures, and it is the people who create a religious community, not the building in which they gather. New immigrant communities in Minnesota in the nineteenth century built simple churches that they eventually replaced as they became more prosperous and established. Many recent immigrants and members of small urban congregations worship in renovated storefronts and other modest buildings or in older churches that have been vacated.

It would have been easy to overload the text with churches from the Twin Cities, which could constitute a volume in itself. There are structures from every corner of the state, with more from urban than rural areas, but not by intent. One reason is that many rural churches are of the white frame Gothic variety and thus become repetitious to a certain extent. While it is not fair or accurate to say that if you've seen one you've seen them all, it is fair to say that many are similar in plan and exterior appearance. A representative selection of these has been made to show the variations on the theme.

It was impossible to weigh the selections fairly among the various denominations, Catholic and Protestant. For one thing, the state is incredibly well endowed with magnificent Catholic parish churches and cathedrals, which are some of the most beautiful to be found anywhere in the United States. On the other hand, thanks to the vast energies of Bishop Henry Whipple (1822–1901) in the last half of the nineteenth century, there is an abundance of elegantly simple Episcopalian churches throughout the state, especially in southern Minnesota. Bishop Whipple, like his counterpart Archbishop John Ireland (1838–1918) of the Archdiocese of St. Paul, played an active role in encouraging the establishment of congregations and the erection of churches.

Neither man flinched from handpicking architects for many of his buildings, with Ireland out-doing Whipple in this regard. If one is to survey even a few of the hundreds of truly outstand-ing Catholic and Episcopalian churches and chapels in Minnesota, it is not difficult to under-stand why there are more of these in the book in proportion to other denominations. Yet, the Lutherans, Methodists, Baptists, Congregationalists, and others are represented as well with su-perb examples of their architectural heritage. Minnesota is also home to several beautiful Jewish temples, two of which are included in the book.

Minnesota is indeed blessed with an abundance of fine religious buildings. This book high-lights a few of them and invites the reader not only to explore the state and visit the structures discussed here but also to seek out the many that are not. It is the author's fervent hope that every reader will develop an awareness of religious architecture and extend this appreciation to other structures as well. Far too many buildings, including churches, have been lost to neglect, and a broad public concern for older buildings is key to an effective historic preservation program. While it is inevitable that buildings will be lost to fires and natural disasters, it is to be hoped that much of the deliberate destruction can be controlled and prevented through public advocacy on behalf of Minnesota's valuable religious heritage.

This book is arranged alphabetically by town or city. Each entry contains a brief history of the parish or congregation. Every church has a story to tell, and these stories have been included in as much detail as space will permit. Accompanying the histories is a description of key architectural features.

Churches of Minnesota

Zion Lutheran Church

924 Bridge Avenue
LeRoy Gaarder, Albert Lea, architect
1958–61

Zion Lutheran may well be LeRoy Gaarder's most successful church. It combines Gothic and Tudor elements in a picturesque blend. Above the entrance rises an abbreviated open bell tower capped by a small copper spire. A stone carving of a ship in an oval frame is set into the base of the tower. The church is constructed of variegated Wisconsin limestone, Gaarder's favorite building material. Half-timbering is set against the stone rather than stucco, which is a resourceful variation on the customary Tudor style.

The congregation was formed in 1945, and the first permanent pastor, Herbert Bussman, arrived early in 1946, after having served as an army chaplain during World War II. Mr. Bussman's first priority was to erect a church, and together with a selection committee, the new congregation settled on ten lots along Bridge Avenue, which it purchased for $15,000. A ten-year development plan was drawn up that included hiring an architect to design the church, constructing a temporary structure, and establishing a fund to pay for a permanent building. In mid-1947, LeRoy Gaarder was commissioned to design the church, and his plans were accepted on July 2. Work on the basement began in August and was completed in February 1948. A temporary wooden building was erected on the basement, and it served for more than a decade. The present church was dedicated on April 9, 1961, but it would take many more years until the interior was completely furnished. Total cost of construction, including furnishings and architect's fees, was $240,000.

Gaarder also designed First Presbyterian Church in Albert Lea, a fine Gothic and Tudor Revival structure, in 1929.

St. Mark's Episcopal Chapel

11283 Kimball Avenue Northwest

North on Minnesota Highway 24; left on 108th Street Northwest; right on Kimball Avenue Northwest

Octavius Longworth, builder
1871–72
National Register of Historic Places

THIS PRETTY LITTLE CHAPEL is made even more idyllic because of its setting amid pine and deciduous woods in rural Wright County. The chapel is a splendid example of the "Bishop Whipple" churches built in Minnesota through the influence of this most energetic of all Episcopal leaders, Bishop Henry Whipple.

Construction of St. Mark's was the direct responsibility of Octavius Longworth and the Reverend David B. Knickerbacker. Both were former members of St. Mark's Church in Brooklyn, New York. Longworth came to Minnesota in 1859 and settled in Wright County. Mr. Knickerbacker became rector of Gethsemane Church in Minneapolis and occasionally visited Longworth's homestead to conduct services. The two men decided to build a church, and Longworth donated land for it. Upon completion in 1872, the chapel was dedicated by Bishop Whipple, who returned fifteen years later to consecrate it as St. Mark's. Throughout its long history, the church has never had a resident pastor.

The small Gothic Revival chapel is rectangular in shape with board-and-batten siding. It has a steeply pitched roof and pointed lancet windows. The interior is composed of a large open space with straight-backed narrow pews facing a raised altar at the west end. The walls are of native wood with wainscoting and planking trimmed with beveled board and batten. There are exposed trusses in the ceiling.

St. Katherine Ukrainian Orthodox Church and Cultural Center

1600 West Highway 96
Oleg Gregoret, St. Paul, architect
1995–97

T HE UKRAINIAN ORTHODOX CHURCH PARISH in St. Paul was founded in 1950 as Saints Volodymyr and Olga. The first permanent pastor arrived a year later. Services were held outdoors at first, in Como and Phalen parks, and for a time the congregation met at Christ Episcopal Church. In 1952 it built its first church at 700 Jenks Street, and when the community outgrew that space, it purchased the former First Methodist Church at Victoria and Portland in 1960. With a seating capacity of one thousand, the building provided the growing parish with a great deal more room.

In 1995 the parish broke ground for a unique (in Minnesota) new structure in Arden Hills. Named St. Katherine Ukrainian Orthodox Church (the parish remains Saints Volodymyr and Olga), the new building was designed in the Ukrainian baroque style, developed in the middle of the seventeenth century by Hetman Bohdan Khmelnytskyj and Hetman Ivan Mazepa. Churches in Kiev, capital of Ukraine, were direct inspirations for St. Katherine. The cupolas are copper-clad, and the walls are finished in white painted stucco with precast artstone trim. The height to the top of the cross on the central cupola is 90 feet, and the church covers 4,000 square feet.

The church accommodates about 250 people on the main floor and choir loft. Flanking the sanctuary are rooms for storage of church supplies and the priests' dressing area. The iconostasis was moved from the former church and installed in the new one. The Cultural Center houses a conference room/library, as well as Sunday school rooms and offices. The Parish Hall can accommodate 300 people in banquet seating and has an elevated stage for programs and performances.

Austin

Church of St. Augustine

405 Fourth Street Northwest
McDonald and Delameter, Minneapolis, contractors
Charles Hall, Minneapolis, brick and stone contractor
1894–96

THE FIRST SERVICES IN THE PARISH of St. Austin's were held on November 2, 1857, when the first priest, Father Michael Pendergast, arrived from Winona. Father Pendergast, as well as priests from Faribault, served Austin at intervals until 1867, when the first resident pastor, Father John McDermott, arrived. Meantime, work began in 1863 on a church; the foundation was built of local stone and the cornerstone was laid in August. The walls, of locally manufactured bricks, were erected in 1865, and services were held within them, even though the roof and floor were not installed. The parishioners sat on crude wooden benches with grass at their feet and the sky overhead. The church was finished in the fall of 1866, and dedicated on June 15, 1868. It was initially named St. Austin's.

The present structure was begun in the spring of 1894, the cornerstone was laid in May and dedicated on Thanksgiving Day, 1896. St. Augustine is certainly one of the most imposing churches in southern Minnesota and probably one of the most overlooked. It is a large, Gothic Revival structure built of red pressed brick with red sandstone trim quarried at Bayfield, Wisconsin. The facade is dominated by two projecting towers, the left one taller than the right one, each topped by hexagonal spires and gilded crosses. The taller spire is 170 feet high. This large church measures 77 feet in width and 169 feet in length.

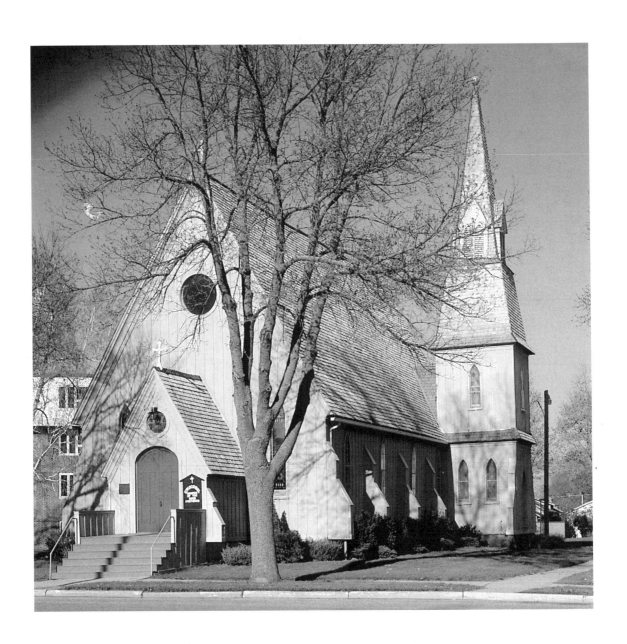

Church of the Good Shepherd Episcopal

Eighth and Moore Streets
Solomon Stephens Burleson, Blue Earth, architect
1872
National Register of Historic Places

M INNESOTA SEEMS TO BE BLESSED with a number of outstanding little Episcopal churches—thanks to the missionary zeal of Bishop Henry Whipple. While it is difficult to find one that stands above the rest, this elegant frame church is surely among the finest.

Faribault County was created by the Sixth Territorial Legislature in 1855. The first settlement in the newly formed county occurred in the same year, when Moses Sailor built a cabin on the Blue Earth River south of the later town site. The next year, Blue Earth City was platted and settlers began to arrive. Most were Methodists, but others, including Episcopalians and Presbyterians, also entered the community.

The first Episcopal service was held in Blue Earth on December 10, 1867, in the Presbyterian church that had been constructed that year. Three years later, the Reverend Solomon Stephens Burleson, rector of the parish in Northfield, visited Blue Earth at the request of Bishop Whipple to consider serving the parish. Burleson was an illustrious missionary priest who established churches in Northfield, Dundas, and Cannon Falls. Whipple and Burleson returned to Blue Earth in 1871, and the bishop offered the parish $3,000 for construction of a church if the congregation would provide the rectory. The offer was accepted; Burleson resigned his parish in Northfield and moved to Blue Earth. He designed the church himself, and it was completed on Easter, March 21, 1872. Bishop Whipple consecrated the structure on August 13.

The Church of the Good Shepherd is rectangular, with a steeply pitched roof and a tower and shingled steeple located at one side. It is clad with board-and-batten siding, painted gray, and there are engaged wooden buttresses placed against the walls of the nave and tower. The interior is intact with its exposed beam ceiling, board-and-batten interior surfacing, and original furnishings. The pews are of wood peg construction. Stained glass windows are from Switzerland; the center sacristy window is a gift of Old Christ Church in St. Paul.

Bramble (Koochiching County)

Saints Peter and Paul Orthodox Church

North of Togo on Minnesota Highway 65

Architect and builder unknown
1915–18
National Register of Historic Places

I T MAY AT FIRST BE STRANGE to find a Russian Orthodox church in the middle of no-where in one of the state's least developed counties, but in view of the fact that the southeast corner of Koochiching County was settled by immigrants from Russia, this church does not seem at all out of place.

The small gable-roofed frame structure, capped by a tower and massive tin-covered double onion dome painted gold, was erected in 1915–18 by local labor. Land for the church was donated by William Lucachick, an area farmer. The first mass in the new structure was celebrated by a Russian Orthodox priest from Chisholm.

The interior contains an iconostasis installed in 1926. In keeping with Russian Orthodox tradition, there are no pews; benches along each side of the nave are provided for the elderly and infirm, who sit after the most sacred part of the mass. The rest of the congregation stands throughout the service. The church is heated by a wood stove at the rear of the nave.

In the 1930s the church fell into disuse. It was rescued and restored through the efforts of Father Paul Berg, an Episcopal minister from Grand Rapids. He discovered the deserted little building and raised money and local interest in its restoration. It was rededicated in 1968.

Browerville (Todd County)

Christ the King Catholic Church
(originally St. Joseph's Catholic Church)

720 Main Street North
Boehme and Cordella, Minneapolis, architects
1907–9
National Register of Historic Places

T HIS BAROQUE CHURCH WAS BUILT by a Polish Catholic congregation that had split from the German group in 1895 over financing of a school erected in 1890. The church was begun in 1907 with the aid of special assessments and completed for Easter services in 1909. The contractors were Hirr and Zierton of St. Cloud.

The church's most distinctive feature is its 70-foot-tall tower, topped by a drum surrounded by a series of eight columns and surmounted by an onion dome and cross. The tower bears an emblem of an eagle, the symbol of Poland. The building is faced in cream-colored brick with an asphalt shingled roof. It measures 151 feet long and 70 feet wide. The detailing is classically inspired, but the overall style is German baroque. The main entrance is approached by a set of monumental steps. Altogether, it is an extremely handsome church.

Next to it is a remarkable grotto made of boulders, constructed by Joseph Kiselewski, Browerville native and designer of the Good Conduct Medal for the U.S. armed forces.

St. Joseph's suffered declining membership by 1979 and merged the following year with the local German parish. The united parish was renamed Christ the King and holds services in this church.

Burnsville

Prince of Peace Lutheran Church

200 Nicollet Boulevard East
Bentz/Thompson and Associates, Minneapolis, architects
1974–75

T HE PRINCE OF PEACE CONGREGATION held its first meeting on January 16, 1964, in the Burnsville Funeral Home at Nicollet Avenue and Burnsville Parkway. In 1975 it relocated to the Ridges Campus in conjunction with Fairview Hospital and then moved into the present building.

When the congregation of Prince of Peace decided to build a new church, it was more interested in a structure that would be modern and utilitarian, not traditional or monumental. As the pastor told the architects, "We worship God, not a building."

The result was a distinctive triangular building designed by Milo Thompson, two stories in height and 220 feet long on each side. The exterior is featureless except for crosses embedded in the precast panels on each side. The upper level of the interior space is a spacious and inviting multipurpose sanctuary that can seat sixteen hundred but can also be divided into four smaller triangular spaces by three movable walls to suit special functions. Large exposed steel trusses form a triangle that supports the metal ceiling. The carpet carries on the triangular motif with a grid for aligning chairs in rows along the church's three axes. Ramps link the upper and lower levels. The lower level houses offices and ancillary spaces.

The church was designed for both outdoor and combined indoor-outdoor services. It was also designed to be added to; an extension, planned soon after the original structure was completed, houses a choir room, stage, gymnasium, locker rooms, and offices.

Cannon Falls

Church of the Redeemer

123 Third Street North
Christopher Doner and Lester Bancroft, Cannon Falls, builders
1866–67
National Register of Historic Places

T HE CHURCH OF THE REDEEMER is one of the oldest extant churches in the state and the first church built in Cannon Falls. It is also one of the finest examples of the purity and simplicity of line that characterizes many Episcopal churches.

Unlike many other congregations, this is the first and only church that the Episcopal community in Cannon Falls has had. For about eight years, the families met for services in private homes, and their minister commuted by foot or horseback from Hastings, eighteen miles away.

In 1866 the decision was made to build a church. A building committee bought three lots and met with Christopher Doner to draw up plans. Doner was responsible for the carpentry, and Lester Bancroft was the mason. Construction began in late winter or early spring of 1866. Buff Platteville limestone was quarried from the Bremer family farm north of Cannon Falls and hauled to the site. Bishop Henry Whipple laid the cornerstone on June 28 and returned on May 1, 1867, to consecrate the church. The entire cost, including land and furnishings, was about $3,500.

The exterior of this small building remains almost intact. Four Gothic-arched windows line each side wall, and a small wooden bell tower rises from the front of the roof. A limestone addition at the rear that provides entrance to the basement was built when a furnace was installed. The nave has been redecorated with a tile floor over the original boards and fiber board on the original wood walls. The butternut wainscoting is original.

It is unfortunate that much of this little gem is today obscured by vines. One would hope that they will be removed to reveal this fine little church in all its glory and prevent irreparable damage to the soft stone walls.

Center City (Chisago County)

Chisago Lake Evangelical Lutheran Church

1 Summit Avenue
Architect unknown
1888
National Register of Historic Places (Center City Historic District)

THIS CHURCH, FOUNDED BY SWEDES, is the second-oldest Lutheran congregation in Minnesota—the oldest being First Lutheran in St. Paul, founded only one week earlier in 1854. (The third oldest is in Scandia.) By 1905 the congregation numbered 1,495, the peak of its membership.

The present church, built in 1888 in the Romanesque Revival style, is faced in buff-colored brick, with a gable roof, rectangular entrance tower with louvered belfry and spire capped by a gold cross and clocks on each face above the belfry, round-arched stained glass windows, decorative brickwork that defines the bays on the sides of the nave, and corbeling under the eaves. The northeast side was added to in 1976.

The congregation was organized by the Reverend Eric Norelius, who also founded the Vasa congregation, among many others, and Gustavus Adolphus College. Mr. Norelius was a divinity student when he came to Center City and served for three months before returning to seminary. The first permanent pastor was appointed in 1855, and the first frame church was built in 1856. It was enlarged twice in later years. Its bell was purchased for $50 from a steamboat. The second church was erected in 1881–83 using 300,000 Chaska bricks at a cost of $25,000. A new bell finally replaced the old one in 1888, but a few weeks later the church was struck by lightning and burned. The congregation immediately rebuilt it, using the same masonry contractors—Jonas Norell and Louis Johnson—as the previous one. The bell was added in the steeple in 1890, and the clock was installed in 1907.

The interior has been remodeled several times, but it manages to retain the flavor and feel of a nineteenth-century church, with its metal ceiling and columns, ornate apse and altar, and exquisite stained glass. The church's site is atop a hill above Chisago Lake nestled in trees and with a broad expanse of lawn, creating an extraordinarily picturesque setting.

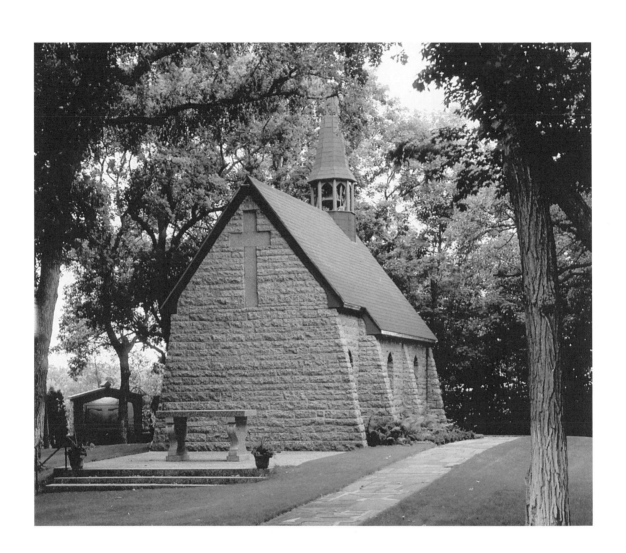

Cold Spring (Stearns County)

Assumption Chapel

Minnesota Highway 23 to the eastern edge of Cold Spring; south on Chapel Street about ¼ mile

Architect and builder unknown

1951–52

A SSUMPTION CHAPEL WAS BUILT AS A MEMORIAL to the grasshopper plagues that struck the Cold Spring area in 1876–77. The infestation of Rocky Mountain grasshoppers was so savage that farmers harvested virtually no crops for two summers. Stories tell of the destruction: grain stalks were consumed down to the ground; cattle were attacked and many died of blood poisoning; pastures were wiped clean, as were gardens. Even clothes left hanging outside were eaten by the ravenous hordes.

The farmers resorted to whatever measures they could improvise to fight back. Some made "hopperdozers" of sheets of tar-covered metal fastened to runners. Horses dragged these through the fields and the grasshoppers would stick to the tar. The farmers burned off the tar along with the hoppers, retarred the dozers, and started over again. Others used large burlap bags to trap them: one farmer collected eighteen bushels of grasshoppers from a ten-acre field. A four-year-old boy gathered hoppers at three cents a bushel and saved enough to buy a two-dollar pair of boots.

The settlers watched nervously as the spring and summer of 1877 approached, knowing that the millions of eggs laid by the grasshoppers the previous year would hatch. They appealed to Governor John S. Pillsbury to declare a Day of Prayer for April 26, 1877. The plague continued through the summer but gradually abated. The Day of Prayer was extended to the months through which the hopper menace lasted.

Father Leo Winter of Jacobs Prairie and St. Nicholas believed the plague was a punishment from God and decided to build a chapel for people to pray in and repent of the sins that had brought on the calamity. Construction began on July 16, 1877, and the chapel was finished on August 15. It was a frame building, 16 feet by 25 feet, with an altar and a statue of the Virgin Mary and Child. Mass was said there every Saturday during the plague, which began to abate even as the chapel was being built. By September the grasshoppers had disappeared. Services continued in the chapel until 1894, when a tornado destroyed it. Only the statue was salvaged.

Bishop Peter Bartholome of the Diocese of St. Cloud rebuilt the chapel in 1951 and named it Assumption Chapel. The new structure is as much a monument to the local granite industry as to the grasshopper plague. It is built of pink-gray granite and roofed with red shingles. Engaged buttresses divide the walls into three bays. Over the entrance is a relief of Mary with two grasshoppers kneeling at her feet as if in humble submission to her power. Inside, the ceiling is redwood, the walls polished agate and carnelian. The floor is of polished pink, agate, and gray granite. The altar is greenish black granite, and behind it is the statue of the Virgin Mary that stood in the original chapel.

The chapel stands on a high hill outside of Cold Spring and is illuminated at night. As a tourist attraction, it has drawn visitors from all parts of the United States, Canada, and Europe.

Collegeville

St. John's Abbey Church, St. John's University

Interstate 94 to exit 156; south 1½ miles on County Road 159

Marcel Breuer, New York, architect
Frank Kacmarcik, St. Paul, art coordinator
Traynor and Hermanson, St. Cloud, supervising architects
1954–61

S T. JOHN'S ABBEY WAS FOUNDED by Benedictines in 1857, and several buildings were constructed after that time (mainly around 1880) to serve as housing and educational facilities. An abbey church was built in 1879–80 (which resembled Assumption Church in St. Paul) and served until the present structure was completed.

In 1954 Marcel Breuer, a distinguished New York architect, was commissioned by St. John's officials to draw up a master plan for the campus. He was selected from a list of notable architects that included Richard Neutra, Walter Gropius, Eero Saarinen, Pietro Belluschi, and Barry Byrne. Breuer drew up a campus plan for one hundred years that called for nineteen buildings. Most would be erected in a system called "shadow building," whereby the new structure would be built in the shadow of the one it was replacing.

The set piece is the church, with its striking bell wall or bell banner that stands in front as a distinctive symbol to be remembered by visitors. The five exposed electrically operated bells are situated so as to be heard by the monks at work. The church dominates the hilltop campus and is the first object one sees when approaching the college. The building has already become a landmark, making it one of the most significant religious structures in the state. Behind the bell tower is a honeycomb facade of concrete and glass (see Plate 3). Both have now weathered to a nutty brown and are much more attractive than when the concrete was raw and new. Pier Luigi Nervi, Breuer's collaborator on the UNESCO world headquarters in Paris, was an adviser on the structure.

Inside, there is an immense cantilevered balcony, cast in reinforced concrete, which hovers over the main floor almost expectantly, seeming to defy gravity. The altar is the focal point of the dramatic space.

Val Michelson of St. Paul worked on the general campus plan and supervised the construction of the church. It was the offer to supervise the construction that brought Michelson to Minnesota. He later said that Breuer was a good person to work for, an architect who "let you know what he wanted by talking and did not put much on a page." He would sketch an idea and then ask his staff for input so that, in a sense, his work was a team effort.

Danvers (Swift County)

Church of the Visitation

201 County Road 14

From Benson, seven miles west on U.S. Highway 12 to County Road 14

Glynne Shifflet, Minneapolis, architect

1931

THIS DELIGHTFUL BRICK-AND-STONE CHURCH was erected in 1931 to replace an earlier one dating from 1892 that was destroyed by fire. It was designed by Glynne Shifflet, who was working in Cyril Pesek's firm in Minneapolis. Pesek said years later that Shifflet studied architecture in France and came to admire small country churches. He was fortunate that the priest at Danvers, Father Joseph O'Neil, had also traveled in France and was of similar mind. Shifflet created a little gem whose beauty is enhanced by its setting amid an 8½-acre site of spreading lawn and an adjacent tree-lined cemetery. Total cost of construction was about $30,000.

The church is faced with a combination of soft dark red brick and rough yellow limestone blocks and pieces. The roof is covered with unevenly laid slates and pierced by triangular vents. Stone crosses adorn the peak of the roof and entrance gable. There is a two-story square tower on the north end of the building topped by a small metal spire.

The interior has white plaster walls and ceiling and heavy dark timber beams. The only alterations took place in 1975, when new entrance doors of glass replaced the original wooden ones. The adjacent one-story rambler rectory was erected in 1962.

Danvers was platted in 1899, but the parish of Visitation began twenty years before as a mission of the church in nearby Clontarf, one of the Irish Catholic settlements in western Minnesota promoted by Bishop (later Archbishop) John Ireland of St. Paul in the 1870s. The first mass in the area was said in 1885 by the Reverend A. Oster of Clontarf, who was responsible for having the first church built. The parish was served from Clontarf until 1898, then attached to Benson until 1915, when the first resident priest was assigned.

Church of St. Bridget

501 Third Street South
Edward J. Donohue, St. Paul, architect
1901
National Register of Historic Places

THE CHURCH OF ST. BRIDGET was another of the parishes founded in the late nineteenth century by Bishop John Ireland of St. Paul as part of an ambitious program to move large numbers of Irish Catholic settlers onto lands in Swift and adjacent western counties that he had purchased for the church. The official name of the settlement organization he founded in 1876 was the Catholic Colonization Bureau of Minnesota. Ireland's idea was to place people on some 369,000 acres of land contracted for with the railroads. He sponsored a number of settlements, including Graceville, Clontarf, Currie, Minneota, Ghent, Iona, Avoca, Fulda, and De Graff, which was the first parish established as part of that mass colonization effort. Many Irish families were brought from the East to farm the region, but being by and large city folks, they preferred to migrate to the towns. Thus, Ireland's scheme, though not a failure by any means, fell short of being the roaring success he had hoped for.

The Church of St. Bridget was designed in 1901 by Edward J. Donohue of St. Paul, who specialized in work for the Catholic Church, and was erected by Melrose builder E. C. Richmond. It is 115 feet long, 50 feet wide, and the corner bell tower is 3½ stories tall. It is faced with red brick from Twin Cities brickyards, trimmed in Kasota limestone on a St. Cloud granite foundation. The style is Romanesque Revival, best seen in the arched twin doorways and massiveness of the tower.

The interior is largely intact, with exposed wooden beams and an ornate Gothic oak altar. Large murals painted in 1939 by J. James Tissot and E. J. Hartung serve as the stations of the cross. The adjacent rectory was built in 1937.

Duluth

First Presbyterian Church

300 East Second Street
Traphagen and Fitzpatrick, Duluth, architects
1890–91
National Register of Historic Places

THIS MAGNIFICENT ROMANESQUE REVIVAL CHURCH has the finest group of Tiffany-designed stained glass windows of any church in the state (see Plate 6). One of the reasons for this lavish furnishing of Tiffany windows is that Duluth had, for a number of years, its own resident Tiffany designer, Anne Weston.

The church was built of brown, quarry-faced sandstone for $92,000. It has a triple-segmented arched entrance and a corner tower and spire that is 125 feet high. A matching addition on the rear was built in 1912–13.

The congregation is one of the city's oldest, organized before 1870. The first church stood diagonally across Second Street from the present one. It was built in 1870 for $16,000, and after the congregation moved into the present church in 1891, it was used by the Messiah Lutheran congregation until it was demolished in 1970.

First Unitarian Church

1802 First Avenue East
Anthony W. Puck, Duluth, architect
1910–11

T HIS FINE LITTLE CHURCH, built in the Tudor Revival style, is a picturesque structure sitting unobtrusively on a corner in a residential neighborhood in the shadow of an adjacent apartment house. Constructed of the local "black granite," or gabbro, from the Arrowhead region, it has a square, squat corner tower topped by a hexagonal shingled flared steeple. The corners of the tower have engaged stone buttresses. The upper half of the front facade is stucco and half-timber.

Unitarianism began in Duluth in about 1885, when C. F. Dole of the American Unitarian Association of Boston visited the town at the request of a small group of residents. He evidently recommended to the home office that a Unitarian Society should be established, for on April 10, 1887, a meeting was held to organize a liberal religious society in Duluth. The following month, incorporation papers were prepared, signed by eighteen people, and in the fall, a minister named West was called from the Unitarian Society in Geneva, Illinois. He served in Duluth for about nine months. After Mr. West's departure, the group had no minister for almost two years until the arrival of T. Jefferson Volentine and his wife from Iowa in 1890. Around this time, the Unitarians purchased the old Pilgrim Congregational Church building and moved it from its original location at East Second Street and First Avenue East to East First Street and Eighth Avenue East. It was refurbished with carpet, wallpaper, and a pedal organ.

Mr. Volentine seems to have been an ambitious man, for the paint and wallpaper were scarcely dry when he began proposing that the congregation apply for a $5,000 loan to build a "real little church," as he put it, that would triple the seating capacity of the present one. The congregation rejected the measure since the group was already in debt for the costs of fixing up its building, and Mr. Volentine was voted out. He was succeeded, in the fall of 1892, by Franklin Chester Southworth, who stayed five years, during which time the little church was moved yet again to a donated lot a block away at East First Street and Ninth Avenue East.

The intervening years between the final move of the church and the construction of a new one saw the expansion of the congregation and the coming and going of two more ministers. During the tenure of a third, George Gebauer (1908–17), a lot was purchased for $4,000 at East First Street and Eighteenth Avenue East. Anthony W. Puck, a church member since 1905, was chosen as architect. Construction began late in 1910, and the building was finished and ready for services by the following September. Total cost of construction and furnishings was about $20,000.

Recently, a Quaker congregation has been using the church.

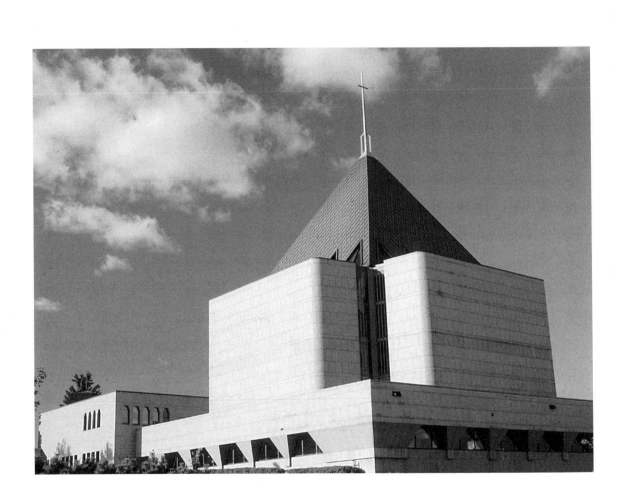

First United Methodist Church

230 East Skyline Parkway
Pietro Belluschi, Boston and Portland, Oregon, architect
Melander, Fugelso, and Associates, Duluth, associated architects
1964–66

METHODISM CAME TO THE FLEDGLING VILLAGE OF DULUTH in November 1869 with the arrival of the denomination's first resident pastor, Harvey Webb, his wife, Jemima, and their small daughter. Mr. Webb helped establish the First Methodist Episcopal Church and conducted its initial service in the local schoolhouse within a few days of his arrival. The following year, a church building was begun on a lot at the corner of Third Avenue West and Second Street, donated by the Western Land Association. The frame building, costing $800, was dedicated in 1871, and the church had about fifty members. Two years later, the Panic of 1873 fell hard on Duluth, and the church lost about half its members, who moved elsewhere in search of livelihoods.

As good times returned to the city, so did the population, and the growth of the congregation forced members to begin planning for a new, larger church. A lot was purchased a block away, at Third Avenue and Third Street, in 1887, and in 1889 plans were drawn for a new building by Weary and Kramer of Akron, Ohio, with McMillian and Radcliffe of Duluth as associates. The church was based on the First Methodist Episcopal Church in Burlington, Iowa. Construction began in 1891, and the building was enclosed by winter that year; interior furnishing was not completed until early 1893, when the church was dedicated. Total cost was $120,000. It was constructed of local brownstone and featured an $8,000 organ (replaced in 1932). A Duluth newspaper described the church as "imposing in appearance, commodious in size, convenient in arrangement, artistic in finish, and comfortable in furnishings." The old frame structure was demolished and the lumber transported to Virginia, Minnesota, where the building was reassembled for a Methodist congregation.

The present church was erected on Skyline Parkway after estimates to upgrade the old church and provide off-street parking in the downtown location proved to be too costly. Although the church no longer served a downtown population, its planners still felt that it needed to be in a location that was accessible to everyone in the city. In 1959 seven acres were purchased on Skyline Parkway for a new church that would be visible from many areas of the central core as well as have a commanding view of Lake Superior. Pietro Belluschi was employed as architect in 1963 and designed a church of "sculptural simplicity." Construction began in 1964 and was finished in 1966 at a cost of about $1.4 million. The old stone church was sold and torn down in 1967.

The building is 150 feet from grade to the top of the cross. The nave is 88 feet from the floor to the peak of the ceiling. The exterior is sheathed in Texas pink granite, and the pyramidal dome is covered with copper. Design flaws plagued the church with leaks for years (a not uncommon phenomenon in many religious structures), and only recently has this situation begun to be stabilized through extensive and well-planned restoration. The altar and sanctuary floors are of Travertine marble, and all interior millwork is oak. The church seats 790 in pews designed by Belluschi and manufactured at Chatfield, Minnesota. The organ in the sanctuary has 4,256 pipes; the organ in the balcony was given in memory of Chester A. and Clara B. Congdon in 1968 by their children and grandchildren.

Duluth

St. Paul's Episcopal Church

1710 East Superior Street
Cram and Goodhue, Boston, architects
1911–12
National Register of Historic Places

T HIS ELEGANT CHURCH is the only religious structure in Duluth designed by the famous team of Boston architects, Cram and Goodhue, although they created other buildings in the city. Bertram Grosvenor Goodhue was principally responsible for the design, which came at a time when he was breaking away from his partnership with Ralph Adams Cram. Goodhue successfully created a church whose Gothic flavor is seen in the delicate dressed stone trim, blue gray slate roof, and the pointed arches over the windows. A crenelated tower looms over the building but does not seem out of scale or to dominate it, rather complementing and enhancing the ensemble. The windows have wood-and-concrete frames, a cost-saving measure, but are executed so skillfully that the tracery appears to be cut stone. In 1947 three bells cast by Gillett and Johnston of Graydon, England, were installed in the tower.

The interior is sensitively finished in stone and highly crafted oak woodwork. A 1928 three-story el addition by Duluth architects Abraham Holstead and William J. Sullivan houses offices, classrooms, and church parlors, and carefully matches the original church.

The church is built of local stone quarried near the site and stands in the once fashionable Endion neighborhood on the east side. Its style is derived from English Gothic, not surprising considering that the architects—Cram in particular—were leaders in promoting the virtues of the Gothic style in America in the early twentieth century. Its rusticity recalls but does not copy country churches and is so carefully and purposefully crafted as to appear less sophisticated than it truly is.

Goodhue lavished the same degree of Gothic care in his designs for the Hartley office building at 740 East Superior Street (1914) (Hartley was a parishioner of St. Paul's and, as chairman of the building committee, probably played a key role in securing Goodhue the commission) and the Kitchi Gammi Club, 831 East Superior Street (1912). He also designed a mansion for Cavour Hartley, 3800 East Superior Street (1915), in a style that is difficult to type but seems to have elements of Tudor and Craftsman mingled in what emerges as a very elegant work.

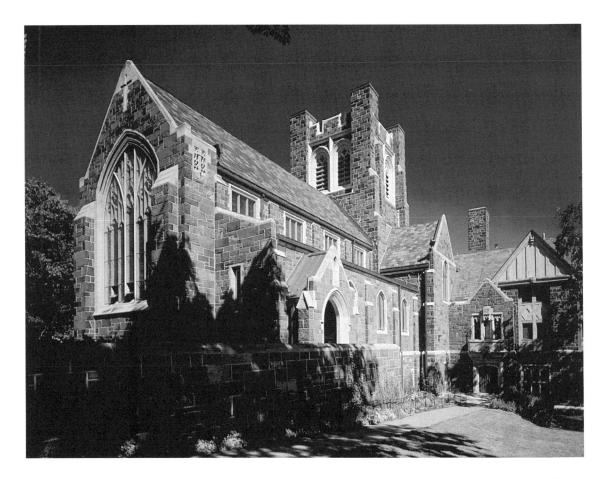

The first Episcopal services were held in Duluth sometime before 1866. Toward the end of the decade, General George B. Sargent was sent to Duluth by Jay Cooke to act as his financial representative and to have charge of Cooke's operations. Both Cooke and Sargent were Episcopalians, and Sargent was also commissioned to start a church. Cooke donated money for its construction, which occurred in 1869 at Second Street and Lake Avenue. It was called "Cooke's Church" for about a year until being renamed St. Paul's. It was a sizable frame church and, according to photographs, featured exquisite timber trusswork inside.

In 1895 the Diocese of Duluth was created and plans were discussed for the construction of a cathedral. In 1905 the bishop generated a furor when he decreed that all of Duluth east of Eleventh Avenue East would be part of the new cathedral parish, Trinity, which was to be constructed at Twentieth Avenue East and Superior Street. The parish of St. Paul's decided to build a new church and selected a lot at Seventeenth Avenue East and Superior Street in 1909. Clearly, this was an effort to break the bishop's decree and it worked: two years later he abolished the arbitrary line and said that both parishes could serve the whole city. The congregation of St. Paul's went ahead with construction of its church in 1911; the building was completed in 1912 at a cost of $115,000.

Eden Prairie

Wooddale Church

6630 Shady Oak Road
Bentz/Thompson/Rietow, Minneapolis, architects
1984–90

WOODDALE (BAPTIST) CHURCH IS AN ENORMOUS STRUCTURE that sits amidst almost thirty-two acres of wooded and landscaped property in the southwest metro area. The complex is dominated by a huge central worship center that seats 1,000 on the main floor and another 1,000 in the balcony. The choir loft accommodates 125 members. It is 70 feet from the floor of the worship center to the base of the skylight. Rising from the top of the sanctuary is a 193-foot spire topped with a six-foot-tall cross. The spire is constructed of steel lit by twenty-seven metal halide light fixtures.

The focal point of the interior of the worship center is a monumental tracker organ built by Visser-Rowland Associates of Houston, Texas. It has 6,294 pipes, the largest of which is 32 feet in height. For those interested in and knowledgeable about organs, this one has two consoles, 74 stops, and 114 ranks. It weighs forty tons and took five months to install in 1990.

Wooddale Church started as a Bible study group in the 1940s, occupying facilities at Seventy-first Street and Nicollet Avenue in Richfield until 1984. The congregation—then numbering about 1,100—was frustrated by lack of expansion space and moved to a new facility in northeastern Eden Prairie. The first phase of the complex was a multipurpose worship center, offices, classrooms, and nursery. The second phase, which was occupied in November 1985, contained more classrooms and offices, as well as a gymnasium, shower, and locker area. The third phase—the most ambitious—was the construction of the large worship center, begun in October 1988 and dedicated on the first Sunday in January 1991. Later expansions added to the office and education space, and more classrooms are planned. The approximate cost of construction, including furnishings, parking, consultants, the organ, and other fees, is $9.7 million. The result is certainly one of the state's most outstanding contemporary churches.

Eitzen (Houston County)

Portland Prairie Methodist Episcopal Church

From Caledonia, south on Minnesota Highway 76; west on County Road 27

Mr. Tuttle, New Albin, Iowa, builder
1876
National Register of Historic Places

THE CHURCH IS ONE OF THE BEST EXAMPLES of the Eastlake style in Minnesota, named for Charles Eastlake and characterized by fineness of detail as well as careful attention to the use of decorative wood trim. It is a wood frame structure, clad in clapboard with a steep gable metal-clad roof, and stands on a stone foundation. It is painted cream with dark brown trim. The main entrance is to the right, under a gable roof that projects from a short tower just behind it. Balancing the entrance and tower on the left is the chimney, clad up to the roofline with nicely detailed wood. A secondary entrance is just to the left of the chimney, tucked under the gable end of the roof. In the center, between the tower and chimney, is a large window. The interior is intact, despite a hailstorm in the spring of 1996 that damaged many of the windows, including the large one in the front facade. They have been replaced. There were no stained glass windows in this modest little church.

The area was first served by a circuit rider from Caledonia, between 1855 and 1876. The congregation was composed mostly of Yankees from New England and New York; hence their desire to build a church with English antecedents. In 1876, working from plans obtained in St. Paul (whether from an architect or not is unknown), a Mr. Tuttle from New Albin, Iowa, erected the building at a cost of $1,540. In 1935 the active congregation moved to Caledonia, but the church is used a few times a year, notably on the Fourth of July, when there is a service and celebration in the large yard.

Fairfax

Fort Ridgely and Dale Evangelical Lutheran Church

From Fairfax, west 4 miles on Minnesota Highway 19; 1¼ miles south on 430th Street

Architect and builder unknown
1886

THE HISTORY OF THE CONGREGATION OF THIS CHURCH is indeed an interesting one. It was organized in 1868 as the first Lutheran congregation in the county. Soon afterward, the congregation's district divided on the issue of where to build a new church: the northern half became Dale and the southern half became Fort Ridgely.

Before the church could be built, however, the congregations split once more, this time over a doctrinal issue. Each lost half its members, and what remained of Fort Ridgely and Dale agreed to build a church together but not to unite (that step was not to occur for sixty years). The church was erected in 1886 and dedicated on May 28, 1893, after the installation of the altar, pulpit, pews, and bell. A parsonage had been built much earlier, in 1878, for the first resident pastor.

The church is said to have a log core, but this has not been confirmed. It is a simple rural church, covered with clapboard and having the usual projecting tower entrance centered at the front of the church. It is still heated by a wood stove and is maintained in very good condition. The sacristy was added in 1899.

The Fort Ridgely and Dale congregations finally united in 1946 and today are part of Central Lutheran Church of Fairfax.

Faribault

Cathedral of Our Merciful Savior Episcopal

515 Northwest Second Avenue
James Renwick, New York, architect
1862–69
National Register of Historic Places

B Y FAR THE OLDEST EXTANT CATHEDRAL IN THE STATE, Our Merciful Savior Episcopal was built as the seat of the diocese of Bishop Henry Whipple beginning in 1862. It is constructed on the Latin cross plan in the English Gothic Revival style of native blue limestone from Fall Creek Quarry east of Faribault, with a square tower set back in the northeast corner of the church. The base of the tower was completed in 1868, but the belfry was not finished until 1902, at which time the interior was slightly modified. The nave, however, which is 45 feet wide and 90 feet long, remains essentially the same as when first built with exposed timber trusses. It seats six hundred people.

James Renwick designed a number of prominent buildings, including the Smithsonian Institution in Washington, D.C. (the "Castle"), and St. Patrick's Cathedral in New York City. He probably was either an acquaintance of Bishop Whipple's or was recommended to Whipple by some of his eastern friends, because architects from the East Coast were not usually employed for work in the Upper Midwest without such contacts.

Chapel of the Good Shepherd
Shattuck–St. Mary's School

1000 Shumway Avenue
Henry M. Congdon, New York, architect
1871–73
National Register of Historic Places

T HE FULL NAME FOR THIS VERY INTERESTING BUILDING is the Eunice Shumway Memorial Chapel of the Good Shepherd. It was named after the daughter of Mrs. Augustus Shumway of Chicago and is the only building surviving from the old Shattuck campus. The chapel was built at the time when the Bishop Seabury Mission Divinity School was moved to a temporary site following the destruction of Seabury Hall by fire (1872) and separated from Shattuck School.

Construction began in June 1871 and was finished in September 1872. Although Mrs. Shumway suffered extensive property loss and some financial difficulties due to the great Chicago fire of October 1871, she stood by her pledge of $20,000 to build the chapel. It was designed by the noted New York architect Henry M. Congdon, who was also the designer of the Church of the Holy Communion in St. Peter. Bishop Henry Whipple was well connected on the East Coast and perhaps either obtained Congdon's services through influential friends or may have known the man himself and hired him to design both the church in St. Peter and the chapel at Shattuck.

Of the two, the chapel is by far the more elaborate design and is, of course, much the larger. It is in the English Gothic (once called Pointed Gothic) style, built of local blue limestone with a rough quarry face except where it is used as trim around doors and windows. The chapel has two remarkable and unusual features: first, the bell tower and steeple are constructed entirely of quarry-dressed stone, conical in shape, but appearing light and delicate without the heaviness that stone can convey; second, the seating in the chapel faces the center aisle rather than toward the front. The floor tile, pulpit, lectern, and windows were manufactured in England.

The baptismal font was carved by Carmella Fontana of Carrara, Italy. On the front facade is a shedlike narthex with a Gothic-arched doorway flanked by double lancet windows on each side. In its parklike setting, the chapel is indeed an elegant and sophisticated building. Total cost of construction was about $30,000.

Fourth Avenue United Methodist Church

(originally First Methodist Episcopal Church)

219 Fourth Avenue Northwest
Kenyon and Maine, Minneapolis, architects
1915

M ETHODISM IN FARIBAULT BEGAN with the appointment of the Reverend Thomas Kirkpatrick to the Cannon River Mission of the Wisconsin Conference. His residence was in Red Wing, but he traveled through a wide region in southeastern Minnesota, arriving in the tiny settlement of Faribault in 1855. Mr. Kirkpatrick established the Methodist Episcopal

Church, and meetings were held in Nutting's Hotel (also known as Faribault House). In 1856 the Minnesota Conference was formed and the first permanent minister was appointed.

A church building was begun in 1856 but not finished until 1860, when it was dedicated and called by the parishioners "The Little White Church." An addition to the frame structure was built in 1865, and an organ was installed. The church was replaced by a redbrick building erected on the same site at the corner of Third and Cherry Streets from 1876 to 1879. It was heavily damaged by fire in 1901, but was repaired and served until the present structure was built in 1915 at a cost of $35,000 by William O'Neil of Faribault.

Fourth Avenue United Methodist Church (called First Methodist Church of Faribault until 1968) is classical in form with a large metal-sheathed dome over the sanctuary. The entrance is framed by a pediment supported by six columns. The building is clad in tan brick and trimmed in limestone. A local newspaper article published in November 1915 called the form a "new type of [building] being used extensively throughout the country, presenting a striking and pleasing form of architecture." An education wing at the rear of the church was added in 1964.

Freeport (Stearns County)

Church of the Sacred Heart

110 Third Avenue Northeast
Parkinson and Dockendorff, La Crosse, Wisconsin, architects
1904–15

T HE CHURCH OF THE SACRED HEART is one in a line of magnificent churches that are visible from Interstate 94 north of St. Cloud, beginning with the Seven Dolors at Albany and ending at Melrose with the Church of St. Mary. These churches hint at the many splendid religious structures to be found in Stearns County.

The German Catholic parish of Freeport was at first part of the New Munich parish. In 1881, the parish applied to the Diocese of St. Cloud for a priest, and Father Simplicius Wimmer was sent to them. He built the first church, a small frame structure that was dedicated in 1882. It was 36 feet wide and 70 feet long and had a steeple on the front. It stood on the site of the present rectory and cost $4,000, including furnishings. A rectory was constructed in 1890. The old church was donated to the parish of St. Rose and moved five miles north. It stands to this day, mostly unrecognizable by being brick veneered and enlarged.

The parish soon outgrew this modest little church and decided to build a new one in 1896. It was brick veneered, measured 66 feet wide and 154 feet long, and seated one thousand people. Being more than double the size of the original church and much more elaborate in its appointments, it cost more than $30,000 to erect. The main altar alone was $2,000. A new rectory to accompany the new church was built in 1902.

In 1904, a lightning strike and subsequent fire destroyed the church. The parish immediately decided to rebuild and everyone pitched in, including the priest. The third church was even larger and more ornate than the preceding one. Some thirty-eight boxcar loads of brick were required to build it. The main altar and side altars were manufactured by the Daprato Statuary Company of New York at a total cost of $4,400. The stained glass windows were made by Ford Brothers Glass Company of Minneapolis for $4,900. In 1915 a clock was purchased from Hoffman-Pollhaus Clock Manufacturing Company of St. Louis and installed in the steeple

along with a chime of four bells. The total cost of the church was about $115,000 by the time it was finished in 1915.

The beautiful cemetery next to the church has been enlarged several times since it was established. The wall was built by Michael Gresser, and the steel gates and pickets were installed in 1948.

Frontenac (Goodhue County)

Christ Episcopal Church

29036 Westervelt Avenue Way West

From U.S. Highway 61, east on County Road 2; south on Westervelt

Nathaniel Collins McLean, Frontenac, builder
1868
National Register of Historic Places (Old Frontenac Historic District)

F RONTENAC HAS ONE OF THE MORE COLORFUL HISTORIES among small river towns
in Minnesota. It started as a trading post operated by James "Bully" Wells in the 1830s and
continued to operate until 1852, when Bully transferred his holdings to Evert V. Westervelt, a
Dutch immigrant and trader. Westervelt ran the post for a couple of years, until Israel and Lewis
Garrard arrived in town.

The Garrards were descendants of one of the founders of Cincinnati and had come to Frontenac (then called Waconia) to hunt. Lewis stayed only a short time, but Israel decided to stick
around and built a hunting retreat in 1855 called St. Hubert's Lodge. Two years later, Garrard
and Westervelt bought 4,000 acres of land along the Mississippi at this point and set aside 320
acres of it for a town site to be called Westervelt. In 1859 the village was renamed Frontenac after
a seventeenth-century French governor of Canada. Westervelt by this time had sold out half his
holdings to Lewis Garrard and the other half to Israel, but he remained active in town affairs
until his death in 1888.

Israel Garrard began to develop the village in 1858–62. The Civil War cut short much of the
building effort, but not before Garrard had brought a small army of craftsmen from Cincinnati to
erect houses and stores for the town. He entered the Civil War at the head of a unit of volunteers
and emerged from it a general.

After the war, General Israel Garrard resumed the development at an accelerated pace, determined to create an exclusive vacation community. In 1871 the railroad threatened to destroy the
little paradise, and Garrard donated land three miles to the southwest so that the railroad would
bypass the town. Frontenac Station was built along the railroad to serve the town.

A number of prominent acquaintances of Garrard's stayed in the town for varying lengths of time. Two were the architects Christopher LaFarge and George Hines, who gained the commission for the immense Cathedral of St. John the Divine in New York City in the 1880s. The men used yellow sandstone quarried at the Frontenac Stone Quarry for that magnificent church.

Another associate of Garrard's was General Nathaniel Collins McLean, a Civil War veteran and stepbrother of the Garrards'. McLean funded and, along with Henry Hunecke, supervised the construction of a church in 1868. The result is a very pretty little frame structure clad in board-and-batten siding, built in the English Gothic style with a large square tower on the front reminiscent of English country churches. The interior is largely intact with original stained glass windows and simple brown stained wood paneling. The only significant changes have been the placement of a larger altar and the installation of electric lights to replace the original kerosene fixtures. It is said that the front door has never been locked since the church was built, both to encourage its use and as a symbol of the church as a refuge at all times for all people.

Garden City (Blue Earth County)

First Baptist Church

109 South Jackson Street
Architect and builder unknown
1868
National Register of Historic Places

THIS CHURCH IS THOUGHT TO BE THE EARLIEST STRUCTURE in the state constructed of concrete block or artificial stone. It bears unmistakable Greek Revival characteristics in the turned eaves and pilasters dividing the side and front bays. The concrete blocks have a texture that resembles brick. It is thought that the belfry on the front of the church was added later. A more recent concrete block addition on the back forced reorientation of the entry, so the main entrance is now through the new addition at the rear of the church and the altar is situated where the old entrance was.

Garden City was originally called Fremont and was platted in 1856 on the Watonwan River. A number of towns were platted along the river at this time, but Garden City survived because the railroad ran through it. The congregation of Baptists formed in 1858, and eight years later the church was formally organized. In 1867 a split occurred in the group between those who wanted a more aggressive evangelical mission and those who did not. One of the groups moved ahead with plans to construct a church, and the men went up and down the river buying logs, which a local mill operator offered to saw free of charge if they could float them to his mill. Winter intervened before the logs could be delivered to the sawmill, and high water in the spring swept them all away.

Not to be discouraged, the congregation immediately laid plans to build a larger church of concrete blocks manufactured in the town by the firm of Geist and Hentzelman, which had recently relocated to Garden City from Illinois. The structure was built at a cost of $4,100, measuring 33 by 55 feet and seating 250 people. It was dedicated on January 17, 1869, and the two schismatic groups reunited to use it jointly.

Hanska (Brown County)

Nora Unitarian Church
(originally Nora Free Christian Church)

12333 155th Avenue

Minnesota Highway 257 east from Hanska; south on 155th Avenue

Architect and builder unknown
1883
National Register of Historic Places

T HIS SIMPLE FRAME GOTHIC COUNTRY CHURCH seems to epitomize what small rural churches in the Midwest are supposed to look like: quaint, simple, and peaceful. Yet, despite its peaceful appearance, Nora Free Christian Church has had a rocky history.

The church was formed by a group of dissenters within the Norwegian Lutheran community in Brown County. They asked Kristofer Janson to be their minister, and he answered the call in 1882. Janson was a dissenter himself who had parted company with the rigid doctrines and conservatism of Lutheranism in his native Norway. He visited the Midwest on a lecture tour in 1879–80 and spoke to packed halls in many towns and cities, including in Minnesota. Although he was popular with the common people, the church leaders in the state warned that he was preaching dangerously heretical ideas.

After organizing the Free Christian Church of Minneapolis (later known as the Nazareth Church), Janson left for Brown County's Linden Township in January 1882 to minister to the congregation of Nora Free Christian Church. In the months that followed, the liberal church members were criticized and even shunned by their more conservative neighbors. One of their leaders, Johannes Mo, announced in a Norwegian newspaper that his group's cemetery would be open to anyone regardless of creed.

By the fall of 1882, the congregation had raised enough money—some of it from East Coast Unitarians—to build a church. The following spring it was erected along with an attached parsonage for Janson and his family. Only two services were held (July 8 and 15) before the structure was demolished by a tornado on July 21, 1883. Critics immediately declared it was God's punishment on the dissident group.

The church was rebuilt with a separate parsonage. Its dedication on July 13, 1884, was attended

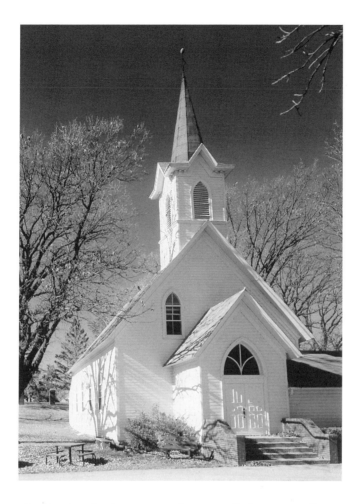

by four hundred people. Services in the summer became all-day events: Janson would conduct the morning service, preach a sermon, and then the worshipers would have a picnic with a band concert, social hour, an afternoon literary reading and discussion led by Janson, ending with evening prayers and hymns. From 1883 to 1893, the Jansons (who had seven children) spent their summers at the Nora church and wintered in Minneapolis, declaring Nora to be a refuge from city life and a "paradise." At his paradise, Janson wrote novels, stories, poetry, and articles, and produced his own monthly magazine, *Saamanden* (The sower).

In 1893, Janson resigned and returned to Norway, where he continued to minister and to write and speak. He never returned to the United States but did maintain contact through correspondence with his former congregation. He died in Copenhagen in 1917.

By then, the Nora Church was well established, strong, and independent. Under Janson's successor, Amandus Norman, it continued to grow and flourish well past his death in 1931. Today, the church has a thriving congregation and is beautifully maintained. The parsonage dates from 1906 (probably the 1883 structure enlarged and rebuilt), and the nearby gazebo was built about 1930.

Greenfield Lutheran Church

235 Main Avenue South
Andrew Roth, La Crosse, Wisconsin, architect
1912–13

HARMONY SITS IN THE MIDST of a mostly Norwegian-populated area. The first settlement was Greenfield Prairie, which began in 1854. A small community grew up with a few buildings, including a post office; it was named Peterson after Knud Peterson, the first postmaster. The name subsequently was changed to Windom (in honor of U.S. Senator William Windom), then to Harmony in 1872.

The congregation of Greenfield Lutheran was organized in 1864, and the first church was built in 1866 of locally made brick. It stood one-half mile from the present structure and measured 48 feet long by 36 feet wide and 18 feet high, with a 75-foot-high steeple. By 1911 the old church was in such a dilapidated condition that the walls had to be held together with cables strung from side to side. The steeple had also been split by lightning, but fortunately no fire resulted from the strike. The congregation decided a new church was required and after much debate chose a site in town, where construction began shortly after the contract was awarded on June 10, 1912, to contractors Riseland, Roheim, and Steen of Harmony. The building was dedicated in September 1913.

It is in the Gothic and Romanesque styles with the taller steeple being capped with a gold cross that is 100 feet above ground level. The church is constructed of red pressed brick trimmed in Bedford (Indiana) limestone over a full basement.

First Presbyterian Church

602 Vermillion Street
Charles N. Daniels, Faribault, architect
1875–1881
Harry W. Jones, Minneapolis, architect
1907–9
National Register of Historic Places

FIRST PRESBYTERIAN CHURCH is one of the earliest Romanesque Revival churches in the state. The congregation was established in 1855 by the Reverend Charles LeDuc, brother of William LeDuc (1823–1917), prominent agriculturalist and Civil War figure. It was formally organized the following year, and the first church, built of stone, was erected at the same time. The church has had the distinction of having many of the town's business leaders as members.

In 1875 the congregation decided to build a new, larger structure, and work began that year. The superstructure was erected in 1876, but because of financial difficulties the church was not entirely finished for seven years, although it was completed to the point that services could be held in it by 1881, the year of its dedication. Total cost of construction amounted to $15,000.

The church is built of reddish brown brick on a base of smooth-dressed, buff-colored limestone. It has two towers of matching height today, but originally both were capped by truncated hipped roofs covered with wood shingles and metal cresting. In 1887 the top of the north tower was replaced with a wooden belfry and very tall, slender spire, which reached a height of nearly 125 feet, making it the tallest steeple in the state. The church itself measures 87 feet long and 52 feet wide. A parsonage, built in 1884, used to stand next door. It was razed in 1972.

In 1907 lightning struck the tall steeple and the subsequent fire gutted the church, leaving only the walls standing. The congregation determined to rebuild immediately and hired the prominent Minneapolis architect Harry W. Jones to design the restoration. Jones was given the task of rebuilding the church to look as much like the original as possible. The result of his work is the church as seen today, both inside and out.

The only alterations since Jones's restoration have been the addition of an education wing in 1962 and replacement of the coal furnace with a modern gas-fired heating plant in 1945.

Hay Creek (Goodhue County)

Immanuel Lutheran Church

24686 Old Church Road

Minnesota Highway 5; east on Old Church Road

Architect and builder unknown
1897
National Register of Historic Places

T HIS FINE LITTLE COUNTRY CHURCH is tucked in a picturesque setting amid the hills of southern Goodhue County. It stands in an area settled by German Lutheran farmers, who organized the congregation in 1858.

The present structure replaced an earlier church. It measures 36 feet wide and 58 feet long with a 12-foot-square tower projecting 6 feet from the front of the church. The four-sided louvered belfry is topped by a tall pedimented steeple. The front facade features a stained glass rose window. It is in the Gothic Revival style.

In 1975 an office and entry addition was built on the northeast corner, but by incorporating matching materials and a window removed from the old church, it does not detract from the appearance of the building, thus demonstrating that additions can be sympathetic when thoughtfully designed. The polygonal apse was restored by a parishioner a few years ago, giving the interior much more of the feeling of the original church.

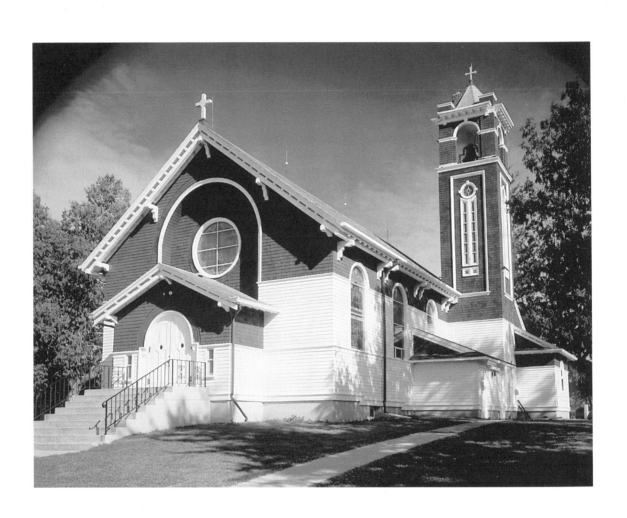

Church of the Annunciation

4996 Hazelwood Avenue (County Road 46)
John H. Wheeler, St. Paul, architect
1913
National Register of Historic Places

T HIS BEAUTIFUL CRAFTSMAN CHURCH is made even more picturesque by its bucolic setting in northern Rice County. It has clapboard-and-shingle siding with bands that divide the massing into three parts. Brackets, exposed rafter tails, round arches over the windows, and a highly ornamented corner tower are the principal design features. The tower is especially noteworthy for its detail: there is an open belfry with wood keystones, corner piers, brackets, and modillions. It is capped with an octagonal roof and metal cross. The front facade has a large circular stained glass window framed with a semicircular trim strip.

This church was built after the previous one was struck by lightning and burned to the ground on June 24, 1913. The architect, John H. Wheeler, designed a traditional masonry Catholic church for the mother parish, St. Dominic's in Northfield, and elected to create a more delicate structure in wood here. It was built by contractor Joseph Kump of Northfield at a cost of $12,000.

The first mass in the Hazelwood area was offered in private homes as early as 1850. The parish was organized as a mission of St. Dominic's in 1861, and a twenty-acre site was selected for the church. The men of the parish built a frame church in 1863, which was enlarged in 1874. A tower and belfry were built in 1884, and in 1903 the church received a new floor, new pews, and stained glass windows. All was lost in the fire of 1913, but from the ashes arose this wonderful country church, surely one of the finest in the state.

Church of the Sacred Heart

Ninth Street and Fourth Avenue
Parkinson and Dockendorff, La Crosse, Wisconsin, architects
1919–21
National Register of Historic Places

T HE AREA THAT WAS TO BECOME HERON LAKE in southwestern Minnesota was first settled in the 1860s. The town was platted by the St. Paul and Sioux City Railroad in 1872. As more people entered the area, the need for a church to serve the Catholic settlers, mostly Austrian and German immigrants, became more apparent. A frame structure was built about 1880 across the street from the present church, but it was demolished soon after in a windstorm. A replacement built a block away was of such poor construction that it had to be torn down, and services were held for a time in a private home.

In 1884 Father Anthony Ogulin arrived to become the first resident priest in Heron Lake. He brought with him two freight car loads of lumber donated by Bishop John Ireland for the construction of a church. William Timmons of Adrian built it in November and December, on the present site of Sacred Heart School. During the pastorate of Father Ogulin's successor, a tower was added to the church in the early 1890s.

When Father Mathias Jostock arrived in Heron Lake in December 1914, almost the first thing he heard from the parishioners was, "We want a new church." Father Jostock was from Trier, Germany, and he visualized a church in the baroque style of his homeland. The parish voted in October 1916 to build a new structure, but World War I and its attendant shortage of materials forced it to delay construction until 1919. Otto Neitge of Mankato was hired as contractor.

In April 1920, a huge celebration was held to mark the laying of the cornerstone. All the businesses in the town closed for the day, and there were band concerts, speeches, and a banquet. Another ceremony was held on January 12, 1921, when three bells were installed in the twin towers. One of them was cast in 1910 and had been salvaged from the old church; a second was donated by a local men's club in 1920; and the third was purchased from Breck College in Wilder, which was moving to St. Paul. This bell was cast in 1890 in Cincinnati, Ohio.

On July 21, 1921, as the interior was being finished and the dedication was being planned, the balcony collapsed, killing two workers and injuring two others. It was rebuilt and the dedication was held on August 24, officiated at by Bishop Patrick R. Heffron of the Diocese of Winona.

The church cost $150,000 to build. It is one of the most outstanding religious structures in southwestern Minnesota, designed in the Central European baroque style with neoclassical touches. Built of reinforced concrete with a brick veneer trimmed in stone, it is dominated by twin three-stage open bell towers with copper-covered octagonal caps topped by tall metal crosses. The double entrance doors are flanked by two pairs of Ionic columns that support an ornate pediment. Below the pediment is a colorful tile mosaic of the Virgin Mary. Thirteen stained glass windows, a crystal chandelier, and ornate communion rail were imported from Europe. The walls and ceiling of the nave are elaborately decorated with symbolic paintings. A mural over the altar unites the Old World and the New—St. Peter's in Rome and Sacred Heart in Heron Lake; the Roman Gate (Perta Nigra) of Trier, Germany; and Heron Lake's grain elevator, painted by a brother of Father Dobberstein, who built the famous Grotto of the Redemption in West Bend, Iowa. Later, when the mural was restored, the wooden grain elevator pictured in the original was replaced by a modern concrete grain terminal. Stone walls around the front of the church and the cemetery were added in the late 1920s.

Hibbing

Our Savior's Lutheran Church Pilgrim's Chapel

501 East Twenty-third Street
Robert Y. Sandberg, Hibbing, architect
1958

T HIS DISTINGUISHED LITTLE CHAPEL is one of the most visually interesting of any of the structures discussed here. It was built in 1958 from a design by Robert Y. Sandberg, as was the accompanying education wing. The chapel is an A-frame with its north end wall of stained glass forming the backdrop for the altar. The exterior consists of prefabricated metal panels that feature large triangular-shaped mosaics forming a triad of Christian symbols. Other mosaics on the adjacent education wing of the main church relate the story of Christ on earth. All were designed by Cyrus Running, director of art at Concordia College, Moorhead. The chapel was preconstructed and dismantled for shipment and reassembly at the site.

Our Savior's Lutheran Church was begun by pioneer Norwegian women whose families settled in the Hibbing area in the 1890s. The congregation was organized in 1903, and the following year the name was changed from Tabor to Our Savior's. It was incorporated in 1910, and in 1911 the first resident pastor arrived. Services were held in other area churches as well as in private homes and the public library. The first attempt to build a church ended in failure in 1920 owing to a lack of funds, and in the next two years the pastor recommended dissolving the congregation. In 1922, however, loans were taken out to buy an existing church in south Hibbing, Alice Union Church (Methodist), at Third Avenue West and Twenty-third Street. The building was extensively remodeled and redecorated in 1925, a basement dug under it with a cornerstone placed, and a parsonage was purchased. In 1945 lots were acquired for a new, larger church at Fifth Avenue East and Twenty-third Street, and in 1952 construction began on a building designed by Minneapolis architects Hills, Gilbertson, and Hayes. The rectilinear church with its 64-foot rectangular tower was finished a year later.

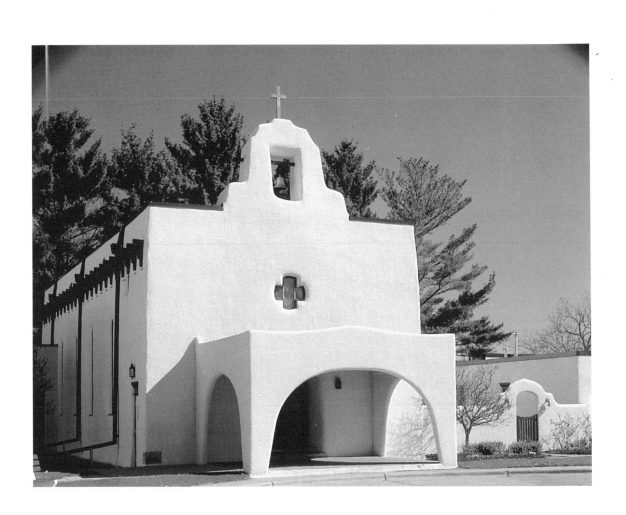

Lake St. Croix Beach

St. Francis of Assisi Catholic Church

16770 Thirteenth Street South
Bard and Vanderbilt, Minneapolis, architects
1938

ONE MAY WELL ASK what a Southwest Mission–style church is doing in eastern Minnesota amid pines and greenery near a picturesque river. Yet, here is just such a church, remarkably well preserved, and a very good copy of the simple Mission adobe structures that once thickly dotted the Southwest. It was designed at the insistence of the parish priest by Bard and Vanderbilt, the architects of Mayflower Community Church at Diamond Lake Road and Stevens Avenue in south Minneapolis (1928). It is entirely possible that the priest saw this Spanish colonial–style building (now a funeral home) and liked it and asked the same firm to create St. Francis.

The building is stuccoed and painted a gleaming white. It is rectangular with four slit windows on each side of the nave and sanctuary and faux beam ends protruding through the sides in the fashion of the adobe brick vernacular structures of the American Southwest. The entrance features an arched porte cochere. There is a bell tower on the front of the church and a cross-shaped opening in the middle of the front facade.

Lenora (Fillmore County)

Lenora United Methodist Pioneer Center

(originally Lenora Methodist Church)

Junction of County Roads 23 and 24
Architect and builder unknown
1856–66
National Register of Historic Places

METHODISM SPREAD TO MINNESOTA at a very early time. In 1845, the Minnesota conference was organized, and by 1854 a Methodist missionary, the Reverend Benjamin Crist, was including the as yet unplatted future town site of Lenora on his circuit between Chatfield and Brownsville. Meetings were conducted in homes until the next minister, Elder John L. Dyer, envisioned a town of Methodists and a grandiose church with an academy in the basement built on forty acres he donated from his claim. Work began on a stone building in the fall of 1856 and continued the following spring, with money raised from the sale of town lots in Lenora. But the Panic of 1857 fell hard on the region, and many people, discouraged by the difficult pioneer life and financial problems, pulled up stakes and returned to their former homes back east. Dyer, too, left and eventually ended up in Colorado, where he became known as the "Snowshoe Preacher."

Further work on the church was abandoned, leaving half-completed stone walls that stood for the next eight years. By 1865 prosperity had returned to the area, and work was resumed by a stonemason who used the material from the large uncompleted church. This much smaller structure was completed in 1866 and dedicated by the Reverend Daniel Cobb. In the 1870s, contrary to hopes and expectations, the railroad bypassed Lenora and the community declined.

The church has been preserved in a condition very close to its original frontier appearance. Only the roof and entry have been replaced (replicating the older one that fell into disrepair). There is no electricity: lighting is provided by two ceiling oil chandeliers and oil lamps in wall sconces. A wood stove is used for heat, there is an old-fashioned reed pump organ, and the original pews are still in place. At the front of the church is a raised dais with a spindle communion rail and a pulpit. The walls and ceiling are of painted tongue-in-groove bead molded boards. The church still has monthly services in the summer months, conducted by a pastor from Rochester.

Episcopal Church of Our Savior

113 Fourth Street Northeast
John Sutliff, Chicago, architect
1903

T HIS IS THE CONGREGATION'S THIRD CHURCH. The first was built about 1858, when the first Episcopal services were held in Little Falls. The second church was erected in 1869, and this one replaced it.

The church is a mixture of Gothic and Tudor styles, with fieldstone employed for the lower walls' foundation, and stucco (with embedded pebbles for decorative accent) and half-timbering on the upper portion. The corner tower is mainly of fieldstone, with quoined corners, and the entrance is through the base. The belfry is capped by a flared shingled roof surmounted by a cross.

Inside, the furnishings and decorative detailing are reminiscent of medieval Gothic. The altar paneling is in a triptych arrangement. The ceiling has exposed rafters interspersed with massive hammer beams.

The church was constructed by Louis Triplett, a local builder.

Our Lady of Lourdes Church

208 West Broadway
Victor Cordella, Minneapolis, architect
1922–23

T HIS BAROQUE-STYLE CHURCH is another distinguished product of Victor Cordella, who also designed Saints Cyril and Methodius and St. Mary's Ukrainian Orthodox Church in Minneapolis, Christ the King in Browerville, Saints Peter and Paul in Gilman, and probably St. Francis Xavier in Buffalo. Cordella seemed to specialize in working for Polish or Slavic congregations. He himself was from Poland and so knew well their customs and traditions and the styles of ecclesiastical architecture of Central Europe.

Our Lady of Lourdes parish was formed in 1917 by 120 Polish families living on the west side of the Mississippi River in Little Falls. They purchased the old Antlers Hotel that same year for $4,400 and used it for services, a rectory, and nuns' quarters. (It was demolished in 1951–52.) Cordella was employed as architect after the parish saw his church at Browerville. In 1922 construction began on the present church, and it was completed the following year. It seats about five hundred and measures 131 feet long and 80 feet wide at its widest point. The church is faced in light brown pressed brick trimmed in gray granite, resting on a concrete-and-stone foundation. The stained glass was manufactured by Witte Glass Company of St. Paul, and the sculpture was by St. Paul Statuary Company. In 1924 three bells were installed in the west tower (electrified in 1989). Wicks Organ Company of Highland, Illinois, built the pipe organ in 1941.

In 1952 a school and convent were built, and a year later the rectory was constructed adjacent to the church.

Mankato

First Presbyterian Church

220 Hickory Street East
Warren H. Hayes, Minneapolis, architect
1893–96
National Register of Historic Places

MANKATO IS ONE OF SEVERAL CITIES IN THE STATE that is rich in ecclesiastical architecture. It has numerous nineteenth- and early-twentieth-century churches that beautifully represent a variety of styles. Among them, First Presbyterian is one of the finest.

The church is built of locally quarried buff limestone. The style is Romanesque, which seemed to be the favorite choice of its designer, Warren H. Hayes. The result is a somewhat chunky edifice that looks and feels massive. It has a tall square corner tower and octagonal spire, with a smaller pyramidal tower and central lantern. Additions were made in 1927 and 1959, with a chapel being the last modification. The church's bell was purchased in 1857 by the Church Women Society and hung in two earlier buildings.

Inside, the church originally featured an Akron plan layout, with movable partitions between the auditorium and Sunday school rooms. In this church, these were replaced in later remodelings by permanent walls. The seating arrangement in the auditorium is semicircular with the altar in the northwest corner, another typical feature of Akron plan churches and Hayes's designs in particular. The Akron plan is said to have been devised in 1868 in Akron, Ohio, by a Methodist Sunday school superintendent named Lewis Miller and architect Jacob Snyder. Hayes adopted the design and used it repeatedly in his churches to good and lasting effect. One may see it today not only in First Presbyterian but also in First Congregational Church and Wesley United Methodist Church in Minneapolis and in Central Presbyterian Church and Zion Lutheran Church, both in St. Paul, all dating from the late 1800s.

Mankato was founded by families from St. Paul in 1852. General John C. Fremont, the famous army explorer and onetime candidate for president, camped at the town site in 1857. The town subsequently became a major railroad, lumber milling, and manufacturing center. The region north of town was discovered to be rich in limestone, and several quarries have flourished there, providing building materials for literally thousands of structures throughout the state.

Church of St. Mary

(originally Church of St. Boniface)

211 Fifth Avenue Southeast
A. E. Hussey and George Bergmann, St. Cloud, architects
1898
National Register of Historic Places

Stearns County has the largest percentage of catholics of any county in the United States. This is clearly evident in its numerous Catholic churches, many of them of grand proportions. St. Mary's is one of the largest in the Diocese of St. Cloud, which covers the center of the state.

The area around Melrose was settled by Irish railroad workers, who established the first parish, called the Church of St. Patrick, in 1872. German farmers followed them, and by 1876 a second parish, St. Boniface, was formed. In 1898 the Germans erected this church, either to outdo the Irish or in hopes that the diocese would relocate to Melrose if a big enough structure were built. They may have succeeded in the former goal, but not in the latter. The diocese remains in St. Cloud.

The church dominates the skyline and is in turn dominated by its distinctive twin towers topped by metal domes and crosses, which are 130 feet in overall height. It is built of red brick trimmed in local gray granite above the three entrance doors on the front facade, and a foundation of the same granite. It is 180 feet long and 70 feet high, and is in a mixed Gothic and high baroque style with Bavarian antecedents. The adjacent rectory was built at the same time of the same materials.

Interior furnishings are impressive, as one would expect in a church of this magnitude (see Plate 2). The arched ceiling was designed for excellent sound convection. It is painted in blue with cream-colored columns and walls trimmed in gilt. The high altar and side altars were built in Germany and assembled on-site. They are brown with gilt trim. The sixteen stained glass windows in the nave are spectacular, including an intriguing Eye-of-God window on the south side.

In 1958 the Irish and German parishes merged, and the name changed from St. Boniface to St. Mary's. Statues of Saints Patrick and Boniface are enshrined on the high altar, with that of St. Patrick being mounted on a small platform to put him at the same height as St. Boniface.

Millville (Wabasha County)

Swedish Evangelical Lutheran Church

Bridge Street
Congregation-built
1874
National Register of Historic Places

MILLVILLE WAS ORIGINALLY CALLED LONG CREEK, and the area was settled by Swedes in the 1860s. The congregation was organized in 1869, but because of depressed farm prices, it could not afford to build a church. Finally, in 1874, enough money had been scraped together to purchase minimal materials—stone and lumber—for this church. It was erected by the men of the congregation, using buff-colored Oneota stone quarried on the land of one of the members. All interior furnishings were made by hand. The total cost of materials was $802.60, a staggering amount for this poor rural congregation. Miss Elisa Hack of Wabasha lent $400 to help pay for the church, but the congregation remained so poor that it saw no hope of ever repaying her. One of the members was dispatched to Wabasha in 1879 to persuade Miss Hack to cancel the debt, and she did.

The little church continued to have a rather rocky history. The congregation dwindled in the 1880s and 1890s as families moved farther west in search of new, richer lands. Many of the original Swedish members were replaced by Norwegians who used the church until 1914. It continued to be used by other groups up to 1967, when it was finally abandoned and sat derelict until being purchased and restored by the Millville Historical Association in the late 1970s. It is not now used on a regular basis, but is well maintained in near-original condition by the historical group.

The church is classified by historians as "functional Gothic Revival," which means it is so simple and unrefined in its Gothic accoutrements as to be almost totally unitarian in appearance. It is symmetrical in plan and massing, its one room lighted by eight windows with pointed arches. The main entrance is a double door made of wood planks; a "pastor's entrance" opens at the back near the pulpit. The church is heated by a wood stove exhausted through a brick chimney straddling the rear of the gable roof. The building measures 40 feet by 28 feet by 12 feet high, and the stone walls are 2 feet thick. The handmade pulpit and pews are original.

About 1881, a board fence was put up around the church after the congregation was bothered by cows from the adjacent pasture sticking their noses in the windows during services. A small cemetery is at the rear of the lot. A stone over the entrance reads: "Swedish:Ev:Luth: Church.1874."

Minneapolis

Basilica of St. Mary

88 North Seventeenth Street
Emmanuel L. Masqueray, St. Paul, architect
1908–25
National Register of Historic Places

T HE BASILICA OF ST. MARY IS VERY MUCH A LANDMARK in Minneapolis. It occupies a prominent site at the southwest end of the downtown business district, alongside Interstates 94 and the beginning (or end, depending on your direction of travel) of 394. Along with the Cathedral of St. Paul, it is a potent reminder of the strength and power of the Catholic Church in the Twin Cities, past and present.

The new church was proposed by Archbishop John Ireland in 1905, while Emmanuel L. Masqueray was preparing the plans for the Cathedral of St. Paul. Masqueray had been handpicked by the archbishop to design the cathedral and was asked if he would also design the Pro-Cathedral of the Immaculate Conception (as the basilica was named until its dedication in the mid-1920s). The site was donated by the Donaldson department store family, and the cornerstone was laid on May 31, 1908.

The style selected by Masqueray, a devoted practitioner of beaux-arts tenets, is late French Renaissance, as best seen in the broad-naved cathedrals at Albi and Cahors. The exterior is Renaissance and baroque, evident in the twin entrance towers and the major tower and dome over the sanctuary. Masqueray strayed from the simplicity he so admired in the French cathedrals by introducing a certain degree of exaggeration in the treatment of details and overall form, which characterized much of the turn-of-the-century beaux-arts architecture in the United States.

The foundation is of Rockville granite, and the 70-foot exterior walls are sheathed in vibrant white Vermont granite, a building material three times stronger than marble and the same stone used on the Wisconsin State Capitol. A colonnaded portico forms the main entrance, flanked by twin towers. The east tower holds a 3,000-pound bell—dedicated by Bishop Ireland in 1877—transferred from old Immaculate Conception Church, which the basilica replaced. Above the entrance is a rose window 15 feet in diameter, and at the roofline is a gable containing a figure of the Virgin Mary, to whom the church is dedicated. Five arched windows in bays on each side of the nave provide light; there are sixty stained glass windows in the basilica.

The dimensions of the structure are as awe-inspiring as the design. It measures 120 by 278 feet; the entrance towers are 22 feet square and 133 feet in height; the dome is 61 feet square and soars to a height of 187 feet; the nave is 140 feet long, 42 feet wide, with a ceiling height of 75 feet. The nave vault is not supported by the interior cornice, but rather is hung from five iron girders that support the concrete roof. The interior is lighted by the huge rose window in the front (street) facade and round-headed windows in each of the bays of the nave (see Plate 12). A new lighting system was designed and installed in the 1980s by Rambusch Studios of New York that is subdued yet beautifully highlights the interior details.

The exterior was finished in 1915, but another decade was required to complete the interior furnishings. Masqueray died in 1917 and did not live to see either this church or the Cathedral of St. Paul completed: both were finished by Maginnis and Walsh of Boston, one-time competitors for the cathedral commission.

The church has been subject to several restorations of varying degrees. The recent ones appear to have successfully addressed the persistent roof leaks that often plagued many Masqueray churches. He seems never to have understood that one could not transfer the steep, oblique roof angles of churches in his warmer native France to the harsh Minnesota winters and avoid the damaging ice dams and subsequent leakage.

On the same block as the basilica is a priests' residence built in 1927, a three-story school dating from 1912–13, and a convent of more recent vintage. In a sharp departure from tradition, the inner-city congregation has initiated rock music concerts on one weekend in the summer, and they have proved to be effective fund-raisers.

Photograph by Michael Jensen

Minneapolis

Christ Church Lutheran

3244 Thirty-fourth Avenue South
Saarinen, Saarinen, and Associates, Bloomfield Hills, Michigan, architects
Hills, Gilbertson, and Hayes, Minneapolis, associate architects
1949–50
National Register of Historic Places

C HRIST CHURCH LUTHERAN is among the finest modern church designs to be found anywhere in Minnesota. It was one of the last buildings designed by Eliel Saarinen (1873–1950) with his son, Eero (1911–61), and is their only church structure in the state.

The Reverend William A. Buege persuaded the congregation to build a simple, "honest" church instead of the "mini-Gothic cathedral" they had wanted. He contacted Eliel Saarinen at Cranbrook Academy to design a church and then traveled to Michigan to personally seek his acceptance of the commission. Saarinen agreed and designed the church in what was to be the last year of his life. By a strange stroke of fate, Eero Saarinen created the adjoining education building in the last year of his life, 1961.

The distinguished historian and critic Henry-Russell Hitchcock called the church "cool, clear, and rational." It has strong rectilinear form, almost verging on the severe. Because of the necessity to keep costs as low as possible, the Saarinens designed a relatively simple structure, from which almost all exterior ornamentation is stripped. It sits quietly, unobtrusively, in its residential neighborhood. Even the 88-foot bell tower does not attract attention.

The sanctuary, which can seat up to 750, is a rectangular box of brick and Mankato stone on the exterior with a brick interior. It has been acclaimed both for the excellence of its acoustics as well as for the "quietly dramatic" natural light that enters through narrow windows. Energy is thus conserved by the limited use of glass in the sanctuary. The 16-foot cross over the altar is lighted by a window hidden from the congregation, so that its shadow falls on the light brick walls. There are no parallel surfaces in the interior walls; each of them either curves, slants, or undulates, and thus cleverly eliminates echoing or "flutter" produced by sound bouncing off parallel walls (see Plate 5). The ceiling is composed of acoustical tile and is suspended from the roof by metal hangers. The choir loft and organ are located in the rear, above the chapel. The adjacent rectangular tower is

connected to the sanctuary by a glass-enclosed link, and the sanctuary is connected to the 1962 classroom addition (also by Eero Saarinen) by a courtyard and gallery.

Victor Gilbertson, who supervised the work locally for the Saarinens, later said that they only visited Minneapolis to inspect the job. Their young students at Cranbrook drew the plans and made many mistakes that Gilbertson's firm had to correct.

A problem arose during the interior decoration concerning the painting of the brick wall behind the altar. The specifications called for it to be painted white, and Joe Lacey, the Saarinens' representative, said that a lead-and-oil-base off-white paint should be used. Two coats were applied to provide an adequate cover. When Eero Saarinen visited the site shortly thereafter, he saw the wall and protested, "This won't do at all." He said that he wanted the bricks to show through the paint and did not intend them to be completely covered. Gilbertson put four men to work for a week with paint remover and scrapers and brushes to remove the paint. He said that other architecture firms later called him to ask how that finish had been specified. Gilbertson would laugh and say, "Are you sitting down? Are you ready for this?" and then would proceed to tell them it had evolved from a mistake.

A few years after its completion, a panel of thirty-five architects and church leaders named Christ Church Lutheran their first choice for architectural excellence among all U.S. churches built since 1930. It also won a twenty-five-year award in 1977 from the American Institute of Architects.

Minneapolis

Church of Saints Cyril and Methodius

1315 Second Street Northeast
Victor Cordella, Minneapolis, architect
1916–17

T HE CHURCH OF SAINTS CYRIL AND METHODIUS began in 1891 with the incorporation of the parish. It followed by three years the formation of the Saints Cyril and Methodius Lodge, a benevolent fraternal society, which started a fund for a church. A site for the new structure was purchased on the southeast corner of Sixteenth Avenue and Main Street Northeast, and construction had already begun when the lodge was told it needed the permission of Archbishop John Ireland. A delegation met with Ireland, who granted his permission for their incorporation but refused to allow the church to be named for *two* saints, saying one was enough. Thus, the parish initially was called the Church of St. Cyril, and the name seems not to have been officially changed until the 1980s.

Ireland was also responsible for recruiting the parish's first priest, the Reverend John Zavadan. Father Zavadan arrived in January 1893, and immediately moved ahead with plans for the construction of a church; a wood frame structure was erected that year. A rectory was built in 1904, which, along with the church, was moved in 1909 to the southeast corner of Thirteenth Avenue and Third Street Northeast because of expansion of the Northern Pacific Railroad yards in the area. That church was demolished in 1922.

The rapid growth of the parish mandated a larger building, and in 1916 construction began on the present structure. It was dedicated in September 1917 by Bishop James O'Reilly of the Diocese of Fargo.

The style of the church is described as classic Renaissance. It is clad in dark brown brick with a tall central tower topped by a copper belvedere. This church is a virtual duplicate of St. Francis Xavier Catholic Church in Buffalo, Minnesota, built about two years earlier. The interior features a barrel-vaulted ceiling with a modern altar table and a minimum of decorative detail compared with what existed up to the 1950s. The lighter colors and less ornate ornamentation relieve the church of the heaviness that originally characterized it.

Minneapolis

Hennepin Avenue United Methodist Church

511 Groveland Avenue
Hewitt and Brown, Minneapolis, architects
1916

T HE CONGREGATION OF THIS CHURCH BEGAN as part of Centenary Methodist Episcopal Church, which stood on Seventh Street between First (later, Marquette) and Second Avenues South in Minneapolis in 1866. In 1875 part of the congregation broke away and formed Hennepin Avenue M. E. Sunday School (soon after voting to rename themselves a "church"); they built their first structure, a wooden "tabernacle" at Eighth Street and First Avenue North, in 1876.

The following year property was donated on the southwest corner of the intersection of Tenth Street and Hennepin Avenue to which the tabernacle was moved. It continued in use until 1881, when the growing congregation built its "Red Brick Church," designed by Jacob Snyder of Akron, Ohio. The tabernacle was sold to Portland Avenue Church of Christ and moved to Grant Street and Portland Avenue, where it remained for several years until being demolished to make way for a new structure. The Red Brick Church was always unpopular with the congregation because of its inadequate ventilation and heating—too hot in summer, too cold and drafty in winter. In the 1890s, it had part of its front entry trimmed off during the widening of Hennepin Avenue.

In 1911 the church was sold to real estate developer Harry Pence. Hennepin Avenue Methodist Episcopal Church bought the building occupied by Fowler M. E. Church on Dupont near Franklin Avenue (designed by Warren Hayes of Minneapolis in 1898), and the two congregations merged. T. B. Walker donated part of his homestead above Loring Park as the site of a new expanded church. The firm of Hewitt and Brown of Minneapolis was retained to design it (Edwin Hewitt was the design partner—he had earlier served as architect of St. Mark's Episcopal Cathedral just a block away), and the church was finished in 1916. The old Fowler church was sold to the Scottish Rite of the Masonic Order; it still exists as one part of a much-enlarged structure at Dupont and Franklin.

Hennepin Avenue United Methodist Church is built in the English Gothic style. It is modeled on Ely Cathedral in England, which Hewitt himself journeyed to study before designing this church. The inspiration for the spire rising directly above the crossing is borrowed from Ely; when built, it was the second-tallest structure in Minneapolis (only the clock tower on City Hall was

higher). It is 238 feet from the sidewalk to the top of the spire. The exterior is faced in soft gray Bedford limestone; the interior ceiling and walls are lined with Gustavino tile for sound absorbency. Pews, altar, and balconies are of white oak (see Plate 11). The main auditorium is based on the Akron plan, with radial seating for 1,600 set at an angle to the walls. The building measures 220 feet in length, 130 feet at its greatest width. When completed, it cost $420,000.

In the late 1960s, a tunnel was constructed adjacent to the church to carry Interstate 94 under the intersection of Hennepin and Lyndale Avenues and Lowry Hill. To ensure that the tunnel walls would not collapse during construction and thus threaten possible structural damage to the church, the ground around the tunnel was frozen with special refrigeration equipment. The process was successful, and the church did not suffer any structural damage. Time will tell, however, whether the unceasing rumble of heavy traffic through the tunnel will result in problems for the church. In 1999 the always troublesome intersection of Hennepin and Lyndale Avenues was yet again rebuilt to alleviate traffic jams and reduce accidents. The construction, which took place immediately adjacent to the church, seems not to have affected it.

Lakewood Cemetery Chapel

3600 Hennepin Avenue
Harry W. Jones, Minneapolis, architect (exterior)
Charles R. Lamb, New York, architect (interior)
1908–10
National Register of Historic Places

THIS ELEGANT CHAPEL is situated on the grounds of the largest and one of the oldest cemeteries in the Twin Cities. The site of the cemetery, overlooking Lakes Calhoun and Harriet, was purchased in 1871 by a group of Minneapolis businessmen, including Dorilus Morrison, Thomas Lowry, William D. Washburn, Samuel C. Gale, and William King, to be used by all the citizens of the city.

The chapel was designed by Harry W. Jones, a popular architect of his day, in the Byzantine style and is highly reminiscent of the great sixth-century church of Hagia Sophia in Istanbul. The building is faced in St. Cloud granite, the dome and roof are clad with Gustavino tile, with Spanish roll tile on the outer roofing.

The interior, designed by the New York architect Charles R. Lamb, is modeled after San Marco (St. Mark's) Cathedral in Venice and is covered with ten million tiles forming a rich panorama of mosaic art, designed in part by Lamb's wife, Ellie Condie Lamb (see Plate 9). Six Italian artists were brought to Minneapolis to lay the mosaic tiles. There are twenty-four windows (representing twenty-four hours in the day) that act as a sundial: the time can be told by which window the light is shining through. The dome is 65 feet high and features tiles of gold leaf laid under glass to prevent tarnishing. The chapel seats two hundred and has such excellent acoustics that speakers at the rostrum can be heard almost perfectly everywhere in the room without the aid of a microphone.

An inscription at the base of the dome, executed in Teco pottery and gold mosaics, reads, "Until the day break and the shadows flee away." Teco was a trademark for the finely wrought pottery manufactured by the American Terra Cotta and Ceramic Company of Chicago. The company also made terra-cotta ornaments for building exteriors, which may be seen on such structures as the Grain Exchange at Fourth Avenue and Fourth Street in Minneapolis, the Merchants National Bank in Winona, and the former Farmers and Merchants Bank in Hector.

Plymouth Congregational Church

1900 Nicollet Avenue
Shepley, Rutan, and Coolidge, Boston, architects
1907–9

T HE PLYMOUTH CONGREGATION WAS ORGANIZED IN 1857, predominantly by New Englanders who had migrated to Minneapolis. The following year, they erected their first meetinghouse at Nicollet and Fourth Street. The women of the congregation were energized to the temperance cause by their pastor, the Reverend Henry Nichols, and undertook a crusade to close local saloons. Shortly afterward, the church was burned in a mysterious fire. The old church was quickly replaced in 1863 by a larger structure, which served unscathed until it was outgrown and an even larger and more grandiose building, designed by Russell Sturgis of New York, was constructed at the corner of Nicollet and Eighth Street in 1875. The present Plymouth Congregational Church was built in 1907 when commercial growth in the downtown area made the site of the old church highly desirable property. It was sold for $223,000, which covered all but $7,000 of the cost of construction and furnishing of the new building.

Shepley, Rutan, and Coolidge of Boston were retained as architects. This firm succeeded to the practice of Henry Hobson Richardson, the famous designer of many outstanding buildings in all parts of the eastern half of the United States and progenitor of the widespread Richardsonian Romanesque style that flourished through the 1880s. The architects selected English Rural Gothic as the style for the new church. The Congregational Church at Newton Centre, Massachusetts, was the direct inspiration for Plymouth. Seam-faced granite quarried at St. Cloud was used in construction, and window traceries are of buff-colored Bedford (Indiana) limestone.

The sanctuary is built in the shape of a cross, with an open timber roof of hammer beam construction. Rich oak paneling gives warmth and a feeling of intimacy. As many as eleven hundred people may be seated in the sanctuary. The setting of the pulpit is central and elevated in the spirit of Congregationalist tradition, in which the heart of public worship is held to be the proclamation of the gospel through the preaching ministry.

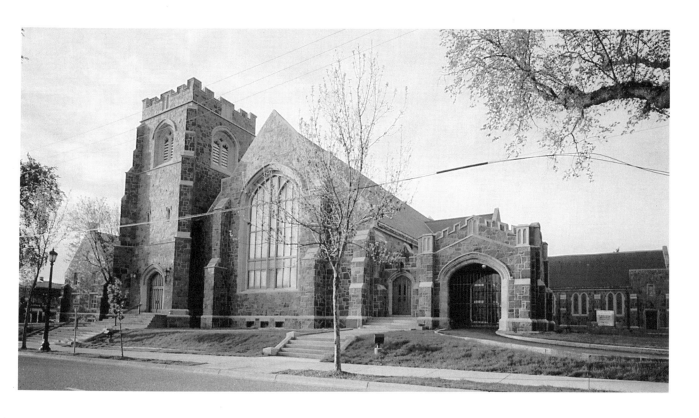

Several additions have been made to the original church and Guild Hall, beginning in the late 1940s. These house classrooms, chapels, a library, dining rooms, recreational space, and offices. All have been built to replicate the style of the original structure and are faced with the same St. Cloud granite.

Redeemer Missionary Baptist Church

(originally Stewart Memorial Church)

116 East Thirty-second Street
Purcell and Feick, Minneapolis, architects
1909
National Register of Historic Places

T HE PARTNERSHIP OF WILLIAM G. PURCELL AND GEORGE FEICK JR. began in
Minneapolis in 1907. Purcell had once worked in the office of the prestigious Chicago architect Louis Sullivan and had absorbed that great man's philosophy of "progressive" architecture, today known as the Prairie School.

Sullivan has been called the "father" of the Prairie School. It was his principles of design that formed the basic tenets of the style: emphasis on horizontality; use of earth tones that mimicked the hues of the prairie; openness in the interior plan; "honesty" (i.e., the requirement that the exteriors of buildings reflect their purpose, or "form follows function"); and judicious use of complex, intricate ornament based on geometrical and vegetative shapes that served to make buildings beautiful, not gaudy.

Stewart Memorial Church was designed by Purcell and clearly demonstrates his ability to work in the Prairie School idiom. It is one of very few Prairie School churches built in America and recalls Frank Lloyd Wright's Unity Temple in Chicago, finished in 1906. Purcell grew up a Presbyterian in Oak Park, Illinois, where he had ample opportunity to watch Wright houses being constructed. He decided on a truly unique building for the congregation that was based, he said, on "my own Presbyterian conscience to crystallize church experience."

Like Unity Temple, Stewart Memorial features the same flat roof, wide overhanging eaves, and a delightful sense of lightness and roominess in the sanctuary—a clear response to the needs of the congregation for versatility and flexibility (see Plate 4). The sanctuary opens directly into the Sunday school wing, which was designed by another firm in 1915. Stewart Memorial exudes warmth through the use of inviting colors and materials. Ornament was kept to a minimum, mainly to save money.

The church was named after the Reverend David Stewart, a pastor at First Presbyterian Church in Minneapolis, from which Stewart Memorial's congregation came. This is the second church on the site. The first was built about 1885 at Third Avenue and Thirty-second Street, then moved one block east between 1890 and 1895, to the back of the lot at Thirty-second and Stevens. The congregation quickly set about raising funds for a new structure and was finally able to go ahead with construction by 1909.

An interesting story connected with the construction of the church concerns the contractor Purcell hired to install the plumbing and heating equipment. The man was blind, and he surprised Purcell by supervising the work every day, climbing over the trenches and scaffolds on the site without falling. His daughter read the drawings to him, pushing his finger over them to locate walls, doors, and pipes. Remarkably, he was able to memorize all the details.

An exact copy of Stewart Memorial was built by the Bohemian Presbyterian Church in Hopkins. It burned around 1930 and was replaced by a more conventional structure designed by Minneapolis architect J. V. Vanderbilt, which Purcell considered a "very good looking church."

Stewart Memorial Church recently underwent an extensive restoration.

St. Constantine's Ukrainian Catholic Church

University Avenue and Fifth Street Northeast
Hills, Gilbertson, and Fisher, Minneapolis, architects
1970–72

S T. CONSTANTINE'S IS A HIGHLY SUCCESSFUL TRANSLATION of ancient Byzantine or Near Eastern Christian buildings into a workable modern style. It is constructed of tan brick surmounted by five domes; the large central dome is covered with polychrome mosaic tile in which religious symbols are worked in golden yellow against a blue background. It is a memorial to the youth of the parish. Victor Gilbertson designed the mosaic tile dome and said he had to use a great deal of long-forgotten mathematics to figure out the size of the pieces. He also said that the church's governing board was so pleased with the building that he has been invited back on special occasions to take part in celebrations.

The first Ukrainian immigrants arrived in Minneapolis in 1878, and in succeeding years they worshiped in halls or in other churches. In 1912, with about fifty families in the city, a small group met to discuss organizing the first Ukrainian Greek Catholic parish. A short time later, they rented a hall at Twenty-second Avenue and Fifth Street Northeast to serve as a temporary place of worship. The following year, they purchased a lot at the corner of Sixth Street and University Avenue Northeast and began building a church in the summer of 1913. This original structure was designed by the Minneapolis architect Victor Cordella at a cost of $20,000 to build and furnish. A school was constructed in 1956.

In 1964 the parish was told by city officials that its old church had to be remodeled to conform to building codes or it would be condemned. The parishioners decided that rather than spend a sizable sum to rejuvenate the old structure, they would raise money for a new one. A site at University Avenue and Fifth Street Northeast was purchased in 1968. Ground was broken for the new church on November 1, 1970, and it was completed two years later. The cornerstone from the old building was repolished and engraved with the name of the church in English and Ukrainian and installed in the new building.

St. Mary's Orthodox Cathedral

1701 Fifth Street Northeast
Boehme and Cordella, Minneapolis, architects
1905–6

S T. MARY'S ORTHODOX CATHEDRAL is based on the cathedral in Omsk, Russia, and
others in the former Soviet Union, and initially it served a population of Carpatho-Russian
immigrants in Minneapolis, who began arriving in 1877. Most found work in the railroad shops
and flour and lumber mills, and by 1887 they numbered about eighty people in all. They came
from a religious tradition called Uniate or Greek Catholic, which was Orthodox up to the late
sixteenth century when it was forced to unite with the Roman Catholic Church. However, the
Uniate Church retained the Byzantine rite (meaning it did not use Latin in its ritual) and allowed
clergy to marry, a sharp departure from the Roman Catholic or Latin rite.

The Carpatho-Russians lacked a church of their own in Minneapolis until 1887, when construction began on a simple wood frame structure on the site of the present church. It was
completed in 1889 and served until it burned in 1904. In 1889 Father Alexis Toth arrived from
Czechoslovakia to become the first resident priest and immediately ran afoul of Archbishop John
Ireland for having been married (Toth was widowed by this time) and not adhering to the Latin
rite of the Roman Catholic Church. Ireland refused to give him jurisdiction to work in the archdiocese, to which Toth responded that he did not need it under the laws of the Catholic Church.
Thus, St. Mary's became Orthodox and has remained so to the present time.

The new church, designed by Victor Cordella, rose on the site of the old, built at a cost of
about $40,000, of which $1,029 was donated by Czar Nicholas II. For more than a year, the
building stood as an empty shell, lacking furnishings, decoration, and even boilers for heat. In
addition, the parish was deeply in debt because of the cost of the new building. Gradually, the
church was furnished and decorated, and central heating was installed after the winter of 1907–8.

The church is clad in brick with a tall tower in the center of the front facade, topped by a copper-
clad spire. (The spire was blown off in a windstorm in 1967 and replaced.) Over the crossing is
a hexagonal drum capped by a hexagonal dome with a gold cross. The interior seats six hundred
(pews were not installed until 1934) and underwent a major redecoration in 1982. A chapel, named
for St. Andrew, was built alongside the church in 1966, and new front steps were installed in 1979.
The parish hall, designed by architect Benjamin Gingold of Minneapolis, was erected in 1957.

Minneapolis

Wesley United Methodist Church

Marquette Avenue and Grant Street
Warren H. Hayes, Minneapolis, architect
1891
National Register of Historic Places

T HE PARISHIONERS OF WESLEY UNITED METHODIST CHURCH call it the "Mother Church of Minneapolis Methodism" because it gave rise to ten United Methodist churches in the city.

Methodism first appeared in the fledgling settlement of St. Anthony in 1852. A small congregation was founded by the Reverend Alfred Godfrey, brother of pioneer sawmill operator Ard Godfrey, whose frame house stands today in Centennial Park at the corner of University and Central Avenues in southeast Minneapolis.

The cornerstone of the present Wesley United Methodist Church was laid on March 2, 1891. On that day, a procession led by board members walked from Centenary, the old church at the corner of Seventh Street and First Avenue South, to the site of the new one five blocks south at Grant Street and First Avenue South (now Marquette Avenue). Among the marchers was the church's architect, Warren Howard Hayes, one of the leading designers in the city. He was a member of First Methodist Episcopal Church at University Avenue and Second Street Southeast, on the east side of the Mississippi River, in old St. Anthony.

Wesley is highly characteristic of Hayes's later designs. It is strongly Richardsonian Romanesque in style, its solid appearance rendered more dramatic by the use of rugged ashlar-finished Minnesota granite and a greater proportion of wall space to window openings. The interior is oriented around a diagonal or Akron plan. The auditorium is turned about forty-five degrees from true, causing it to run diagonally across the shell of the church. Flexibility is a key feature of the Akron plan, whereby side rooms may be either opened or closed off from the auditorium by means of large overhead doors.

Wesley is one of the best preserved of all Hayes's Minneapolis churches because of a 1990 restoration that brought back much of its original interior and exterior appearance. Original plans called

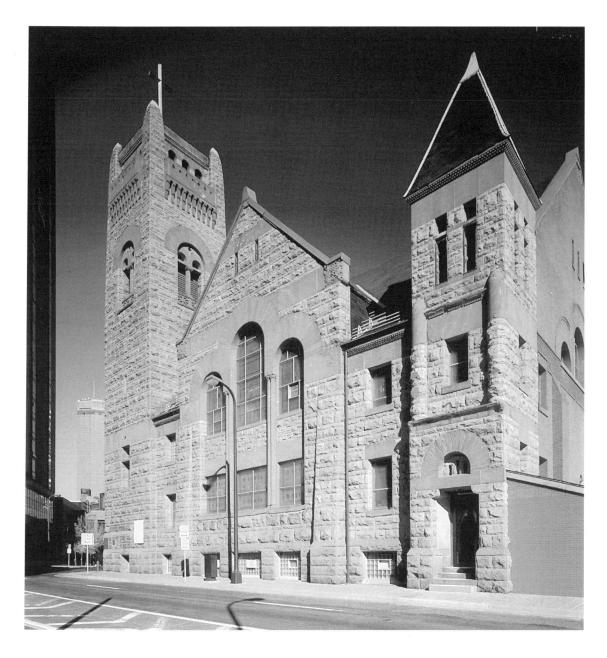

for an enormously ambitious project to erect a "skyscraper church" on an adjacent site in 1928. However, only the first phase of this mammoth project was ever constructed, the Wesley Temple Building, one of a matching pair of office structures flanking a soaring Gothic Revival central tower. The Wesley Temple Building was razed in 1988 to make way for the Minneapolis Convention Center. Fortunately, Wesley United Methodist Church was spared from the wrecking ball.

Minneota (Lyon County)

St. Paul's Lutheran Church

First and Grant Streets
Architect and builder unknown
1895
National Register of Historic Places

THIS BEAUTIFUL LITTLE CHURCH is one of the state's finest examples of Carpenter Gothic ecclesiastical architecture. The building is clean and pure in its pristine whiteness, although appearing a bit stubby because of its higher roofline and the fact that the entrance tower is immediately adjacent to the transept.

St. Paul's serves the second-largest Icelandic community in the United States. Immigrants began entering the area in 1875, and by 1900 there were one thousand living there. Of four churches built in the early 1890s, this is the only survivor.

Although the first pastor, Niels Steingrimur Thorkalsson, arrived in 1887, a building committee was not formed until 1895 and given authority to proceed with construction of a church. Ground was broken that fall and the church was finished in December. Pastor Thorkalsson had resigned earlier that year, and the building was seen to completion by his successor, B. B. Jonson.

The church has a limestone foundation and is of frame construction with lap siding; a square three-story tower and belfry and octagonal steeple rise above the entrance. Inside there is a Gothic altar and semicircular communion rail. The walls were papered until the 1950s, but lack of heat in the church during the week caused the paper to deteriorate to the point of having to be replaced. Celotex (a soundproofing material made of large square tiles of compressed shredded paper) was subsequently used as covering for the walls and ceiling.

Minnetonka Beach (Hennepin County)

St. Martin's By-the-Lake
(originally Camp Memorial Chapel)

2801 Westwood Road
Cass Gilbert, St. Paul, architect
1888

C ASS GILBERT LEFT A RICH LEGACY of churches in Minnesota, and this is certainly among his finest. He executed this church in a mix of Shingle, Queen Anne, and Craftsman styles, creating a very handsome little building that has been lovingly cared for by its Episcopal congregation down to the present day. The building was moved in 1950 from its original location two hundred yards northwest of its present site, and its name was changed from Camp Memorial Chapel to St. Martin's By-the-Lake.

The interior is furnished in dark-stained wood, with wainscoting up to the window sills. The ends of the pews are unusually tall and the backs are formed of horizontal planks with openings between them, evocative of park benches that one might see in a resort area such as Minnetonka. The ceiling is supported by open trusses ending in hammer beams. The windows are small and square and filled with delicate, but not ostentatious, stained glass. A fine trefoil stained glass window is in the peak of the roof above the simple altar. In 1980–81 a choir loft was added at the rear (entrance end). The original porch was removed and then rebuilt when the work was finished.

Camp Memorial Chapel was built by Major George A. Camp (1830–92). Camp was born in Charlotte, New York, and moved to St. Anthony in 1851 to work for his uncle, Anson Northrup, in the lumber business. After the Civil War, Camp returned to St. Anthony and served in the Minnesota legislature until 1876, after which he entered partnership with T. B. Walker in sawmilling. About 1880 the Camp family moved to Lake Minnetonka and, after their first home burned down, lived in a mansion that today stands immediately to the west of the church. Camp decided to build a chapel for the wedding of his only surviving child, Lucy, and hired Cass Gilbert, who was not only an Episcopalian but also a rising star in the architecture field.

When the chapel was moved in 1950, it was relocated to land donated by General Charles McClellan Reeve, commander of a Minnesota unit in the Spanish-American War. Reeve's house was demolished a year later, and the lumber was reused to construct the rectory adjacent to the church. The rectory has also been torn down. General Reeve died in 1947, seven weeks short of his one hundredth birthday. After the church was moved, St. Martin's became first a mission church and finally, in 1954, an independent parish.

Monticello

Community United Methodist Church
(originally Simpson Methodist Episcopal Church)

Lynn and West Fourth Streets
John Gallo, Monticello, builder
1857
National Register of Historic Places

UNTIL RECENTLY, THIS WAS THE OLDEST METHODIST CHURCH BUILDING in continuous use in the state. It was organized in 1855 by the Reverend Samuel Creighton.

The church was intentionally placed in a central location in Monticello. Local carpenter John Gallo contracted to build it at a cost of $945. It was the seventh Methodist church to be erected in Minnesota.

The building is Greek Revival in style, which was dying out back East but still very much in vogue in Minnesota. It has corner pilasters, turned eaves, and a rectangular—almost square—outline with a shed roof, all typical of Greek Revival. This building—like the First United Methodist Church in Taylors Falls (1861) and First Congregational Church in Zumbrota (1862)—possesses that same New England picturesqueness that makes these churches so appealing. They seem especially fresh and clean in their white-painted lap siding and, where present, simple square or rectangular towers and sharply pointed steeples.

There has been a succession of alterations to the church over the intervening 146 years, but none so severe that it has detracted from the integrity of this wonderful little building. The bell tower is clearly of a later vintage because of the bracketing under its eaves, which is not characteristic of Greek Revival structures, and, indeed, it was added in 1880, at the same time that the interior was remodeled and the tiny three-row balcony was removed, a back room added, and a furnace installed. But the congregation had to wait eighteen years for a bell. In 1898 Mrs. Annie McCord donated a bell to the church, and it still hangs in the steeple. In 1913 the building was raised and a full basement was excavated. The sanctuary was remodeled in 1954, and new pews were installed. Seven years later a brick education wing was built, joined to the original church by a narrow concourse. In 1962 the Historical Society of the Methodist Conference recognized

Simpson Methodist Episcopal as the oldest Methodist church in continuous use in the state. The church was vacated by the congregation in June 2000, after its new building was finished. It was sold to Sunny Fresh Foods, which indicated it would keep the church intact and use the classroom area for offices.

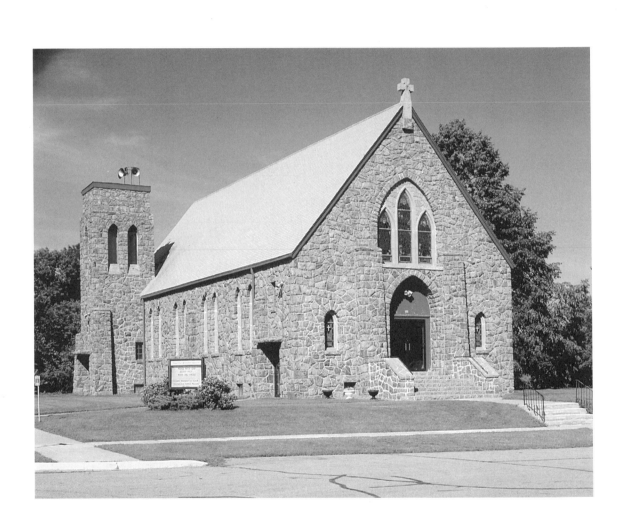

Morton (Renville County)

Zion Evangelical Lutheran Church

Valley Drive and Fifth Street
Thorwald Thorson, Forest City, Iowa, architect
1939

MORTON WAS PLATTED IN 1882 BY THE RAILROAD, which was marching westward across central Minnesota. But the town's prosperity was based on the nearby granite quarries, which were opened in 1886 by T. Saulpaugh and Company of Mankato. The following year, Morton was incorporated.

The congregation of Zion Evangelical Lutheran Church began in Beaver Falls in 1882; however, repeated efforts to build a church there failed and the members moved to Morton, where they organized Zion Lutheran Church in February 1889. That same year, they erected a frame church, 26 feet wide and 40 feet long, with an 80-foot steeple, at a cost of $1,357.43. The church was dedicated in June. A parsonage was built ten years later, but the membership in Morton was so small that the pastor moved to Redwood Falls and the parsonage in Morton was rented out to private families. Finally, in 1916, Candidate Herbert Parisius was installed as pastor to serve only Zion.

In 1939 the old church was razed and the present one erected on the same site. The foundation was put in by volunteers in twelve and a half hours on July 26, and on August 13 the cornerstone was laid. The new church was dedicated on December 10. Its total cost was about $25,000. It is thought to have been designed by Thorwald Thorson of Forest City, Iowa, because of its resemblance to St. Luke's American Lutheran Church in nearby Franklin (1938) and First English Lutheran Church in Ortonville (1939), both of which were designed by Thorson and constructed of Morton and Ortonville granite, respectively.

The church is constructed of Morton granite laid randomly. It is Gothic Revival in style, with four-bay side walls each containing a pair of narrow arched windows. At the left rear is a three-story bell tower. The stained glass windows were installed in 1944.

Nerstrand (Rice County)

Valley Grove

From Minnesota Highway 246, west on County Road 29

Architect and builder unknown
1862 and 1894
National Register of Historic Places

T HIS SITE IS ONE OF ONLY FOUR described here that violate the author's rule to include only active churches. But, in defense of two of them (Swedish Evangelical Lutheran in Millville and Portland Prairie Methodist Episcopal near Eitzen), they, like Valley Grove, are used for religious ceremonies on special occasions, such as weddings or other kinds of celebrations. In any event, this is the only instance in the state where the old and new churches occupy the same site, facing each other across a space of about fifty feet.

Valley Grove originally was called Tyske Grove. The name was changed in 1870. The older of the two buildings is Greek Revival in style, built of locally quarried stone in 1862. It has a stubby square tower and four windows on each side. The interior of wood construction is very plain, having been converted to use as a reception hall for ceremonial occasions taking place in the newer structure. There is a main room in which tables can be set up or dances held, and a spacious kitchen at the rear.

The newer Gothic Revival church was erected in 1894. Shortly afterward, the congregation divided and the second group built an identical church (now greatly altered) in the town of Nerstrand. The church is of frame construction, with lap siding characteristically painted white. The single entrance is through the projecting bell tower.

Regular services in the church have not been held since 1972, when the congregations disbanded because of dwindling membership. The two buildings are maintained by separate preservation groups, the oldest one by the Valley Grove Cemetery Association and a trust, the newer by the Society for the Preservation of Valley Grove Church.

Church of St. Wenceslaus

215 East Main Street
Hermann Kretz, St. Paul, architect
1906–7
National Register of Historic Places

THIS LARGE, IMPOSING REDBRICK CHURCH with its twin towers dominates the city. It is, like so many others of its type, a combination of neoclassical and Romanesque elements and has Central European antecedents—this time, based on a church in Prague, Czech Republic. Indeed, it serves the oldest Czech parish in the state.

The town of New Prague and surrounding area was settled in 1856 by Czech immigrants who had first lived in Dubuque, Iowa. Within two years of their arrival in Iowa, however, cholera had decimated their numbers and they elected to move to a healthier climate. Four men journeyed up the Mississippi to St. Paul, where they consulted with members of the Catholic community about a possible area for settlement. They were told to go to St. Cloud, where the Benedictines from St. John's Abbey were helping Catholics find land and get a new start. But the men lost their way and followed the Minnesota River instead, ending up at Shakopee. There they learned that there was ample land farther south, in the area that was to become New Prague. By October 1856, the four men had purchased land and had brought their families and others to the new country from Dubuque. The following year, more Czechs arrived, and in subsequent years the area became heavily settled by German Catholics as well.

In 1856 the parish of St. Wenceslaus was formed, and the following year the first church was built of logs near the location of the present building. It took two summers to build that first church, using the volunteer labor of farmers who were members of the parish. The first pastor arrived in 1861; three years later fire destroyed the log church. For several years, services were held in the rectory, and then work began on a more permanent brick-and-stone building in 1866. It was dedicated by Bishop Thomas Grace of the Diocese of St. Paul in 1868. A decade later the parish school was built.

Inevitably, growth in membership in the parish forced the construction of a new, larger church to replace the old one. The new church was begun under the direction of Father Francis Tichy. Hermann Kretz of St. Paul was hired as architect, and a contract was signed with A. Kropf to erect the huge building. The initial contract was for $53,000, but cost overruns eventually raised the final figure to $85,000. Discontented parishioners forced Father Tichy to resign in 1906 and the church was finished by Father Jaroslav Cermak. It was dedicated on July 7, 1907, by Archbishop John Ireland. After the present building was completed, a new rectory was added in 1908 and the existing school was built in 1914 with a large addition in 1954. The convent was erected in 1949.

The Church of St. Wenceslaus is of majestic proportions, measuring 165 feet in length and 67 feet in width; the towers are 110 feet in height. The ceiling of the nave—which is of tin—is 39 feet from the floor. The exterior is sheathed in red brick, trimmed in cream-colored metal. A statue of King Wenceslaus, patron saint of the Czechs, is in a niche above the main entrance. The sanctuary has a main altar and two side altars, all hand carved, including the statuary. A figure of King Wenceslaus is on the main altar; the side altars are dedicated to the Blessed Virgin Mary and St. Joseph. There is a large pipe organ in the balcony, manufactured in 1979 by the Hendrickson Organ Company of St. Peter, Minnesota. The nave seats one thousand. The church underwent restoration in 1999, which brought back much of its original splendor.

New Trier (Dakota County)

Church of St. Mary

8433 East 239th Street

Between U.S. Highways 52 and 61 on Minnesota Highway 50

George J. Ries, St. Paul, architect
1909
National Register of Historic Places

S ITUATED ATOP A HILL AMID FLAT FARM COUNTRY south of the Twin Cities, this finely crafted redbrick beaux-arts classical (Central European baroque) church can be seen for miles around.

The first settlers from Trier, Germany, began arriving in 1854 and three years later built a log church. A priest was assigned to them in 1858, and, with the growth of the congregation, a larger stone church was built in 1864 on a hill overlooking the town. This church, in the Gothic style, had a single tower and spire rising above the main entrance. A frame convent was built in 1870 for Benedictine sisters, who came to run the school, but they left after the railroad bypassed the town and School Sisters of Notre Dame took their place. The old convent was replaced in 1950 by a brick building.

In 1909, after deciding to build a new and larger church, the congregation employed architect George J. Ries of St. Paul to design a new building. Ries also designed the splendid St. Agnes Catholic Church in St. Paul's Frogtown in 1897–1904. His output was not prolific, but these two churches clearly demonstrate his outstanding facility in ecclesiastical architecture. Two remnants of the old church were incorporated into the present one: the cornerstone, installed in the vestibule, and a five-foot painted statue of the Blessed Virgin Mary made in 1862, which occupies a shrine over the main entrance.

Alterations have been few since 1909: the domed upper portion of the original belfry has been removed; the entrance steps have been rebuilt of concrete; and the soft original white glazed brick trim has been replaced with a harder variety.

The New Trier parish was the mother church for those at Cannon Falls (1866), Miesville

(1873), Vermillion (1882), and Hampton (1900). Of these, Hampton's St. Matthias Catholic Church is perhaps the most interesting. It was built in 1900 of red brick in the Romanesque Revival style, designed by Hermann Kretz of St. Paul, a leading architect of German Catholic churches in his day.

1. The decor of St. Agnes Church in St. Paul beautifully replicates the baroque churches of Central Europe in its lavishness and exuberance. The succession of vaults decorated with frescoes forms an awe-inspiring ceiling.

2. Of the many extraordinarily large and impressive Catholic churches in Minnesota, the Church of St. Mary in Melrose is among the most beautiful and carefully proportioned. The arched ceiling, painted in blue with cream-colored columns, was designed for excellent sound convection. The nave features sixteen spectacular stained glass windows, including an intriguing Eye-of-God window on the south side.

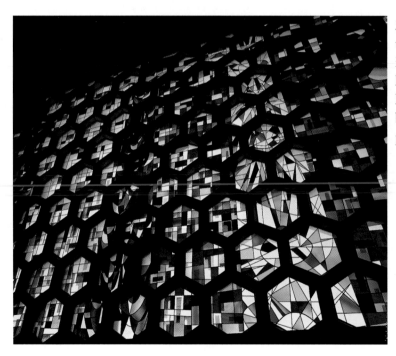

3. An outstanding feature of the St. John's Abbey Church in Collegeville is its large honeycombed wall filled with 430 hexagons of stained glass designed by Bronislaw Bak, a former art professor at the college.

4. Originally Stewart Memorial Church, Redeemer Missionary Baptist Church in Minneapolis remains the only Prairie School church in the state. The sanctuary admirably characterizes the main features of the Prairie School: the absence of unnecessary ornament, emphasis on horizontality, and sharply defined linear elements.

5. Lighting, wall treatments, and furnishings all work together perfectly in creating the quiet drama of the interior of Christ Church Lutheran in Minneapolis. There are no parallel surfaces in the interior walls; each either curves or slants or undulates, thus cleverly eliminating echo or "flutter" produced by sound bouncing off parallel walls. Christ Church Lutheran is among the finest modern church designs in Minnesota and clearly demonstrates the masterful craftsmanship of the Saarinens.

6. The Tiffany stained glass windows at First
Presbyterian Church in Duluth contribute greatly
to the extraordinary ambience of the sanctuary. The
windows were designed by Anne Weston, a resident
Tiffany designer in Duluth for several years.

7. The beautiful Church of St. Mary, Help of Christians in Sleepy Eye is an outstanding example of Gothic Revival. This cathedral-sized parish church seats 975 and has 100-foot ceilings in the nave. The magnificent butternut altar was crafted by E. Hackner of La Crosse, Wisconsin, in 1905.

8. The Cathedral of St. Paul's grand baldachin, shown here, was designed by architect Whitney Warren of New York and was installed between 1922 and 1924.

9. The sanctuary of the Lakewood Cemetery Chapel in Minneapolis is modeled after St. Mark's Cathedral in Venice and is encrusted with ten million tiles forming a rich panorama of mosaic art. The inscription at the base of the dome, executed in Teco pottery and gold mosaics, reads, "Until the day break and the shadows flee away."

10. The unusual circular sanctuary of Vinje Lutheran Church in Willmar is illuminated by ribbons of stained glass designed by William Saltzman of Minneapolis. The pattern in the glass consists of abstract swirls made from two thousand square feet of antique handblown glass from Germany. The choir loft, with a twenty-three rank organ, appears to float above the congregation.

11. The interior ceiling and walls of Hennepin Avenue United Methodist Church in Minneapolis are lined with Gustavino tile for sound absorbency. The ceiling of the sanctuary is a starburst pattern of ribbing executed in stone. The overall plan of the church is based on medieval Ely Cathedral in England.

12. The nave of the Basilica of St. Mary in Minneapolis was planned to be awe-inspiring and spacious with unobstructed views of the altar. Five arched windows in bays on each side of the nave provide light, and there are sixty stained glass windows, including a rose window above the entrance that is fifteen feet in diameter.

Photograph by Michael Jensen

13. The comfortable interior space of Danebod Lutheran Church in Tyler features a Star of Bethlehem in the ceiling, a hand-carved baptismal font, and a ship model, indicative of the seagoing tradition of the Danes who constructed the church in 1895.

Northfield

All Saints Episcopal Church

419 Washington Street
Architect unknown
1866
National Register of Historic Places

Bishop Henry Whipple was one of the state's truly remarkable figures, a tall man from New York who was appointed Episcopal Bishop of Minnesota in 1860. When he came to Minnesota, it was still the frontier with relatively few people living outside of Minneapolis and St. Paul. During the next forty-one years, he traveled thousands of miles through the state in the course of his mission and became famous for championing the cause of the Indians in matters of education and religion as well as working tirelessly for his own church. Literally hundreds of Episcopal parishes were formed in those years, and Whipple visited each one—often several times—and dedicated their churches.

This delicate little building may have been designed by Whipple himself, although there seems no way to prove it. He was known to have taken an interest in architecture and commented on structures he saw during his extensive travels in the United States and abroad. Whoever it was created a very simple but picturesque little church, now framed with old evergreens and beautifully maintained.

The church is in the Gothic Revival style, its wood frame sheathed in board-and-batten siding, painted white trimmed in gray with typical red entrance doors. The church consists of a nave, smaller chancel, entry tower and belfry, and vestry. The nave originally measured 20 by 50 feet, but was enlarged to 60 feet in 1879. At that time, the chancel was moved back and attached to the larger nave. There are six stained glass lancet windows on each side of the nave. The present belfry and spire replaced the original gable-roofed belfry about 1879, at the same time that the nave was enlarged. The interior has been remodeled but retains most of its original woodwork and furnishings.

The parish was formed in 1858, three years after Northfield was founded by J. W. North, who built both a flour mill and a sawmill on the Cannon River. In 1857, John Sidney Archibald and his brother George arrived from Ontario and platted the town. They also built a dam and gristmill on the river, which was the largest such operation in the state until Washburn built its huge "A" mill in Minneapolis in 1879.

For the first few years after the formation of the parish there was no pastor or church. In May 1866, the townspeople were stimulated by the Reverend Solomon S. Burleson to raise money for a new building, and work began on the church. S. B. Hoag and Charles Anderson were the carpenters and Henry B. Martin did the masonry work. Mr. Burleson pitched in and wielded a hammer along with the rest of the church members. Construction was finished in time for Christmas services. It cost $1,620. Three years later, a bell was purchased.

In 1868 the parish at Dundas broke away and built the Church of the Holy Cross, a stone building that was intentionally planned to outshine All Saints. It ended up costing the astonishing amount of $7,000 and is indeed a very fine structure. Like All Saints, it was dedicated by Bishop Whipple.

Skinner Memorial Chapel, Carleton College

First Street between College and Winona Streets
Patton, Holmes, and Flinn, Chicago, architects
1916
National Register of Historic Places

CARLETON COLLEGE WAS FOUNDED IN 1866, and this elegant chapel was built half a century later as a gift of Mrs. Emily Willey Skinner in memory of her husband, Miron, a trustee of the college, who died in 1909.

The architects, Patton, Holmes, and Flinn of Chicago, developed a campus plan around 1910, which, as usually happens, was greatly modified in succeeding years. Between 1914 and 1928, they designed nine buildings for the college, including the chapel, Music Hall, a classroom building, stadium, and five dormitories.

The very dignified chapel is in the English Gothic Revival style, built on the Latin cross plan of reinforced concrete faced with Bedford limestone. Its most prominent feature is the tall bell tower that would seem massive and heavy were it not for the feeling of lightness conveyed by the tracery openings on all sides. The interior features dark beams and a dark wood ceiling set in contrast to the light gray stone walls. Relatively small windows do not permit much light to enter, yet the effect is not by any means unpleasant, but rather instills in the visitor a feeling of coolness and tranquillity.

First Baptist Church

123 East Main Street
Warren B. Dunnell, Minneapolis, architect
1892–93

THE CONGREGATION OF FIRST BAPTIST CHURCH was founded in 1857 and the present church was built in 1892–93. The Romanesque Revival building has changed little in the time since it was erected.

The church is built on a cross-gabled plan. Its main facade is dominated by a tall tower and steeple on the right side, set forward of the facade. It is topped by an octagonal colonnaded belfry and spire. At the left corner of the front gable end is a much smaller tower and steeple. The church is constructed of red brick with light stone foundation and lower base of the tall tower. The gable ends are shingled.

This elegant church has one of the oldest pipe organs in southern Minnesota.

St. Paul's Episcopal Church

Cedar and Mill Streets
Congregation-built
1867, 1884

S T. PAUL'S HAS THE DISTINCTION of being the oldest church in continuous use in Owatonna. The first Episcopal service in town was held in 1859; the congregation organized the following year. In 1867, it built this, its first church, for $1,500. It is of wood frame construction and was called the Guild Hall.

In 1884 the congregation built the structure on the corner for $5,000. It was consecrated by Bishop Whipple in 1885. The church is clad in board-and-batten siding, with fishscale shingles and stained glass windows set in pointed-arched Gothic windows. A square tower is on the left of the front facade, slightly set back from the facade itself. It is topped with a cylindrical belfry and conical roof. Until 1974, the tower lacked a bell.

The church and the Guild Hall were separate buildings until 1929, when the hall was turned ninety degrees, attached to the back of the church, and renamed Tanner Hall after the Reverend George Tanner, who led the effort to build it in 1867. The original organ was also replaced in 1929. Fifty years later, there was a large amount of renovation work, including the installation of air conditioning and new parquet flooring in the nave. But the church remains essentially intact as originally built.

Pierz (Morrison County)

St. Joseph's Church

68 North Main Street
Architect and builder unknown
1886–88
National Register of Historic Places

T HE TOWN AND PARISH OF PIERZ was called Rich Prairie until 1894, when it was named after Father Francis Pierz, a pioneer Catholic missionary who came to Minnesota in 1838. Father Pierz first worked in Indian missions in northern Minnesota and then, after 1852, in central Minnesota; he was instrumental in keeping the Chippewa from joining the Indian uprisings of the early 1860s. In 1871, in declining health, he retired from the mission field to become the first resident priest of the newly organized parish of St. Joseph's. Father Pierz donated his large farm to the predominantly southern German immigrants who populated the parish and oversaw the construction of their first church.

The present structure is the second church of the parish, erected in 1886–88. It is a large Gothic Revival building with a tall tower and spire topped with an iron cross that dominates the church and the town. The spire was raised to its present height of 160 feet in 1902. The church is wood frame with a cream-colored brick veneer. A reddish brick is used to frame the windows and the piers, for the crosses above the side windows, and for the "1888" date on the front of the tower.

Inside, the church has remained virtually intact. It has a barrel vaulted ceiling in the nave and columns that form side aisles. Only a few alterations have been made, including an addition to the apse in 1907 to provide space for several offices. The exterior walls of the apse were pushed out to join the side walls of the nave. Two years later a basement was excavated for a chapel, and the interior was redecorated in 1913 with stenciled motifs painted on the walls and apse. These remain to the present time.

Good Shepherd Lutheran Church
(originally St. Paul's Episcopal Church)

221 Fourth Street Southeast
Sioux Valley Stone Company, builder
1892–95

P IPESTONE IS CENTERED IN A REGION noted for its abundance of Sioux quartzite. The nearby quarries have provided materials for building and road construction since the 1870s, and one may see many buildings throughout southwestern Minnesota and eastern South Dakota that are constructed of this highly durable stone.

The cornerstone of St. Paul's Episcopal Church was laid in ceremonies led by Minnesota Archdeacon Thomas Henry Montague Villiers Appleby in 1892. The building was completed three years later, and an addition was erected in 1922 by contractor J. G. Hunt.

The church is of the local Sioux quartzite on the first floor and base of the tower. The rectangular windows are defined by limestone lintels, mullions, and sills. The same stone is also used to form a Gothic arch over the main entrance, which is through the tower, and as belt courses at the basement or foundation line and lower portion of the wall. The cross gables and part of the tower base are covered in fishscale shingles. A shingled spire rises from the tower. Small gabled vents project from the steeply pitched roof. The church style is based on English Gothic, but except for the louvres in the tower and the entrance, the openings do not have Gothic arches. There is a trefoil window in the gable facing the street.

The church served an Episcopalian congregation until 1988, when Good Shepherd Lutheran Church began holding services in it. They have, however, maintained the building in near-original condition.

Rochester

Calvary Episcopal Church

111 Third Avenue Southwest
Architect unknown
1862–63, 1868

T HE FIRST EPISCOPAL SERVICES IN ROCHESTER were held in 1858 by the Reverend Jackson Kemper, the first missionary bishop of the Protestant Episcopal Church. Two years later, Bishop Henry Whipple visited the small community and appointed the Reverend Charles Woodward of St. Paul as Missionary of the Domestic Board at Rochester. Woodward began holding regular Episcopal services, and that same year a congregation organized itself as Calvary Parish.

In 1861 Bishop Whipple offered $500, matched by his friend Bishop Morton Dix, toward a church on the understanding that the parish would contribute $500. Land was donated and construction of the church began in 1862. The contractor was J. B. Alexander of Winona. Brick for the church was made in a local kiln. The original structure measured 27 feet by 55 feet, built in English Gothic style at a cost of $600. It seated about one hundred people. The first service was held in July 1863, although the stained glass windows were not yet installed. An organ was purchased in Chicago, and a bell, donated by B. B. Sherman of New York City, was installed in 1864.

In 1868 an addition of 22½ feet was built onto the nave, and a partial basement was excavated for a furnace. A chancel was constructed on the north side along with a robing room. The plain glass windows were replaced by stained glass; a new round window was installed at the south end of the church, and the building was renamed Calvary Church. A Guild Hall constructed of Winona brick was erected in 1891 and a tower entrance was added. In 1900 a kitchen and dining room were added to the Guild Hall. A number of stained glass windows, including three Tiffany windows, were installed in the years 1905 to 1907.

Many other alterations have been made since that time. In 1924 local architect Harold Crawford was commissioned to design a larger tower and enlarge the altar. In 1950 a new lych gate was built. In light of the arrival of IBM in Rochester, the parish deliberated whether or not to abandon the downtown site and move to the northern part of town, where the new industry

was situated. The rapidly expanding Mayo Clinic offered to buy the church and land for $261,500 in 1957, but the congregation ultimately decided not to sell and, instead, elected to build a Calvary Mission Church on the north side of Rochester. It was dedicated in 1961. Later additions to Calvary Church included an ambulatory on the east side of the chapel in 1983, necessitating the move of four stained glass windows to its outer wall. A columbarium adorned by a Celtic cross was built in 1984, designed by Harold Crawford.

Rollingstone (Winona County)

Holy Trinity Catholic Church

83 Main Street
Charles Wender, Rollingstone, builder
1869
Nicholas Arnoldy, Rollingstone, builder
1893
National Register of Historic Places

T HE COMMUNITY OF ROLLINGSTONE was founded by German immigrants from Luxembourg who brought their solid Catholic faith with them. It is preserved in this church, which has served as the center of the community for well over a century.

Rollingstone was settled in 1855. By 1861 its founders had built their first church and established a nearby cemetery. The original wood frame church was replaced by the present stone structure in 1869, and when that became too small nearly twenty-five years later, the parishioners added onto their building rather than replace it, as did many other parishes. The addition doubled the seating capacity. From the beginning, the parishioners provided the labor and financial support for their church.

Built of local, rough-cut limestone in the Gothic Revival style, the church was erected by Charles Wender in 1869. The addition in 1893 was the work of Nicholas Arnoldy. Both of these men were probably local carpenters and stonemasons. The original building measured 35 feet wide and 60 feet long; the 1893 addition was of exactly the same dimensions. A transept chancel was built at the same time that measured 35 feet long and 24 feet wide, creating a cruciform plan. The tower base is stone and the spire is wood frame covered with shingles. The interior has been substantially altered over the years, so much so that virtually nothing of the original remains.

St. Charles (Winona County)

Trinity Episcopal Church

807 St. Charles Avenue
Architect and builder unknown
1874
National Register of Historic Places

T UCKED UNOBTRUSIVELY IN THE MIDDLE of a residential neighborhood is this tiny white frame Episcopal church. The building is clad in board-and-batten siding, with lancet windows and a delicate little open belfry above the entrance. The church is remarkably intact, both inside and out. Only in the 1920s did it receive electricity.

Trinity was built in 1874, a decade after the congregation was formed and six years after its formal organization. It was probably built with local labor, possibly by the parishioners themselves, in the Gothic style that epitomizes Episcopal churches erected during the tenure of Bishop Henry Whipple.

St. Joseph

Church of St. Joseph
12 West Minnesota Street
Leonard and Sheire, St. Paul, architects
1869–71, 1884
National Register of Historic Places
(St. Benedict's Convent and College Historic District)

THIS FINE RHINELAND GOTHIC CHURCH STANDS ADJACENT to the College of St. Benedict. Seen from nearby Interstate 94, the spire of the church and the dome of Sacred Heart Chapel dominate the skyline of the community.

The area was settled by Germans about 1854. Father Francis Pierz served the population at first, as he did many others in central Minnesota, and urged them to build a church. They erected a log structure in 1856, which was replaced in 1863 by a frame building. By that time, the Benedictine fathers had arrived to minister to the parish.

There soon was need of a larger church, and in 1867 the decision was made to erect a new building. Local granite was quarried 4½ miles east of St. Joseph for the church's twenty-foot-high walls, and field boulders were brought in by local farmers for the foundation. Construction was finished in 1871, and a matching rectory was built in 1874. The tower went unbuilt until 1884, when funds became available. A pulpit was added in the 1880s, and in 1903 four bells weighing a total of 11,000 pounds were placed in the steeple. A clock was installed in 1906, and stained glass windows were added in 1909.

The church is a bit unusual in appearance because the main entrance is directly at ground level and not approached by the customary flight of steps. Nonetheless, it has a most commanding appearance and is one of the oldest churches of its type in the state.

St. Joseph

Sacred Heart Chapel, College of St. Benedict

Minnesota Street and College Avenue
George Stauduhar, Rock Island, Illinois, architect
1912–14
Hammel, Green, and Abrahamson, Minneapolis
Traynor, Hermanson, and Hahn, St. Cloud
Frank Kacmarcik, St. Paul, architects
1981–83
National Register of Historic Places
(St. Benedict's Convent and College Historic District)

THIS LARGE AND IMPRESSIVE BEAUX-ARTS CHAPEL is the dominant architectural object in this small college town. The chapel's most prominent feature is a massive ribbed dome that rises to a height of 135 feet and is pierced with oculus windows on a base surrounded by fluted Ionic columns. The main altar is directly beneath the dome. Sixteen granite columns on Kasota stone piers once supported the roof.

An extensive renovation in 1981–83 resulted in rearrangement of the seating and removal of eight of the sixteen supporting columns. The rest were incorporated in the Gathering Place, an addition to the west entrance of the chapel. The addition is of matching white sand–lime brick on a buff-colored brick foundation. Unlike many additions to existing churches in the state, this one does not damage the atmosphere or feel of the old chapel, but rather, complements it by creating a large restful space for socializing before entering the sanctity of the chapel.

The convent is the largest community of Benedictine women in the world. It was founded in St. Cloud in 1857 by nuns from the St. Mary's, Pennsylvania, community (founded in 1852). The motherhouse was moved from St. Cloud to St. Joseph in 1863.

St. Louis Park

Beth El Synagogue

5224 West Twenty-sixth Street
Bertram Bassuk, New York, architect
1968–70

THE BETH EL CONGREGATION began on the north side of Minneapolis in 1920. The north side had always been the center of Jewish settlement in the city. Initially, it was in a district along Lyndale Avenue, straddling Glenwood Avenue and Olson Memorial Highway, beginning in the 1890s. Gradually, the neighborhood shifted north and westward to an area centered on Penn and Plymouth Avenues. There the first Beth El Synagogue was erected in 1925–26, at 1349 Penn Avenue North (demolished in 1995).

By 1960, most of the congregation had moved out of the area, chiefly to St. Louis Park, and the synagogue followed. Ten acres of land were purchased on West Twenty-sixth Street beside Highway 100 in 1961, and an activities building was constructed within a year, followed by the synagogue eight years later. The congregation selected Bertram Bassuk, a New York architect, to design it.

The building is a highly unusual design, consisting of a prominent sanctuary with a sharply curved ceiling formed by laminated wood beams that swoop upward from all sides of the room to converge at the apex directly over the altar, which is situated in a corner of the sanctuary. The high vertical wall behind the altar contains beautiful stained glass, as do the triangular side walls. The sanctuary thus rises dramatically from the one-story base structure that houses offices and classrooms. A freestanding metal tower in front of the main entrance is an abstract representation of the tablets containing the Ten Commandments.

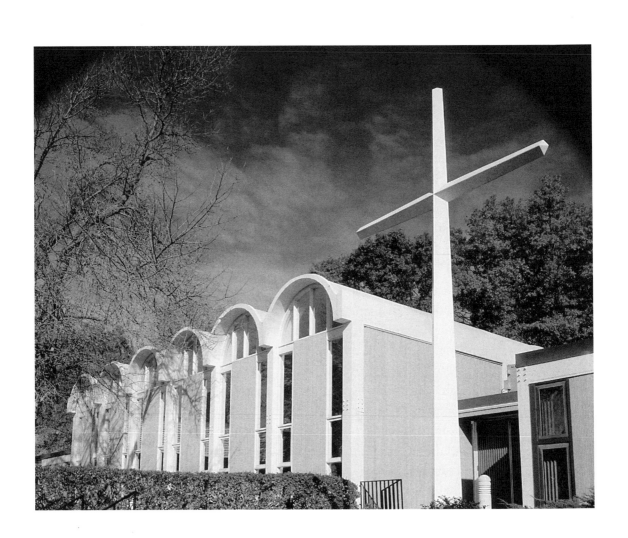

St. Louis Park

Lutheran Church of the Reformation

2544 South Highway 100
Hammel and Green, St. Paul, architects
1958
Hammel, Green, and Abrahamson, St. Paul, architects
1969

T HIS CHURCH WAS ERECTED IN TWO PARTS, the latest being ten years after the original portion was completed. The first part contained the sanctuary, identified by six transverse barrel vaults that form the ceiling and roof. The vaults and the frame are reinforced concrete; the walls are wood sheathing. In 1969 a new sanctuary was added on the north side and connected to the older portion by a passageway housing classrooms. The old sanctuary was converted into a commons area, made extremely pleasant and airy by the abundant natural light that floods in through tall vertical windows. The design won a Merit Award from the Minnesota Chapter of the American Institute of Architects in 1959. The present sanctuary has exposed wood trusses with a lightly stained wood ceiling above the trusses. It seats 325. The original church was built at a cost of $75,000; the addition, which also included administrative offices, a kitchen, choir room, and freestanding bell tower, cost $220,000.

In 1954 a group from Gethsemane Lutheran Church in Hopkins began talking to the regional director of the Board of American Missions about starting an Augustana Lutheran Church in St. Louis Park. A previous attempt, in 1925, failed after two years. In 1956, the Board of Missions purchased 3.7 acres of land between Twenty-fifth and Twenty-sixth Streets, and bordered by Vernon Avenue on the west and Highway 100 (then called the Belt Line) on the east, as a site for a new church. The first service of the new congregation was held in the St. Louis Park Theatre on March 10, 1957, and in June of that year the congregation formally organized as Evangelical Lutheran Church of the Reformation with a membership of 206. Ground breaking for a new building was held in May 1958, and it was finished in September of the same year. The first services were held in December. The dedication of the 1969 addition took place in February 1970.

St. Michael

St. Michael's Catholic Church

22 Main Street North
Adolphus Druiding, Chicago, architect
1890–91
National Register of Historic Places

THE SETTLEMENT OF ST. MICHAEL was established by German Catholic immigrants in 1856. Families from Germany had begun arriving in Wright County the previous year, many coming from St. Louis, McHenry, Illinois, and various parts of Wisconsin.

The founders of St. Michael set about building their first church of logs soon after arriving. This first crude edifice was two miles east of the present church and was replaced by a larger frame church in 1866. This church was moved to near the present site and demolished after the new structure was completed. The pastor, Father Rudolph Deustermann, was highly influential in planning this large, imposing brick church. It was dedicated by Bishop James McGolrick of Duluth on September 29, 1892, and the parish became the "mother church" for all others in Wright County.

The style is Gothic Revival with Romanesque elements and built of yellow Chaska brick trimmed in stone. A conspicuous tall tower and spire with a clock and filigree ornament rises above the center of three bays that comprise the front facade and is visible from all parts of town. There are triangular dormers in the shed roof and a corbeled gable over the entry containing a sculptured niche for a statue of the Virgin Mary. The church seats six hundred.

The adjacent cemetery was started in 1867, and in 1876 a parochial school was opened by the School Sisters of Notre Dame.

St. Paul

Cathedral of St. Paul

250 Summit Avenue
Emmanuel L. Masqueray, St. Paul, architect
1906–42
National Register of Historic Places

N O BOOK ON MINNESOTA RELIGIOUS ARCHITECTURE would be complete without including the Cathedral of St. Paul, the grandest church structure in the state. It is a monument in every sense of the word and a tribute to the ambition of Archbishop John Ireland, whose long-standing vision of a cathedral on a hill above the city of St. Paul was finally realized in this building. It is also a tribute to the design skill of Emmanuel Masqueray, a little-known French-born, École des Beaux-Arts–trained architect whom Ireland commissioned to create his dream cathedral.

The Diocese—and, many years later, Archdiocese—of St. Paul had humble beginnings in a log chapel built at the inspiration of Father Lucien Galtier on a bluff above the river in the settlement known originally as Pig's Eye. The chapel, which measured about 25 feet long, 18 feet wide, and 10 feet high, was dedicated on November 1, 1841. Ten years later, the log chapel—enlarged by Galtier's successor, Father Augustin Ravoux—was proclaimed the Cathedral of St. Paul with the creation of the diocese under Bishop Joseph Cretin. Cretin immediately set about building a larger church to accommodate a fast-growing congregation. The new three-story building was of brick, with a library, kitchen, dining room, parlor, schoolrooms, and storage facilities on the first floor, the church on the second floor, and offices and living quarters on the top floor for Cretin, seminarians, and members of the Brothers of the Holy Family. The bishop soon realized that even the new building was inadequate for the needs of the diocese, and in 1853 he initiated plans for a new cathedral. Construction began the following year and was finally completed in 1858, having been temporarily halted both by the death of Cretin as well as the Panic of 1857. This edifice, erected at the corner of St. Peter and Sixth Streets, was of stone and measured 175 feet long by 100 feet wide, but was bereft of all ornament, including the planned 250-foot-high steeple, to save money. In 1859, Cretin's successor, Bishop Thomas Grace, added transepts to strengthen the walls and add visual interest to the starkly barren building.

Ireland served under Grace as coadjutor and was shown a site on a hill above St. Paul where Grace hoped to build a larger fourth cathedral. Ireland took up Grace's dream of a new cathedral even though he looked at a number of sites before settling on the one that his predecessor had chosen. Standing on the site, however, was a large Italianate residence formerly owned by Norman Kittson, a prominent St. Paul steamboat magnate. In 1903, two St. Paul businessmen, Charles Smith and A. B. Stickney, offered to purchase the deteriorating mansion and use the land to erect a residence for Ireland. The archbishop turned down the offer on the grounds that the public might react adversely to this show of pretense. Instead, Ireland said that the property would be ideal for the new cathedral and so it was purchased in 1904. A building committee was formed to plan for the new structure and select an architect. After a short-lived competition, Ireland intervened and handpicked Masqueray, whom he had met at the Louisiana Purchase Exposition in St. Louis earlier that year.

Masqueray designed an enormous church, working with a budget of $1 million. He based his design on French churches at Périgueux and Paris, creating a beaux-arts edifice that drew heavily on Renaissance and classical themes and featured a massive dome that seemed out of scale for the stubby Greek cross plan. The dimensions are truly grandiose: the nave is 60 feet wide and 84 feet high; the sanctuary in the apse behind the nave is 65 feet by 60 feet; the enormous dome is 96 feet in diameter at the base and 175 feet high on the interior. There are six chapels honoring apostles of countries from which settlers in Minnesota had come. The cathedral seats 2,500 in pews and has space for 1,000 removable chairs (see Plate 8).

Ground was broken in 1906, and the cornerstone was laid on June 2, 1907. By 1914, the church was finished to the point that it could be occupied for services, though the interior had been only roughly finished. That same year, the old cathedral downtown was razed. The new cathedral was dedicated by Ireland in 1915. Interior finish work continued into the 1940s, long after Masqueray's death in 1917 and Ireland's a year later. The original plans and subsequent details were carried out by architects Maginnis and Walsh of Boston.

In 2001 major roof repairs were undertaken, including replacement of all the copper sheathing. At the same time, the stone was cleaned and remortared.

St. Paul

Church of the Assumption

51 West Ninth Street
Eduard von Riedel, Munich, architect
1870–74
National Register of Historic Places

ASSUMPTION PARISH IN ST. PAUL dates to 1856, when the German Catholics separated from the Cathedral parish. At about the same time, they constructed a frame church on a site across the street from the present building. In 1858 the Benedictine fathers took charge of it; they built a school for boys in 1860 and a rectory in 1867. The frame school burned down in 1863 and was replaced by one of stone in 1867.

Membership grew until Assumption was the largest Catholic parish in the state. The old church rapidly became too small, and by 1869 plans were made for a larger and more grandiose structure. Father Clement Staub, the parish priest, looked to the Old World for an architect and contacted Eduard von Riedel, the court architect for the ruling Wittelsbach family of Bavaria. Riedel had worked under Friedrich von Gaertner, one of the prominent German architects of his day, and so it was not unnatural that he chose to copy one of his master's churches— Ludwigskirche in Munich—in designing Assumption. At the time Riedel was commissioned to design Assumption, Bavaria was ruled by King Ludwig II (reigned 1864–86), whose lavish expenditures on new public buildings led to an enormous public debt and precipitated the imposition of a constitutional monarchy in 1890.

Ground was broken for Assumption in 1870, and in June of the following year the cornerstone was laid. The masonry work was contracted to Schlick, Erd, and Bahnholzer of St. Paul. As construction progressed, visiting clergy and parishioners became alarmed at the size and cost of the building, and Father Staub himself suffered a nervous breakdown. The church was finished in 1874 and consecrated on October 18 of that year by Bishop Thomas Grace.

Assumption is on a grand scale. It is 185 feet long and 85 feet wide, built entirely of local limestone, the sides divided into eight bays by pilasters of dressed limestone blocks. The windows have rounded arches, in the Romanesque style. Twin towers dominate the main (south) facade, standing 210 feet and capped with shingled steeples topped by iron crosses. The west tower has a clock (nonoperational), and the east tower houses four bells. The roof is slate.

Inside, the nave is 145 feet in length, 38 feet wide, and 60 feet high. There are side aisles flanking the nave. The four-tiered wooden altar, pulpit, and shrines were installed in 1873. At the rear is a choir loft, in which stands a monumental wood-cased pipe organ and above it an elaborate rose window.

St. Paul

Church of St. Columba

1305 Lafond Avenue
Barry Byrne, Evanston, Illinois, architect
1949–51

THIS REMARKABLE CHURCH is dedicated to one of the greatest of the early Christian church leaders of Ireland. It was designed by Barry Byrne of Chicago, who came out of a strong Prairie School background and who effectively combined Prairie School and sleek late-moderne horizontality with French Norman verticality to create a streamlined showcase that imparts a cool elegance and vitality to the whole.

St. Columba's is faced in 12,000 cubic feet of buff Indiana limestone. The large cross above the entrance doors is of red Cold Spring granite, and the exterior steps and platform at the entrance are of Winona limestone. Flanking the entrance is a tall, oval stone-clad tower.

The interior is perhaps one of the most dramatic spaces to be found in any Minnesota church. Great sweeping curves in the ceiling of the nave, concealing recessed lighting, converge at the altar and remind one of art deco/moderne motion picture theaters of the late 1930s. The nave features slitted vertical clerestory windows. The piers and wainscot are of Winona limestone, the floor and steps to the altar are of Kasota Fleuri marble. The altar and baptismal font, also designed by Byrne, are of Italian marble.

The church is angled to make it seem less crowded on the somewhat cramped urban lot. Still, it suffers today from a sense of being squeezed into a setting that does not readily permit the viewer to gain a perspective of the entire building.

Byrne received this commission on the reputation of having designed a similarly moderne structure for the St. Francis Xavier congregation in Kansas City, Missouri, a couple of years previously.

The parish began in a small store on the corner of Hamline Avenue and Thomas Street in St. Paul on September 16, 1914. The following year a frame church was built and was replaced by the present structure, which was dedicated by Archbishop John Murray on June 11, 1950. By coincidence, the priest of St. Columba's at the time was Auxiliary Bishop Byrne, of the same name as the church's architect. It is not known if they were related.

St. Paul

First Baptist Church

99 Wacouta Street
W. W. Boyington, Chicago, architect
Monroe Sheire, St. Paul, supervising architect
1872–74
National Register of Historic Places

T HE CONGREGATION OF FIRST BAPTIST CHURCH began as a Sunday school in 1847 led by Harriet Bishop. She traveled from Vermont to undertake the role of teacher for about thirty children who, she had heard, had no school or teacher. The first quarters for the school were in a former blacksmith shop. Not long after her arrival, however, Miss Bishop succeeded in having a new school building erected.

The first minister, John Parsons, arrived in 1849 and set in motion a program to build a meeting-house. More funds were required than the congregation could raise locally, and so Mr. Parsons journeyed to New York in 1851 to seek donations. Unhappily, after raising $2,300, he was mugged in New York City, robbed of the entire amount, and left unconscious on the street. He spent a couple of months recuperating from his injuries and, while returning to St. Paul, died on a riverboat north of St. Louis. The congregation had, meantime, erected its first church on money borrowed in anticipation of Parsons's arrival with funds to pay off the loans. Ironically, the first service held in the new church, which was built on Mount Pisgah approximately where Mears Park is now located, was the funeral for Mr. Parsons. The hill came to be referred to as Baptist Hill.

The first little frame church was replaced in 1862 by a much larger stone structure, called the Wacouta Street Church for its location. This structure was soon outgrown by the rapidly expanding congregation, and in 1872 W. W. Boyington of Chicago was commissioned to design a new church, to be built nearby at the corner of Ninth and Wacouta. The old church served as a Sunday school until 1885 and then was sold and turned into a factory. Monroe and Romaine Sheire were the contractors and also members of the congregation. Monroe, who was more of an architect than his brother, acted as local supervisor of construction.

The present church was substantially altered in 1945 by the removal of its steeple, which soared 165 feet above the ground. The steeple was dismantled when it became evident that its stone

base was sinking into the marshy soil and causing a structural strain on the rest of the building. Also removed were the belfry and clock. The latter was returned to its donors, the Thompson family of St. Paul. A far less lofty steeple without a belfry or clock was erected on the tower base in recent years, but it seems to lack the drama of the original one. The ornate original porch was also removed after it began settling away from the facade and was replaced with a new stone front that made for a flat and far less interesting appearance. The beautiful interior decorative elements, especially the trusses and hammer beams, are of black walnut and butternut. All the interior woodwork was made by the Sheire brothers' construction workers.

The Living Word Church

(originally Prince of Peace Lutheran Church for the Deaf)

205 Otis Avenue
Ralph Rapson, Minneapolis, architect
1958

RALPH RAPSON, longtime head of the School of Architecture at the University of Minnesota, studied under Eliel and Eero Saarinen at Cranbrook Academy in Michigan and took away with him their appreciation of spareness and sophistication in building. Prince of Peace Lutheran Church for the Deaf, as this structure was originally called, is Rapson's attempt to design a church that would convey the Saarinens' dramatic sense of space and light and an understated elegant simplicity. Rapson himself said it was "one piece of work of which I am very proud." When completed, parishioners gave him a slap on the back in their silent appreciation of what he had given to them.

The small building is situated in a quiet residential neighborhood just off busy Marshall Avenue in St. Paul. It sits more exposed today because of the removal of large trees that once shaded it. It has tan brick walls and a white-painted concrete cornice, between which is inserted a very narrow glass clerestory. The interior is plainly finished, and the decoration is at a minimum. The new predominantly African American congregation has maintained much of the character of the original structure, down to the three freestanding metal crosses that mark the entrance to the building. Rising from the apex of the pyramidal skylight is a triangular metal "steeple" topped by a thin metal cross. The only alterations appear to be new entrance doors and flanking windows, which replaced much more attractive ones with colored panes of glass. A dry moat surrounds the building on two sides, and the entrance is reached across a short steel-and-concrete bridge.

St. Paul

Mount Zion Temple

1300 Summit Avenue
Eric Mendelsohn, San Francisco, architect
Bergstedt and Hirsch, St. Paul, associated architects
1952–54

E RIC MENDELSOHN is generally acknowledged to be one of the most outstanding twentieth-century European architects. He completed many projects in Germany, the Netherlands, England, and Palestine before immigrating to the United States in 1942. This structure is his only completed commission in Minnesota.

Early on in his studies, Mendelsohn said he "rebelled against the . . . prevalent teaching of applied styles because I recognized that the elastic qualities of . . . steel and concrete . . . must by necessity produce an architecture entirely different from anything known or done before." Milton Bergstedt, whose St. Paul firm oversaw the completion of Mount Zion Temple, wrote in 1955 that Mendelsohn's personality was "that of simplicity, arrogance and sometimes impatience, a man who lived and died as an explorer of modern architecture." His best work was in Europe, for after he came to the United States he no longer was a leader in international design. Of Jewish descent himself, he specialized in synagogues, among them those in Cleveland, St. Louis, and St. Paul.

Mendelsohn died within a year after construction contracts were let for Mount Zion. From his sketches Milton Bergstedt and James Hirsch carried out his plans for the interior design and color schemes.

Mount Zion shows some highly distinctive elements of true genius. This is especially the case with the use of space: Mendelsohn designed a modular and flexible interior, providing a folding wall to separate the Temple, foyer, and assembly room or to open them as one grand space for High Holidays. The sanctuary and chapel are divided into ten ribboned sections (five on each side) symbolizing the Ten Commandments.

The rather spartan exterior of salmon-colored brick, glass, and copper is compensated by a rich, warm interior filled with Jewish symbolism. An adjacent wing houses offices and meeting

rooms. The original design called for much more glass, but the outbreak of the Korean War led to an escalation in the price of building materials and a greater awareness of energy costs.

The congregation is the oldest in Minnesota. Formed in 1856 by a group of middle-class German settlers (the first ones arrived in 1849), it has always been the central Jewish institution in St. Paul. The first rabbi was called in 1866, and the first synagogue was built in 1870 at Tenth and Minnesota Streets, followed by a second building at Avon and Holly (1904, designed by Clarence H. Johnston of St. Paul), in the residential area where most of its members lived. After World War II, the congregation began planning its long-overdue new building, which would reflect its "reform" orientation. The Reform movement rejected concepts of Jewish nationhood and emphasized nontraditional elements of religious practice, including Sunday services. The congregation today remains prominent among Jewish liberal organizations in the United States.

St. Paul

St. Agnes Church of

548 Lafond Avenue
George J. Ries, St. Paul, architect
1897–1912
National Register of Historic Places

O F ALL THE CHURCHES IN MINNESOTA, St. Agnes probably comes closest to repro-
ducing the exuberance that characterizes baroque churches of Central Europe. It was
designed and built in what was perhaps the golden age of beaux-arts architecture in the state. It
adheres closely to beaux-arts ideals, which stressed balance and symmetry throughout a structure.
This can be seen not only in the style of St. Agnes, but in its proportions: the 206-foot tower is
balanced by the 201-foot length of the building.

The construction of St. Agnes occupied the congregation for more than fifteen years. Parishioners' desire to create a true work of art for the glory of God and the community in which it
stood led them to devote almost overwhelming resources to its ultimate completion. The result is
nothing short of a masterpiece, fully deserving of far more attention than it receives from historians and the public at large.

St. Agnes is faced in Vermont marble with all the beaux-arts and baroque conceits present:
scrollwork over the door and window openings supported by smooth pilasters and ornately carved
caps; a mansard roof on the main portion of the structure; a single tower at the side and rear topped
by gilded onion domes, pierced by a spiky needle. The interior is considerably plainer than are
baroque ancestors in Europe but still grand and carefully proportioned, with a succession of vaults
decorated with frescoes forming an awe-inspiring ceiling (see Plate 1).

The first St. Agnes Church was designed by George Bergmann, St. Paul architect and member of
the congregation (1888). It stood where the rectory now is located. The present structure was begun
under the Reverend James Trobec, later to become the third bishop of St. Cloud (1897). Competing
designs were submitted by Hermann Kretz and George Ries, St. Paul architects. The latter's design
was selected, and the church was finished under the Reverend J. M. Solnce, in 1912. In a bizarre turn
of events, the rectory was severely damaged by a bomb on the night of November 4, 1917. No one
was seriously injured in what the bomber, John Hitchler, admitted was an act of hostility toward
German priests. The rectory was replaced by a new one sometime after 1937.

St. Paul

St. Bernard's Catholic Church

Geranium Avenue and Albemarle Street
John Jager, Minneapolis, architect
1905–6
National Register of Historic Places

A MONG ARCHITECTS, John Jager was closer to being a modern "Renaissance man" than most of his colleagues. Born in Slovenia and an immigrant to Minneapolis in the early 1900s, he was a linguist, art historian, soldier, writer, city planner, and architect. Yet his is anything but a household name today.

St. Bernard's is built of reinforced concrete with a facade of brick and limestone. It is the only distinctively art nouveau church in the state with tapering, identical beveled towers topped with open belfries and hexagonal conical caps. Embedded stone pieces on the front facade seem to mimic iron joiners used in wooden post-and-lintel industrial buildings of the day. It cost $102,000 to erect and seats one thousand.

The interior has been altered from its original appearance. It was completed in 1914 and features murals, paintings, and two 32-foot semicircular stained glass windows on either side of the altar. In a 1958 renovation, the original pews, altar piece, and light fixtures were removed. In recent years, the parish has attempted to partially restore the interior within the limits of its constrained financial resources.

The parish of St. Bernard was organized in 1890, and a combination school and church was built that same year. A convent was erected in 1893 (replaced in 1911) for the Sisters of St. Benedict who arrived to take charge of the school, and a parish hall and rectory were built in 1896 and 1900, respectively. A new rectory was built in 1939 and a new parish hall in 1950.

St. Paul

St. Clement's Memorial Episcopal Church

901 Portland Avenue
Cass Gilbert, St. Paul, architect
1894–95

T HE PARISH BEGAN AS EMMANUEL MISSION CHURCH in 1893, established by Bishop Coadjutor Mahlon Gilbert (1848–1900; no relation to Cass Gilbert). A frame building was constructed at the corner of Victoria and Laurel Avenues in St. Paul in 1893. Soon afterward, the widow of Dr. Theodore Augustus Eaton, who had served for forty-two years as rector of St. Clement's Church in New York City, notified Bishop Gilbert that she wanted to erect a memorial church to her husband in the Diocese of Minnesota and donated $25,000 for the project. Gilbert picked the district of Emmanuel Mission for the new church and set about finding a suitable site. He eventually bought the corner lot at Portland Avenue and Milton Street, and the mission purchased two other adjacent lots. Cass Gilbert was commissioned to draw plans for the new edifice, which was begun in 1894 and consecrated on October 6, 1895.

St. Clement's resembles an English "close," set back from the street behind a sizable churchyard approached through a lych gate. The church is built of Minnesota golden buff limestone. The interior is furnished in dark oak and has an altar of white marble made to replicate one in St. Clement's Church in New York.

A parish house was added in 1912–13 by Clarence Johnston, who was hired after Cass Gilbert's plan proved too costly to build. The front vestibule was also added at the same time.

St. Paul

St. Louis Church

506 Cedar Street
Emmanuel L. Masqueray, St. Paul, architect
1909

THE PARISH OF ST. LOUIS CHURCH (Église Saint Louis) was founded in 1868 by French Catholics, and their first church was blessed that year by Bishop Thomas Grace. It stood at the corner of Cedar and Tenth Streets. The second church, at Wabasha and Exchange Streets, was purchased from the Universalists and dedicated in April 1881 by Bishop John Ireland. The parish was placed under the pastoral care of the Marist fathers in 1886 by Bishop Ireland.

The present building is the parish's third. It was dedicated on December 19, 1909, by Archbishop Ireland. It is built of tan brick in Renaissance Revival/baroque style, which its architect, Emmanuel Masqueray, a native of France, often chose for his Catholic churches. The church has twin towers topped with matching metal belvederes and is trimmed in limestone. The entrance is framed by large stone columns. The ornate interior has a barrel vaulted ceiling, illuminated by beautiful stained glass. The clerestory is double-vaulted, supported by Minnesota granite columns. The main altar is made of white carrara marble and colored onyx and is flanked by statues of St. Jeanne d'Arc and King Louis IX (St. Louis). It was consecrated by Bishop John J. Lawler on November 30, 1911. Five windows above the altar depict aspects of the life of St. Louis, patron saint of the church. In 1997, the interior was redecorated, the woodwork refinished, including the pews, and new entrance doors were installed. Extensive work was also undertaken to remedy water leakage problems in the ceiling and basement, and, after a hiatus of two years, a new organ was installed in the loft at the rear of the church early in 1998.

The church is affectionately called the Little French Church, and it was Masqueray's favorite. "It is my little gem," he said.

St. Paul

Weyerhaeuser Memorial Chapel, Macalester College

1600 Grand Avenue
Cerny and Associates, Minneapolis, architects
1967–68

THE FIRST CHAPEL AT MACALESTER COLLEGE was located in Old Main. In 1889, after the construction of Macalester Presbyterian Church, chapel services were held in the church until 1925. George Dayton gave land at the corner of Macalester and Lincoln Avenues for a new church in 1924, and the college chapel held its services in the new structure for many years.

The present chapel was built in 1967–68 and dedicated in 1969. It was erected with funding from Mrs. Frederick Weyerhaeuser given in memory of her husband. Its construction was not without controversy: students protested the destruction of numerous old stately trees to clear

the site, and the leaders of Macalester Presbyterian Church objected to having a chapel built that would potentially draw people away from their congregation. In the end, the new chapel was built, despite the opposition.

Duane Thorbeck of the firm of Cerny and Associates created a hexagonal structure with a brick entry and glass walls held together by aluminum sashes and supports. A concrete base holds the building off the ground and creates a dry moat that partially surrounds it. The interior is softly lighted by natural daylight, partially deflected by brick walls that form side aisles and also serve to screen out distractions from outside, thereby lending a feeling of tranquillity and refuge. It is finished in red brick and blond wood, with heavy columns and radiating arms that support the roof and recall the trees destroyed to make way for the chapel.

St. Thomas Aquinas Church

920 Holly Avenue
Ralph Rapson, Minneapolis, architect
1969

T HIS CHURCH "LETS IT ALL HANG OUT," in the idiom of the day in which it was built. Its architectural effect hinges on its vast interior space and the massive, almost brutal, exposed structural system.

Rapson faced the usual problem of providing the maximum amount of space for the least amount of money. The congregation wanted a thousand seats, a chapel, confessionals, a working sacristy, priest and choir sacristies, and an office, all built on a flat corner lot next to the existing school and priest's and nuns' residences.

The church was built on an existing foundation and so was limited in the amount of load that could be placed on it. Therefore, the building has an independent roof structure supported on concrete columns spaced on 23-foot centers. These provide the support for two double transverse laminated wood beams of 155 feet in length, on which rest the secondary laminated wood beams. The exterior wall is non-load bearing, consisting of steel studs covered with rough stucco; above it is a continuous glazed surface topped by the roof structure. Thus, the massive flat roof structure seems to hover above the low base, giving the whole a strong horizontality.

Inside, Rapson sought, in his words, "to make evident the separate elements of worship within the unity of the nave space." For privacy and serenity, a small chapel is provided that is surrounded by a stucco wall of the same height as the wall enclosing the nave.

In 1973 St. Thomas Aquinas won an Honor Award from the Minnesota Society of Architects (now AIA Minnesota); in 1998 it was given the prestigious twenty-five-year Honor Award by the same group.

St. Peter

Church of the Holy Communion

110 Minnesota Avenue North
Henry M. Congdon, New York, architect
1869
National Register of Historic Places

B ISHOP HENRY WHIPPLE SAID OF THIS CHURCH, "It is the most beautiful rural Church I ever saw." It is, at the very least, one of the most elegant of all the Episcopal churches in the state.

The town site of St. Peter was platted by Episcopalians in 1854, and that same year, the first services were held in the settlement by Bishop Jackson Kemper, the first missionary bishop of the American Church. Everyone in town attended, which probably did not amount to more than a few dozen. In 1856 plans were made for the erection of the first church, and because $200 was received from the Church of the Holy Communion in New York City, the little frame church in St. Peter was given the same name. It was built of wood shipped from St. Anthony and seated about 150 people. The church was never consecrated.

In May 1860 the Reverend Edward Livermore arrived to succeed the Reverend Ezra Jones, the first resident minister. Mr. Livermore was called "a grand scholar and noble priest," and he stayed in St. Peter for the next twenty-three years. Among his first acts was to build parochial schools at St. Peter, Ottawa, and Le Sueur, raising money in eastern cities for them. He made plans for another church building, and, on April 13, 1869, the cornerstone of the present structure was laid. The first service in it was held on February 27, 1870, and it was consecrated by Bishop Whipple on July 27 of that same year. Nine visiting clergy were present at the ceremony, and a special train brought eighty churchmen from St. Paul. The new church cost $8,000 to build. The old chapel later became a blacksmith shop and survived for several years.

Mr. Livermore resigned in 1883; four years later, under the direction of the Reverend D. F. Thompson, a rectory was built. In 1892 electric lights were installed in the church, and in 1903 it was further improved by the addition of a new furnace and new organ.

This pleasant little Gothic Revival church, designed by New York architect Henry M. Congdon, is constructed of yellow Kasota stone, quarried just upriver near Mankato, and like

many Episcopal churches in the state, its style is derived from English country churches. It is just over 60 feet in length, and 32 feet in width. Its steeply pitched roof gives it almost an A-frame look, which is pierced by three small gable dormers on each side. Engaged buttresses divide the outside walls into three bays each. At the rear there is a delicate open bell tower, straddling the peak of the roof.

The inside height is 20 feet from floor to roof peak. It is finished in oak and walnut and the roof is exposed plank sheathing supported by square timbers and hammer beams. The overall result is one of the most refined and elegant of the stone Episcopal churches in the state.

The church's roof and support beams were heavily damaged by a tornado that struck St. Peter on March 29, 1998, resulting in extensive damage inside as well as out. Restoration of the interior and exterior was successfully carried out later that year.

St. Peter

Union Presbyterian Church

Third and Locust Streets
Abraham Radcliffe, St. Paul, architect
1871
National Register of Historic Places

PRESBYTERIAN MISSION ACTIVITY IN MINNESOTA seems to have begun at Traverse des Sioux, where, in 1843, the Reverends S. R. Rakes and R. Hopkins, with their wives, established a church and school for the Indians and white settlers in the area. Ten years later, this church became the first free Presbyterian church, organized with fourteen members. In 1858 a stone edifice was erected there that cost $5,000.

Meantime, in 1857 the first Presbyterian church of St. Peter was organized by the Reverend A. H. Kerr with thirteen members. It merged with the church at Traverse des Sioux in 1869, and they decided to erect a common building in St. Peter. The present church was built in 1871 at a cost of $15,000. Prominent St. Paul architect Abraham Radcliffe was hired to design it, and he gave the congregation a very handsome Gothic Revival structure. It was dedicated on April 25, 1872.

The church is constructed of local Kasota stone, which is more smoothly dressed on the front facade than on the other three sides. It has a tall spire rising on the left side, above a corner entrance, and measures 105 feet long and 45 feet wide. The nave has a ceiling height of 26 feet. There are three smaller spires on the roofline. A two-story education building was built in 1962.

On March 29, 1998, the church was severely damaged when a tornado struck St. Peter. The congregation decided to restore the structure, and repairs were completed in the same year.

Simpson (Olmsted County)

St. Bridget's Catholic Church

2123 County Road 16 Southeast

From U.S. Highway 63, east on County Road 16

Architect unknown
1859–60

S T. BRIDGET'S PARISH has been called the mother church of Catholics in Olmsted County. It was organized in Pleasant Grove township in 1853 by Father Michael Pendergast, who came from Winona to serve as the first priest. The parish and settlement was originally called Buckley Settlement after Michael Buckley, who arrived there in 1853 and donated ten acres for the church and cemetery. St. Bridget was the patron saint of the Buckleys. This structure may be, along with Our Lady of Lourdes (originally Unitarian Church) in Minneapolis, one of the oldest existing Catholic churches in the state, serving what was once a thriving railroad community of mostly Irish immigrants.

The church is of yellow stone brought by oxcart from near Winona, sixty miles away. The walls are three feet thick, and the rafters and rafter supports—made of wood also hauled from near Winona—are hand-hewn. Seven local stonemasons worked on the building, finishing it in 1860 at a cost of $1,500. It measures 75 feet long and 40 feet wide and seats 160 people on the main floor and balcony. A rectory was added in 1879 (since replaced), and the church was incorporated in 1881. A parish hall (built in 1872) used to stand across the road and was the scene of a large 1904 temperance meeting.

The church originally faced south, but in 1914 the tower was destroyed by a windstorm, and it was decided to rebuild the tower on the north end of the church so that it would be less exposed. The interior was reoriented 180 degrees as a result of placing the entrance on the north side. The "new" tower is of gray stone, with a niche housing a statue of St. Bridget and topped by a Celtic cross. There are five round-arched windows on each side of the nave.

Sleepy Eye

Church of St. Mary, Help of Christians

636 First Avenue North
Anton Dohmen, Milwaukee, architect
1900–1902

T HE PREDOMINANTLY GERMAN CATHOLIC PARISH of St. Mary was established in 1878, six years after the platting of Sleepy Eye. A church was built in 1876 of frame with a brick veneer, for $3,000, and served until it became too small and the present structure was erected.

In 1900 Father Wendelin Stulz was appointed to the parish by Archbishop John Ireland. Father Stulz made one of his first projects the building of a new church. Most of the property had already been acquired near the old church, and a building committee was chosen. Anton Dohmen of Milwaukee was employed as architect, and Henry Tappendorf of Rock Island, Illinois, was selected as contractor. Tappendorf's crew completed the foundation by the fall of 1900, but the following spring he refused to continue the work for the contracted amount. He was released from his contract, and a new builder, John Geiser of Chanhassen, was hired. Geiser soon found that the footings were not strong enough to hold the weight of the walls and had to be replaced. He finally completed the church in the summer of 1902.

This strikingly beautiful church is an outstanding example of Gothic Revival. It measures 175 feet long and 75 feet in width, and the ceiling of the sanctuary, which seats 975, is 100 feet in height. The basement walls are of dark brown sandstone from the Mankato area, and the red brick of which the church is built came from A. C. Ochs of Springfield, Minnesota. The total cost of the church was $68,000. The church is of such impressive size that when the order for the large stained glass windows was received in Germany, the studio thought they were for a cathedral. The new structure was dedicated on October 16, 1902, by Archbishop Ireland.

The interior is richly ornamented in creams and brownish reds, redecorated in 1976 (see Plate 7). The altars are of butternut, crafted by E. Hackner of La Crosse, Wisconsin, in 1905. Three large bells dating from 1879 were removed from the old church and installed in the south tower of the new one; they were electrified in 1973. The north tower contains a two-deck carillon

controlled from the sacristy, programmed with hymns that may be played for appropriate seasons or occasions.

The adjacent redbrick rectory was also designed by Dohmen and built by Geiser in 1904. The grade school was erected in 1914 from designs by Edward J. Donohue, a St. Paul architect. A gymnasium addition was built in 1939 and the two-story high school in 1951. The Sisters of St. Francis have provided the teaching staff from 1883 to the present day.

St. Michael's Church

611 Third Street South
Edward P. Bassford, St. Paul, architect
1873–75

S TILLWATER BEGAN AS A LUMBER MILLING TOWN on the St. Croix River in 1843 and was incorporated in 1854. The first Catholic mass was offered in 1849 by Father Augustin Ravoux, who traveled from St. Paul, and for a few years services were held in private homes. In 1853 the first St. Michael's Church was built, on the northwest corner of Fourth and Mulberry Streets. It was a small frame structure that swiftly became too small and was enlarged only three years later. Meantime, a rectory was constructed nearby on Fourth Street in 1855.

The present church was built at the urging of Father Maurice Murphy, who arrived in the parish in 1870. He wanted a prestigious church that would stand on a prominent height above the river town. Edward P. Bassford of St. Paul was hired as architect in 1872, and in June 1873 the cornerstone was laid; construction of the church proceeded for the next two years. It was dedicated by Bishop Thomas Grace of St. Paul in August 1875, although the building was not finished until a month later. The total cost was about $80,000.

This splendid church exhibits elements of Romanesque, Second Empire, and Gothic Revival styles. It is built of Stillwater sandstone and trimmed in Kasota stone, and measures 70 feet by 150 feet. The tall spire on the left side of the facade is 190 feet tall. In 1883 the chimes were played for the first time. They fell into disrepair in 1962 and were silent until restored at a cost of $12,000 in 1969.

Taylors Falls (Chisago County)

First United Methodist Church

Basil Street and Government Road
John L. Bullard, Taylors Falls, builder
1861
National Register of Historic Places (Angel's Hill District)

WHAT MINNESOTA LACKS IN ABUNDANCE it makes up for in the richness of its relatively few Greek Revival buildings. Most of these are to be found in the river towns along the St. Croix and Mississippi. The communities with the greatest numbers of such structures are Old Frontenac, Stillwater, and Taylors Falls.

In Taylors Falls, the Greek Revivals are concentrated on Angel's Hill above the main part of town. Arranged roughly around a square block, most consist of private residences, the bulk of which have been lovingly restored and carefully maintained. At the southeast corner of this square, just up the hill from the home of William Folsom (now a historic site maintained as a house museum) is the fine little First United Methodist Church.

Many of the original settlers of Taylors Falls had their roots in New England; this is evident in the houses and especially in this church, which evokes images of small, neat, picturesque New England churches. When these people came to Taylors Falls in the 1850s, they brought their culture and—in particular—their architecture with them. At the time, the predominant style in New England was Greek Revival.

The church is one of the best examples of Greek Revival architecture to be found anywhere in the state and is typical of the New England meetinghouse. It is a simple wood frame structure clad with clapboard on the sides and rear. The front facade is covered with wide, flat boards laid horizontally and scored to give the illusion of stone. It is divided into three bays by four pilasters, tapered so that they are wider at the top than at the base, thus giving the illusion to the observer on the ground of being in proportion throughout their entire height. There are entrances in the two side bays and a window in the center one. In the pediment above the entrance is a triangular date board. Above that rises the rectangular bell tower. The windows on the front and sides consist of three sashes with twelve panes in each and are replicas of the originals.

The interior has also been faithfully restored to preserve the meetinghouse atmosphere. Except for a dropped ceiling and a modernized basement, it is intact.

Thief River Falls

United Methodist Church

104 Horace Avenue North
Jyring and Whiteman, Hibbing, architects
1969

T HE UNIQUE DESIGN OF THIS CHURCH is dominated by a conical sixteen-sided roof that fits tightly down on the concrete-and-glass base, giving the whole a ground-hugging appearance. The roof trusses terminate in concrete anchors at the ground level and join at the top of the cone to form a circular skylight. In 1994–95, the original larger windows were replaced by smaller, energy-efficient sashes with the effect of having the windows lurk in the shadow of the overhanging roof. The roof was struck by lightning in October 1996, setting off a minor fire that caused a ten-foot-square burn mark in the ceiling of the sanctuary. Subsequent repairs included replacement of the original asphalt shingles with cedar ones.

Methodism began in the area in 1885, when seventeen-year-old Helen Wallin, daughter of a government fur trader, started a Sunday school at the post, situated at the confluence of the Thief and Red Lake Rivers. Church meetings began soon after in private homes until, in 1886, James M. Thomas arrived to work with young Miss Wallin in organizing a Methodist Episcopal congregation in the community. In 1892 a frame church was erected on First Street at a cost of $3,000, where it stood until about 1905, when the structure was moved to make way for the Soo Line Railroad tracks. In 1927 the Methodist Episcopal church began a lengthy process of merging with the Presbyterians and started holding services in the Presbyterian church, renamed the Community Church. The Methodist structure was abandoned and eventually sold in 1939 to the Seventh-Day Adventists. In 1939–40, extensive remodeling of the old Presbyterian church was undertaken, and it served until the construction of the present structure, which is on the same site as the old one.

Tyler (Lincoln County)

Danebod Lutheran Church

140 Danebod Court
Unknown Danish architect
1893–95
National Register of Historic Places

THIS IS BY ALL ODDS ONE OF THE MOST DISTINCTIVE CHURCHES in Minnesota and, in its elegant simplicity, one of the most beautiful. It was erected in 1893–95 by volunteer local Danish craftsmen working from plans by a Danish architect who designed a church at Vallekild, Denmark. The present structure was part of the Danebod Colony, established by an organization that became the Danish Evangelical Lutheran Church of America.

The style is Eastlake or Stick style Gothic, built on a Greek cross plan but with a tower turned forty-five degrees to the axis at the crossing. The exterior was resided with aluminum lap siding in the 1980s, but applied to recall the original with wainscoting at the base and careful attention to preserving the lines and details originally in wood. In 1947, the road west of the church was lowered three and a half feet, and the council decided to move the building farther east and to turn it one-quarter of a turn. The main entrance now faces south instead of west. A full basement was added, and a larger narthex replaced a former cramped entry.

The interior is especially striking, with seating on three sides, a three-sided balcony above, and a ship model hanging below the balcony just inside the main entrance, a common element in maritime countries such as Denmark (see Plate 13). There are also porthole windows in the balcony beneath the eaves. The interior is paneled in gleaming hardwood with a large Star of Bethlehem in patterned hardwood in the ceiling. A statue of Christ modeled on a famous one in Denmark by Bertel Thorvaldsen (1770–1844) is in the altar, and the baptismal font was hand-carved from stone by a local mason.

Until 1947 services were held solely in the Danish language; the transition to English was championed by the Reverend Holger Strandskov, who came to Danebod in 1930 as the church's first American-born pastor.

Vasa (Goodhue County)

Vasa Evangelical Lutheran Church
(originally Vasa Swedish Lutheran Church)

15399 Norelius Road

Minnesota Highway 19 to County Road 7, then north ¼ mile

D. C. Hill, Red Wing, architect and builder
1869
National Register of Historic Places (Vasa Historic District)

VASA, AS THE NAME IMPLIES, was settled by Swedes in 1853. It was originally called Mattson's Settlement after Hans Mattson, the twenty-one-year-old leader who went on to become a secretary of state for Minnesota and consul general to India.

In 1855 the Reverend Eric Norelius arrived at Mattson's Settlement, a truly landmark event, for Norelius was one of the most dynamic figures in the early church history of the state and certainly the most outstanding leader of the early Lutheran Church. He founded more than a dozen Swedish Lutheran congregations in southeastern Minnesota and the St. Croix River valley and was a major force in the establishment of the Minnesota Conference of the Lutheran Church–Augustana Synod in 1858. Twice in the next twelve to fifteen years, Norelius brought to Vasa the meeting of the Minnesota Conference and truly put the town on the map. He also founded Gustavus Adolphus College in St. Peter and the Swedish-language newspaper the *Minnesota Posten.*

The present church was erected in 1869 by D. C. Hill, of whose life and career nothing is known. Working from his own plans, he designed this attractive church to replace the original log edifice. It is in the Gothic Revival style, built on a forty-acre tract on a hilltop where it was visible for a long distance. Approximately 350,000 locally fired bricks were used in its construction. The parsonage was built at the same time of the same kind of brick. The total cost of church and parsonage was $31,065.22.

The church stands on a foundation that is 4 feet thick. It is 118 feet long by 50 feet wide, and the walls are 22 feet high. The roof is supported entirely by the walls; there are no columns in the sanctuary to block the view. The pulpit was designed by Mr. Norelius, based on a vision he had one night of a "Bible on a Bible." The base is a Bible closed; the upper portion is a Bible opened,

with the outside (cover) toward the congregation and the inside facing the pastor. The top is a partially unrolled scroll. The Cross of Christ Lutheran Church at Welch has a similar pulpit.

Vasa Swedish Lutheran once housed the second-largest congregation in the synod. From it sprang other churches in Cannon Falls, Welch, Red Wing, and Spring Garden. The community went into decline in the 1950s, and many of the businesses closed. But enough of its original fabric remained that today much of the little settlement is a historic district on the National Register of Historic Places.

Veseli (Le Sueur County)

Church of the Holy Trinity

4938 North Washington Street
Clarence H. Johnston, St. Paul, architect
1905
National Register of Historic Places

THIS CHURCH IS A SKILLFUL EXAMPLE of work by one of St. Paul's leading turn-of-the-century architects. Clarence H. Johnston executed a great many buildings during his career, including a large number for state institutions such as the University of Minnesota, the State School for the Deaf, and the former Minnesota Historical Society building near the state

capitol. For many years, he was architect for the State Board of Control, which administered state institutions and buildings. His output of churches was comparatively low, making this structure all the more interesting.

Veseli is the largest of four Czech settlements in Minnesota. It existed as part of the parish at New Prague until 1874, when it became independent. The new parish erected a frame church between 1874 and 1878 that was replaced by the present building in 1905 at a cost of $30,000. It is Italian Romanesque in style with touches of Craftsman, and measures 110 feet long and 64 feet wide. There is a square 90-foot-high campanile-type tower attached to the left rear of the church. The facade has a round rose window above which is an abbreviated eave almost forming a canopy for the window. The church itself is built of tan brick with darker brick courses running in parallel on the lower portion of the walls. Some minor, mainly cosmetic, alterations were made to the interior in 1951.

The first school was built in 1881 and replaced in 1916. The convent and rectory were erected in 1926.

Vista (Waseca County)

Vista Lutheran Church

North of New Richland on Minnesota Highway 13; one mile east on County Road 20

Architect and builder unknown
1908
National Register of Historic Places

T HIS CHURCH IS AT THE CENTER OF AN AREA predominantly settled by Swedes and Norwegians in 1856 and 1857. It is one of three built by the Scandinavian settlers in this part of Waseca County: one is only a half mile away, the other—Norwegian Le Sueur River Lutheran Church—is three miles distant. Vista lives up to its name, looking out upon miles of rich and beautiful farmland in Waseca County.

Vista is Gothic Revival, built of red brick on a raised stone foundation. It has a single central tower of wood and brick rising above the double-door entrance. Over the doors is an arched window and above that a sign reading, "1858 Vista 1908," commemorating the fiftieth anniversary of the founding of the congregation. There are five stained glass windows on each side of the nave, and two flanking the entrance.

Wabasha

Grace Memorial Episcopal Church

Third and Bailey Streets
Cass Gilbert or Clarence H. Johnston, St. Paul, architect
1901
National Register of Historic Places

T HERE APPEARS TO BE SOME CONTROVERSY over exactly who the architect was for this church. Cass Gilbert is most frequently credited with the design, but Paul Clifford Larson, in his book *Minnesota Architect: The Life and Work of Clarence H. Johnston* (Afton, Minn.: Afton Historical Society Press, 1996), cites evidence that Johnston may have designed it. Because the jury still seems to be out on this question, both architects are named here as possible designers.

Either man could very well have created this little gem. Gilbert was quite capable of working in English Gothic, as he did in St. Clement's Memorial Episcopal Church in St. Paul and St. Martin's By-the-Lake in Minnetonka Beach. On the other hand, some of Johnston's churches—especially the Church of the Holy Trinity at Veseli and his Hamline Methodist Episcopal and Olivet Congregational churches (both in St. Paul)—demonstrate clearly that he could have designed a sensitive small building such as this one.

Grace Memorial Episcopal is built parallel rather than perpendicular to the street, on a modified cruciform plan with its two gabled entrances on the long side facing the street. One has a Tudor half-timber and stucco gable, the other a detailed carved wood gabled eave and exposed wood truss arching over the main entrance. Engaged buttresses are on the front and side facades. A small bell tower, built of stone with a matching carved wood gabled eave, is located directly behind the main entrance.

Inside, the church is simply appointed with dark woodwork and pews and a walnut beamed ceiling. The stained glass, however, is what makes the interior especially striking, for it includes a Tiffany window above the altar titled "Three Marys at the Tomb," executed in soft muted tones that contrast sharply with the vibrant colors of the other windows. The window was manufactured in Philadelphia and shipped to Wabasha on a flatbed train car, which was considered the safest and most reliable method at the time. Four men were hired to accompany and guard the window while it was being shipped.

The parish was organized in 1862 as Grace Church. Until 1865, the congregation used the Baptist chapel for services. Members then purchased the chapel and moved it to a new location, where they painted and repaired it and added a bell tower. The present structure was commissioned by St. Paul lumberman Thomas Irvine (whose mansion on Summit Avenue is today the home of Minnesota's governors) in memory of his wife, Emily Hills Irvine, and her parents, the Reverend and Mrs. Horace Hills. Mr. Hills was the pastor of this congregation from 1872 to 1877. Irvine was a communicant in the church and married Emily Hills in Grace Church in 1876. When his wife died in 1899, Irvine donated money for a new church as a gift to the people of Wabasha and requested that it be named Grace Memorial. It was dedicated by Bishop Henry Whipple on May 22, 1901—his last visit to the parish, for he died on September 22 of the same year.

Warroad

St. Mary's Church
Roberts and McKenzie Streets
Ursa Louis Freed, Aberdeen, South Dakota, architect
1952–53

T HIS BUILDING IS THE LARGEST ALL-WEATHER LOG CHURCH in the world, designed by Ursa Louis Freed to fit in with its North Woods surroundings and to portray the ruggedness of the life of early voyageurs and Catholic missionaries. It serves the northernmost Catholic parish in the continental United States.

St. Mary's is a memorial to Father Jean Pierre Aulneau, a French missionary killed in an Indian massacre on an island in Lake of the Woods in June 1736. The parish began in Warroad in 1904, and the first church was built in 1906, across the river from the present structure. In 1949, the parish, at the urging of Father Emmett Shanahan, purchased a site for a new church in a part of town that had city sewer and water service. Three years later the parishioners contracted with Andrew Hoy of St. Paul to build the church. Hoy contacted Freed, who donated his services to design it. Bricks were supplied by Hoy at no cost. It was later discovered that Hoy had been taking them from a school at Red Lake Falls being constructed by his employer, Hurley Construction Company. The company threatened to sue the church to recover losses of about $4,400, but settled for $1,500 and agreed to donate the rest to the parish. Needless to say, Hoy was fired as the church's contractor.

Logs were donated by the Indians at Pine Island, ninety miles away, and the parishioners hauled them back every weekend during the winter and peeled and treated them on-site. They also split and stained by hand 70,000 cedar shakes for the roof. Ten stained glass windows were purchased from the demolished St. Mary's Church at Red Lake Falls (only eight were installed). All materials and furnishings were either donated or provided at cost by dealers and manufacturers. A 40-foot bell tower stands next to the church, designed to replicate the cross and cairn of stones erected by the Jesuits in 1905 on the island where Father Aulneau was killed. A sculpture of Father Aulneau carved from a block of Winona limestone by Tony Caponi of Macalester College was installed on the tower. The interior is finished in California redwood paneling and seats 280. Through use of donated labor and materials, the church cost about $125,000 to construct but was valued at nearly $200,000. It was dedicated in June 1954.

Waverly

Marysville Swedesburg Lutheran Church

From U.S. Highway 12, north on County Road 9 3½ miles

Architect and builder unknown
1891
National Register of Historic Places

Tᴴɪꜱ ɪꜱ ᴏɴᴇ ᴏꜰ ᴛʜᴇ ꜰɪɴᴇꜱᴛ brick Gothic Revival parish churches in Wright County, and it might be considered one of the finest such structures in the state.

Swedes started arriving in Wright County in 1869. The Marysville parish was organized four years later and, in the pattern typical of many early parishes in the state, built a log church in 1874. The log church served the parish until 1891 when the present structure was erected. It was in use up to 1952, at which time the Zion Church was completed in Waverly and Marysville was abandoned and its bell transferred to Zion Church. For the next twenty years, this little church remained closed and subject to vandalism and neglect.

In 1971 the remaining parishioners, led by local resident Clinton Mattson, talked the directors of the church out of demolishing it and started efforts to restore their old building. After two years of work, primarily by members of the congregation, the structure was returned to good repair and the parish celebrated its centennial.

The church is built of local red brick on a foundation of granite blocks. It is a rectangular structure with a shed roof and a projecting entrance tower and steeple. The interior is simply furnished with wood pews and a carved and white-painted altar, pulpit, and baptismal font. A balistraded communion rail separates the altar from the nave, elevated one step above the main floor. The church is heated by a wood stove.

Waverly

St. Mary's Catholic Church

606 Elm Avenue
Adolphus Druiding, Chicago, architect (?)
1890–92

THE TOWN OF WAVERLY BEGAN AS ZELLINGEN (later Waverly Mills) in 1856, platted by two brothers named Colwell and a third man, A. C. Morris. They built a dam, sawmill, and gristmill and laid claim to the area around the town site. At the same time, other developers were platting the nearby town of Marysville. The first Catholic priests to serve the area were on a circuit from St. Paul that included Shakopee, St. Michael, and Clearwater. The first Catholic church in the Waverly community stood on the north shore of Waverly Lake and was a mission of both Watertown and St. Michael. It was built in 1861 of logs and replaced by a 22-foot-by-30-foot frame building on the same site five years later, while the community was served by the young missionary priest John Ireland. In 1873–74 the growing parish erected a new, larger frame church on the site of the present rectory in the town of Waverly Mills, whose name became simply Waverly in 1899.

Six years after the Reverend Joseph Guillot became the first permanent pastor in 1884, the present church was begun. While no architect has been attributed to it, it could well have been Adolphus Druiding of Chicago, who specialized in designing churches for Catholic parishes throughout the Midwest and who preferred red brick as his construction material. The form of the church, with its two towers of unequal height, was also one of his trademarks, as was the Gothic style. The building measures 138 feet long by 43 feet wide. About 600,000 bricks made in Chaska, Shakopee, and Waverly Mills were used in its construction. The trim is Kasota stone. Stained glass was manufactured by Brown and Haywood of Minneapolis. There are three bells in the north tower, cast by Henry Stuckstede of St. Louis, Missouri. A smaller bell in the south tower, dated 1874 and also cast by the Stuckstede firm, is from the old church and is not used. The church cost about $50,000 to erect and seats 850. The taller of the two towers rises to a height of 141 feet; the other is 98 feet tall.

As the church was being constructed, Father Guillot and the contractor, John Geiser of Chanhassen, felt that the steeples should be a few feet taller to make the building look more

218

stately. Father Guillot traveled to St. Paul to ask Archbishop Ireland for permission to spend the extra money needed to raise the height of the steeples. Ireland refused. About two years later, Ireland visited the parish and remarked that the towers should have been higher. Father Guillot hastened to tell him the reason they were not taller, and Ireland reportedly had no more to say. St. Mary's was dedicated in January 1892, with Bishop James McGolrick of Duluth officiating.

Father Guillot went on to the parish at Marshall, where he was instrumental in building the Church of the Holy Redeemer. He died in St. Paul in 1953 at age ninety-eight.

Welch (Goodhue County)

Cross of Christ Lutheran Church

15112 Highway 61 Boulevard (U.S. Highway 61 and County Road 7)
Charles E. Johnson, Miesville, builder
1878
National Register of Historic Places

MINNESOTA SEEMS TO HAVE MORE THAN ITS SHARE of picturesque Gothic white frame country churches, and this is one of the finest. It was built in 1878 by Swedish settlers, next to three acres purchased in 1875 for a cemetery. One of the settlers, Charles E. Johnson, erected the church beginning on May 1 and finishing later the same year. Lumber was hauled from the Betcher Lumber Company in Red Wing. Each of the male members of the congregation was assessed $3 and each female member was assessed $1.50, which paid for thirty-two pews and two stoves. A four-bedroom parsonage was built the following year along with horse stalls on the western edge of the property and a fence on the northern boundary used as a hitching rail. An organ was added in 1881.

The building measures 40 by 70 feet; it is one story tall with a gable roof and a highly distinctive tower and spire. The tower is square, capped by an octagonal belfry and gabled steeple with a cross at its pinnacle. The bell was manufactured in West Roy, New York, by the Neely Company and was purchased in 1892 for $500. It was so heavy that the steeple had to be reinforced to hold it. There are five Gothic-arched windows on each side of the church and a wide Gothic-arched window above the double-doored entrance. A distinctive feature of this church is the pulpit, made in 1883 of wood in the shape of a vertical, open Bible resting atop another that is lying closed to form the base. The top of the pulpit is shaped like a partially unrolled scroll resting on the open Bible. It represents the Reverend Eric Norelius's dream of preaching from atop a Bible. There is a similar pulpit in the Vasa Evangelical Lutheran Church. The interior of the church was redecorated in 1993.

The congregation was organized as the Swedish Evangelical Lutheran Church of Welch on December 27, 1873, by Mr. Norelius, who is called the father of the Swedish church in Minnesota. Norelius served in Red Wing as early as 1855, then moved to Spring Garden in 1858, Cannon Falls in 1859, and Prairie Island in 1870. He also founded the churches at Vasa and Center City, featured elsewhere in this volume.

Willmar

Vinje Lutheran Church

1001 Southwest Willmar Avenue
Sovik, Mathre, and Madson, Northfield, architects
1962–66

V INJE IS ONE OF THE MOST REMARKABLE and beautiful of the modern churches to be found anywhere in the state, the product of an architectural firm that specializes in contemporary ecclesiastical designs.

The present church is the fourth for this congregation. It is named for a church in Telemark, Norway, the home of many of the first members of the congregation. All of the initial settlers in the area were either killed or driven out during the Great Sioux Uprising of 1862. After the uprising was crushed by army troops and thirty-eight of the leaders hanged en masse at Mankato, the lands were again available to settlement. In 1863 and for several years thereafter, Norwegian immigrants entered the area and organized the congregation of Vinje in 1867.

Not until several years had elapsed was a church built, a typical log structure so familiar on the Minnesota frontier. The first permanent pastor was called in 1869 (a circuit rider served until then), and in 1875 the congregation joined the Synod for the Norwegian Evangelical Lutheran Church of America. That same year, the second church was finished, a Gothic frame building with a single steeple located on the site of the Vinje cemetery at the corner of Becker and Sixth Street East, on the east side of Willmar. In 1904 the third church was built a block away at Becker and Fifth Street. It was a Gothic Revival style clad in brick veneer on a stone foundation with a 120-foot tower and spire rising above the entrance. It cost $20,000 to build and stood until the present Vinje church was completed in 1963. On Palm Sunday, April 7, 1963, the last service was held in the old church, the front door was ceremoniously closed with a cross, and the congregation walked to its new home in southwest Willmar.

Ground breaking for the new church took place in 1961 and, two years later, the twenty-sided drum-shaped sanctuary was completed. It took another three years to finish the ambitious project. The sanctuary stands inside a courtyard formed by the outer one-story square, which houses offices, classrooms, meeting rooms, kitchen, library, and rehearsal spaces. Each of the four sides of the square is named for a New Testament evangelist.

The sanctuary features an oculus or lantern covered with gold leaf and lighted by baby spotlights. The circular space is surrounded by stained glass windows designed by William Saltzman and fabricated by Gaytee Studios of Minneapolis. The pattern in the glass consists of abstract swirls made from two thousand square feet of antique handblown glass from Germany (see Plate 10). A choir balcony with a twenty-three-rank organ hovers over one side of the sanctuary.

Central United Methodist Church

114 West Broadway Street
Lorenzo B. Wheeler, St. Louis, architect
C. G. Maybury and Son, Winona, associate architects
1894–96
Alpha Hensel Fink, Philadelphia; Eckert and Carlson, Winona, architects
1963

T HIS CHURCH IS A PROMINENT LANDMARK on West Broadway, which seems to have more than its share of fine early religious structures. It reminds us that southeastern Minnesota was being settled before the Civil War and that most of the congregations date from the 1850s.

This one is no exception. It was organized in 1856 as Central Methodist Episcopal, and, soon after, the first church was built, a simple frame structure that cost $400. A parsonage was constructed within a short time, also.

In 1872, as the congregation expanded, a second much larger and more elaborate church was built for $20,000. It was clad in brick and executed in an Italianate style. It also contained a $2,000 pipe organ, the first in southern Minnesota.

The second church burned down in January 1895, during a bitter cold spell. Someone spotted smoke coming out of the organ pipes following the end of services. Fortunately, the congregation had already planned to erect an even larger church and had purchased land for $15,000 and started construction the preceding year. Prominent local citizens James and Matthew Norton were financing the new church.

The new building was of buff-colored stone from Bear Creek Quarry near Winona. It had the typical red or brown sandstone trim, as does nearby First Baptist and First Congregational. On the southeast corner stands a tall tower with a central steeple surrounded by smaller towers. The tower contains eleven chimes weighing 11,000 pounds and given by William Keith, a trustee, supplemented by a gift from local philanthropist Matthew Norton. The walls are of brick, some twenty inches thick, faced with six to eight inches of stone. The cost of construction was more than $100,000.

The congregation seemed to have had more than its share of bad luck, however, for this church, too, was destroyed by fire in 1961. Only the tower remained, and this building was reconstructed

to conform in style with the tower. The result is a successful tribute to the work of the Philadelphia architect Alpha Hensel Fink and the local firm of Edwin O. Eckert and James K. Carlson.

Fink was adviser to the National Methodist Church organization and had his office across the hall from their offices. Thus, when the minister of Central Methodist Episcopal went searching for an architect, Fink's name was suggested. He was not registered to work in Minnesota, however, so he drew the plans and sent them to Eckert and Carlson for their signature. They supervised the construction work, with Carlson acting as structural engineer.

Winona

First Baptist Church

368 West Broadway Street
Bullard and Bullard, Springfield, Illinois, architects
1888–93

THE FIRST BAPTIST MINISTER IN MINNESOTA, the Reverend Edward Ely, arrived in Winona on May 4, 1852. When he stepped off the steamboat, he was asked by Captain Orrin Smith and Erwin Johnson, co-owners of the town site, if he would stay in their town and found a church. If he agreed, they would donate land for a church and rectory. Ely accepted and began holding services in various buildings around town. His wife was an artist and painted portraits of a number of the local citizens in the following years. In 1855 the Baptists organized a church and two years later built their first one, a frame structure at the corner of Fourth and Center Streets that seated 250 people. It burned down in 1887, and the congregation, which meanwhile had grown dramatically, decided to erect a larger, much more prestigious building a short distance away at the corner of Broadway and Wilson. This splendid structure is the result.

Built at a cost of $27,500, the church carries stylistic elements from both the Gothic and Romanesque Revivals. It is constructed of dressed native Winona limestone with Fond du Lac sandstone trim, giving it a striking appearance. It has a hipped roof, several cross-gable bays, and a distinctive tall rounded tower on the southwest corner with a conical roof. There is a Gothic-arched main entry in the tower and a large stained glass window on the south elevation.

Winona

First Congregational Church

161 West Broadway Street
William H. Willcox, Chicago, architect
1880–82

THIS IMPOSING ROMANESQUE REVIVAL CHURCH was built at a cost of $30,000, not counting land and furnishings, which added up to another $8,000. It faces north and is constructed of the local buff limestone and Wisconsin red sandstone trim. It has an irregular plan with a large tower on the northeast corner. The steepled tower has a door with a pointed arch and paired Gothic windows with lintels. The northwest corner has a much shorter tower with an identical entrance.

The congregation was organized in 1854 with eighteen members. It was the first church formed in Winona and possibly in southeastern Minnesota and was the third Congregational church in the state.

The first church was built in 1856 for $4,000—an imposing sum for that date and location. The building was moved to another site in 1863 and subsequently enlarged. It was sold in 1882 after the present church was completed.

Fund-raising began in 1879, and ground was broken for the new structure the next year. The building was finished in 1882 and dedicated that same year. It seats 650 people. The chapel for Sabbath school holds 500 and is a large semicircular room covered by a dome.

Winona

St. Paul's Episcopal Church

265 Lafayette Street
Ananias Langdon, Winona, architect
1873–74

T HE CONGREGATION OF ST. PAUL'S was organized on May 13, 1856. Services were held on the second floor of various commercial buildings until 1862, when fire consumed the last one on the Fourth of July. The members decided to erect their own church, which was a frame structure at the corner of Fifth and Lafayette Streets, costing $2,500. The first service in the new church was held on Christmas 1862. In 1870 their lot was purchased by one of the town business-men, and the church was moved about a block to Broadway. Three years later the congregation needed a larger facility and work was begun on what was to be one of the first stone churches in the city of Winona, using locally quarried materials. The cornerstone was laid that year and the first services were held on Christmas 1874. The second church cost $25,000 to erect and furnish. Twenty years later, a crenelated tower costing $1,000 was added.

The church was designed in the traditional English Gothic style. It is cross-shaped and has a steeply pitched gable roof and engaged stone buttresses. The interior is lighted with Gothic-arched stained glass windows, and there is a large rose window in the front facade.

A stone two-story parsonage, built in the 1890s, stands north of the church.

Winona

St. Stanislaus Polish Catholic Church

601 East Fourth Street
C. G. Maybury and Son, Winona, architects
1894–95
National Register of Historic Places

I N A CITY THAT IS ABSOLUTELY CRAMMED WITH OUTSTANDING CHURCHES, this edifice (literally) stands above the rest. It occupies an entire city block and is, in a word, monumental. Erected on the site of the old church, which was built in 1872 and razed for the present structure, St. Stanislaus dominates its working-class neighborhood.

To describe this church without lapsing into a bland, monotonous recitation of numbers is difficult because one cannot convey an impression of its majesty without resorting to at least a few dimensions. First, the style is "Roman with classical detail" (from a contemporary description), which means it is a blend of Romanesque and baroque. The church is basically a Greek cross in plan with a ten-sided center. The overall dimensions are 140 feet from north to south and 124 feet east to west. The front entrance is identified by twin domed metal white-painted campaniles on square towers that are 114 feet high. The sanctuary is roofed in red tile and rises to a height of 100 feet capped by a round drum and dome that, were it not for the statue of St. Stanislaus atop it, could have come from a modest state capitol. The drum is 30 feet in diameter, and the height to the top of the statue is 172 feet. The exterior brick was painted in 1947.

The interior is similarly impressive. The main ceiling is 46 feet above the floor and measures 100 feet north to south and 116 feet east to west. It can accommodate 1,400 on the main floor and 400 more in the gallery. One of the most significant features of the interior is a set of four large central columns of iron beams enclosed in block and plaster and coated with scagliola to replicate French breche gray marble. Wainscoting in the nave imitates German formosa marble. In 1966 lightning struck the dome, setting fire to the church. Subsequent fire fighting resulted in water damage to three of the columns, but the interior was completely restored in the only significant restoration the church has ever had.

Winona was founded by Captain Orrin Smith, who had often sailed past the future town site on his riverboat and came to realize its value as a stopping point between downriver ports and St. Paul. With Erwin Johnson, he established his first claim in 1851 or 1852, depending on which source you choose to believe. Winona was originally called Wing Prairie, then renamed Wabasha's Prairie after a local Indian chief. Soon thereafter, the name was changed yet again, to Winona in commemoration of the Indian maiden Wee-no-nah, who, legend has it, leaped to her death from a projecting crag rather than submit to the unwelcome attentions of a warrior she did not love. The rock from which she was supposed to have jumped is called Maiden Rock to this day. By 1860 the town already had a population of 2,400, and ten years later was a booming milling (lumber and flour) center. In the 1870s and 1880s, Winona changed from being a river port to a railroad hub, the port of entry for transportation farther west. Its population was heavily composed of German and Polish immigrants, who supplied much of the labor for the many industries that located in the town. Winona also became the site of the first teachers' training school west of the Mississippi and the home of the enormously successful J. R. Watkins drug and extract company.

Wykoff (Fillmore County)

St. Kilian's Catholic Church
North Gold Street
Congregation-built
1902

T HIS DELIGHTFUL LITTLE FRAME CHURCH stands unobtrusively on a corner in a residential neighborhood. The dominant church in town is a large frame Lutheran structure a few blocks away, but it has been unsympathetically altered with a new narthex/entry. Were it not for the addition, that church probably would have been a candidate for inclusion here.

St. Kilian's parish was organized in 1880 and mass was offered in private homes until 1887, when the parishioners bought the former Baptist church and converted it for their use. In 1902 they erected the present building on the site of the old one at a cost of $3,500.

The church is Gothic Revival in style, wood frame with a tall tower placed centrally on the front, and pinnacles at the front corners of the gabled roof. It seats three hundred.

The interior was revised in the 1960s under Vatican II so that the altar would face the congregation. This is the only substantial change in the interior.

Zumbrota (Goodhue County)

First Congregational Church

455 East Avenue
Built by local labor
1862
National Register of Historic Places

T HE NEW ENGLAND SETTLERS OF ZUMBROTA fixed on a familiar design for their new church, using the Greek Revival style to recreate the meetinghouses of their Eastern home. This church is one of only a very few Greek Revival churches in the state and, along with First United Methodist in Taylors Falls, one of the best.

It has been said that no community in southeastern Minnesota was more solidly New England in its origins than Zumbrota. The town was laid out in 1856 by Aaron Doty and a partner named Smith. The same year, the Stafford Western Emigration Company, a group set up to help New Englanders migrate west, became interested in the town and merged with Doty and Smith to survey it. They changed the name to Zumbrota.

By 1857 there were enough settlers to organize a church. For the first four years services were held on the second floor of Kellett's store, one of the first commercial buildings in town (on the site of the present bank). By 1861 the congregation had raised enough money—some of it by a member who traveled East to tap fellow congregations—to build a structure.

The church was built by local labor. Lumber was hauled from Red Wing by ox team, and lime was brought from Lake City by similar transport. Ox teams were abysmally slow, and the trip one way took two days. The stone for the foundation was quarried from land owned by a parishioner northwest of town. John Willard of New York donated fifty hymnals to the congregation, and the stovepipe was donated by a Detroit hardware company.

The church is one story, measuring 37 feet wide and 76 feet in length. Its front facade is divided into three bays by four pilasters. Each bay has tall narrow flat-topped windows covered by louvered shutters that hang from the top of the windows. There is a double-door entrance, above which is a round-arched window and, above that, a green-shuttered oculus centered in the pediment.

The bell tower is square at its base and topped by a tall spire. The bell was added in 1868 at a cost of $640 and weighs 1,202 pounds. It was presented to the church by the Ladies Aid Society and was brought by ox team to Zumbrota. The bell was hung by the sweat of the men of the congregation, who thought using teams of oxen or horses to raise it would have been a sacrilege. For years it was the only bell in town and served also as the fire and school bell.

The building was enlarged in 1880 to its present size. Its first musical instrument was a melodeon, which was replaced in 1885 by an organ purchased from the First Congregational Church in Winona when that congregation decided to buy a larger one. A parsonage was built next to the church in 1870, replaced by a new one in 1960 just around the corner.

Other Sites of Interest

Ada
Congregational Church of Ada (now home to the Memorial Educational Museum, Norman County Historical Society)
First Street East and Second Avenue East
Charles Waterbury and A. O. Rolfe, Ada, builders
1900
National Register of Historic Places

Adrian
St. Adrian Catholic Church
Main and Sixth Streets
Henry A. Foeller, Green Bay, Wisconsin, architect
1900
National Register of Historic Places

Aitkin
Bethlehem Lutheran Church
Minnesota Highway 47 to County Road 12; south 4.4 miles to Oriole Avenue; east 1 mile, left on 320th Street (Nordland Township)
Congregation-built
1897
National Register of Historic Places

Albany
Seven Dolors Catholic Church
140 Second Street
Erhard Brielmaier, Milwaukee, architect
1872 (1898–1900 addition and renovation)

Albert Lea
First Baptist Church
335 West Clark Street
Tapager and Hanson, Albert Lea, builders
1906

First Church of Christ Scientist
Clark Street and Adams Avenue West
C. M. Tapager, Albert Lea, builder
1915

First Presbyterian Church
308 Water Street
LeRoy Gaarder, Albert Lea, architect
1929

Grace Christian Church (originally Danish Baptist Church)
501 West College Street
LeRoy Gaarder, Albert Lea, architect
1925

Grace Lutheran Church
918 Garfield Avenue
LeRoy Gaarder, Albert Lea, architect
1951

United Methodist Church
702 Highway 69 South
Hills, Gilbertson, and Fisher, Minneapolis, architects
1955–57

Alexandria
St. Mary's Catholic Church
411 Hawthorne Street
Slifer and Cone, St. Paul, architects
1949–50
Hammel, Green, and Abrahamson, Minneapolis, architects (addition)
1996–97

Arendahl (Fillmore County)
Arendahl Lutheran Church
From Lanesboro, north on Minnesota Highway 250; east 2 miles on Minnesota Highway 30
Architect and builder unknown
1899

Askov (Pine County)
Bethlehem Lutheran Church
Church Street
Jes Smidt, West Denmark, Wisconsin, architect
1914–15
National Register of Historic Places

Austin
Christ Church (Episcopal)
Third Avenue Northwest and Second Street Northwest
LeRoy Gaarder, Albert Lea, architect
1951

Queen of Angels Catholic Church
1001 East Oakland Avenue
LeRoy Gaarder, Albert Lea, architect
1937–38, 1954–56

Avon (Stearns County)
St. Benedict's Catholic Church
212 First Street Southeast
Gilbert Winkelman, Collegeville, architect
1928

Belle Plaine
Episcopal Church of the Transfiguration
Walnut and Church Streets
Architect and builder unknown
1868
National Register of Historic Places

Our Lady of the Prairie Catholic Church
212 North Chestnut Street
Architect and builder unknown
1905

Bemidji
Bethany Free Lutheran Church
1300 Beltrami Avenue Northwest
Architect and builder unknown
ca. 1915

St. Philip's Church
702 Beltrami Avenue Northwest
YHR Partners Ltd., Moorhead, architects
1991

Benson
Christ Episcopal Church (now houses the Benson Senior Center)
310 Thirteenth Street North
Local labor
1879
National Register of Historic Places

Church of St. Francis Xavier
Thirteenth Street North and Montana Avenue
Emmanuel L. Masqueray, St. Paul, architect
1917
National Register of Historic Places

Blooming Prairie
First Lutheran Church
434 First Street Southwest
Charles Sedgwick, Minneapolis, architect
1916

Brainerd
First Presbyterian Church
512 South Eighth Street
A. R. Van Dyke, Minneapolis, architect
1927
Architecture 1, Brainerd, architects (addition and renovation)
1960–61

Trinity Lutheran Church
1420 Sixth Street South
SMSQ, Northfield, architects
1957

Breckenridge
St. Mary of the Presentation Catholic Church
221 Fourth Street West
Ursa Louis Freed, Aberdeen, South Dakota, architect
1952

Brownsville (Houston County)
Church of the Holy Comforter
Main Street
Charles Brown, Brownsville, builder
1869
National Register of Historic Places

St. Patrick's Catholic Church
604 Adams Street
Architect and builder unknown
Date unknown

Buckman (Morrison County)
St. Michael's Catholic Church
Minnesota Highway 25
George Bergmann, St. Cloud, architect
1902

Buffalo
Christ the King Retreat Center Chapel
621 South First Avenue
Carter and Sundt, Minneapolis, architects
1960–61

Church of St. Francis Xavier
9 Northwest Third Street
Victor Cordella, Minneapolis, architect
1912–14

Zion Lutheran Church
1200 Highway 25 South
Armstrong, Torseth, Skold, and Rydeen, Minneapolis, architects
1988

Caledonia
St. Mary's Church
513 South Pine Street
Architect and builder unknown
1920s

Cannon Falls
St. Ansgar's Lutheran Church
7459 Highway 19 Boulevard
Gjelten and Schellberg, Rochester, Minnesota, architects
1970

Caribou (Kittson County)
St. Nicholas Orthodox Church
Northeast of Lancaster on County Road 4 (Caribou Township)
Architect and builder unknown
1905
National Register of Historic Places

Chanhassen
Colonial Church at Heritage Square (originally Church of St. Hubertus)
7801 Great Plains Boulevard
Architect and builder unknown
1887
National Register of Historic Places

Chaska
Chaska Moravian Church
115 Fourth Street East
Architect and builder unknown
1889

The Church of the Guardian Angels
218 Second Street West
Architect and builder unknown
1885

Zoar Moravian Church
From Minnesota Highway 41, 6 miles west on County Road 10 (Laketown Township)
Architect and builder unknown
1863
National Register of Historic Places

Clearwater (Wright County)
Clearwater Assembly of God Church (originally First Congregational Church)
405 Bluff Street
Architect and builder unknown
1860
National Register of Historic Places

Cloquet
Queen of Peace Catholic Church
102 Fourth Street
Holstead and Sullivan, Duluth, architects
1925

Coleraine
Coleraine Methodist Episcopal Church
501 Cole Avenue
Frank Young, Duluth, architect
1908–9
National Register of Historic Places

Episcopal Church of the Good Shepherd
601 Cole Avenue
U.S. Steel Corporation, Coleraine, builder
1908
National Register of Historic Places

Crookston
Cathedral of the Immaculate Conception
North Ash Street and Second Avenue
Architect and builder unknown
1912
National Register of Historic Places

Crosslake (Crow Wing County)
Crosslake Evangelical Free Church
37218 County Road 66. From Minnesota Highway 371, east on County Road 16; south on County Road 66
Architect and builder unknown
1983

Delano
St. Paul's United Church of Christ
201 Buffalo Street
Carpenter-built
1879

St. Peter Catholic Church
204 River Street
Victor Cordella, Minneapolis, architect
1912

Doran (Wilkin County)
Stiklestad United Lutheran Church
From Breckenridge, south on Minnesota Highway 9 to Doran. East on County Road 8; south on County Road 17
Sam Christenson, builder (location unknown)
1897–98
National Register of Historic Places

Duluth
Congregation Addas Israel Synagogue
302 East Third Street
Architect and builder unknown
1902

Glen Avon Presbyterian Church
2105 Woodland Avenue
German and Lignell, Duluth, architects
1909
C. H. Smith, Duluth, architect (east addition)
1950

Our Lady Queen of Peace Chapel, College of St. Scholastica
1200 Kenwood Avenue
O'Meara and Hills, Minneapolis, architect; G. E. Quick, St. Louis, associate
1937–38

Sacred Heart Cathedral
206 West Fourth Street
Gearhard A. Tenbusch, Duluth, architect
1894–96
National Register of Historic Places

St. Mark's African Methodist Episcopal Church
530 North Fifth Avenue East
Architect and builder unknown
1900–1913
National Register of Historic Places

St. Mary Star of the Sea Catholic Church
325 East Third Street
Architect and builder unknown
1906

Dundas (Rice County)
Church of the Holy Cross
205 Second Street South
E. C. Goodman, W. C. Cleland, Dundas (?), architects and builders
1868
National Register of Historic Places

Edina
Colonial Church of Edina
6200 Colonial Way
Hammel, Green, and Abrahamson, Minneapolis, architects
1978–79

Our Lady of Grace Catholic Church
5071 Eden Avenue
Hammel, Green, and Abrahamson, Minneapolis, architects
1984–85

Elgin (Wabasha County)
Trinity Lutheran Church
305 First Street Northwest
Arno Huseman, Winona, architect
1921

Eveleth
Resurrection Catholic Church (originally Holy Family Catholic Church)
307 Adams Avenue
A. F. Wasielewski, Minneapolis, builder
1909
National Register of Historic Places

Fairmont
First Church of Christ Scientist
222 Blue Earth Avenue East
Harry W. Jones, Minneapolis, architect
1898
National Register of Historic Places

Faribault
Congregational Church of Faribault (originally Plymouth Church)
227 Third Street Northwest
Monroe Sheire, St. Paul, architect
1867
National Register of Historic Places

Immaculate Conception Catholic Church
4 Second Avenue Southwest
Joseph Berglehner and Joseph Bauer, Faribault, builders
1858, 1902

St. Lawrence Catholic Church
729 Second Avenue Northwest
Charles Daniels, Faribault, architect
1876
Charles A. Hausler, St. Paul, architect (addition and alterations)
1934

Trinity Lutheran Church
530 Fourth Street Northwest
BE Architects, Lake Elmo, architects
1990

Farmington
Episcopal Church of the Advent
412 Oak Street
John H. Thurston, Farmington, architect and builder
1872
National Register of Historic Places

Fergus Falls
St. James Episcopal Church
321 Lake Side Drive South
Dennis and Knowles, Fergus Falls, architects
1921

Franklin (Renville County)
St. Luke's American Lutheran Church
110 Second Avenue East
Thorwald Thorson, Forest City, Iowa, architect
1938

Freeburg (Houston County)
St. Nicholas Church
East of Caledonia on County Road 249
Architect and builder unknown
1868

Gentilly (Polk County)
St. Peter's Church
From Crookston, 7 miles east on County Road 11
Holstead and Sullivan, Duluth, architects
1914–15
National Register of Historic Places

Gilman (Benton County)
Saints Peter and Paul Catholic Church
10490 Golden Spike Road. From Minnesota Highway 25, west on Golden Spike Road (County Road 3)
Cordella and Olson, Minneapolis, architects
1930
National Register of Historic Places

Grand Marais
Church of St. Francis Xavier
1 mile east of Grand Marais on Minnesota Highway 61
Frank Wishcop, Grand Marais, builder
1895
National Register of Historic Places

Ham Lake
Our Savior's Lutheran Church (originally Swedish Evangelical Lutheran Church)
2200 Swedish Drive Northeast
Per August Gustafson, Anoka, builder
1872
National Register of Historic Places

Hamburg (Carver County)
Emanuel Lutheran Church
18175 County Road 50. From Minnesota Highways 5 and 25, east on County Road 50
Augustus Gauger, St. Paul, architect
1898

Hampton (Dakota County)
St. Mathias Catholic Church
23155 Northfield Boulevard (Minnesota Highway 50)
Hermann Kretz, St. Paul, architect
1900

Hastings
Guardian Angels Chapel
216 Fourth Street East
Architect and builder unknown
1865–68

Life Tabernacle (originally Hastings Methodist Episcopal Church)
719 Vermillion Street
Architect and builder unknown
1862, 1871
National Register of Historic Places

St. Elizabeth Ann Seton Catholic Church
2035 West Fifteenth Street
Hammel, Green and Abrahamson, Minneapolis, architects
1994

St. Luke's Episcopal Church (originally First Baptist Church)
615 Vermillion Street
Architect and builder unknown
1881

Hibbing
First Presbyterian Church
2201 East Second Avenue
Harry W. Jones, Minneapolis, architect
1926–27

Grace Lutheran Church
2104 Sixth Avenue East
Architect and builder unknown
1919
National Register of Historic Places

St. Archangel Michael Serbian Orthodox Church
710 East Fortieth Street
Aguar Jyring Whiteman Moser, Inc., Hibbing, architects
1971

St. James Episcopal Church
2028 East Seventh Avenue
J. C. Taylor, Hibbing, architect
1927

Hopkins
St. John the Evangelist Catholic Church
6 Interlachen Road
Progressive Design Associates, St. Paul, architects
1968

International Falls
Faith United Church of Christ
1001 Fifth Street
Robert Y. Sandberg, Hibbing, architect
1967

Isanti
St. John's Lutheran Church
From Isanti, west on County Road 5 about 3 miles (Bradford Township)
Congregation-built
1882
National Register of Historic Places

Jacobs Prairie (Stearns County)
St. James Catholic Church
25042 County Road 2. From Cold Spring, 2½ miles north on County Road 2
Congregation-built
1930

Jessenland (Sibley County)
Church of St. Thomas
County Roads 6 and 19 (north of Henderson)
Architect and builder unknown
1870
National Register of Historic Places

Jordan
St. John the Baptist Catholic Church
210 North Broadway
Brother Adrian Wewer, O.F.M., Jordan, architect
1889

Kenyon
Hauge Lutheran Church
317 Third Street
Congregation-built
1871–88
National Register of Historic Places

Kettle River (Carlton County)
Kalevala Finnish Evangelical National Lutheran Church
North of Kettle River on Minnesota Highway 73 at County Road 6 (Kalevala Township)
Architect and builder unknown
1915

Lake City
St. Mary's Catholic Church
404 Lyon Avenue West
Architect and builder unknown
1877

Lake Crystal
First Baptist Church
312 South Oakland Street
Geist and Hentzelman, architects and builders
Date unknown
National Register of Historic Places

Lanesboro
St. Patrick's Catholic Church
400 Hillcrest Street
Architect and builder unknown
1872

Le Sueur
German Evangelical Salem Church
6 miles east of Le Sueur on County Road 156
Architect and builder unknown
1870
National Register of Historic Places

Litchfield
First Presbyterian Church
Third Street and Holcombe Avenue North
Architect and builder unknown
1905

St. Philip's Catholic Church
Third Street and Holcombe Avenue North
Alden and Harris, St. Paul, architects
1921

Trinity Episcopal Church
400 Sibley Avenue North
After Richard Upjohn, New York, architect
1871–72, 1879
National Register of Historic Places

Luverne
Holy Trinity Episcopal Church
Cedar Street North and Luverne Street East
W. E. Greene, builder (location unknown)
1891
National Register of Historic Places

Luxemburg (Stearns County)
St. Wendelin's Catholic Church
22714 Highway 15. Between St. Cloud and Kimball on Minnesota Highway 15
Architect and builder unknown
1872–75

Mankato
Bethany Lutheran College Chapel
734 Marsh Street
KSA Architects, Inc., Mankato, architects
1995

St. John the Baptist Catholic Church
632 South Broad Street
A. J. Ross and Associates, Mankato, architects
1951

St. Peter and Paul's Catholic Church
105 North Fifth Street
Edward P. Bassford, St. Paul, architect
1871

Mantorville (Dodge County)
St. John's Episcopal Church (now houses the Dodge County Historical Society)
615 North Main Street
Architect and builder unknown
1869
National Register of Historic Places

Maple Lake
St. Timothy Catholic Church
8 Oak Avenue North
Damon, O'Meara, and Hills, St. Paul, architects
1922

Marine on St. Croix (Washington County)
Christ Lutheran Church
150 Fifth Street
Carpenter-built
1872–75

Marshall
Church of the Holy Redeemer
Lyon and Fifth Street
Emmanuel L. Masqueray, St. Paul, architect
1916

St. James Episcopal Church
101 North Fifth Street
Architect and builder unknown
1890

Marystown (Scott County)
St. Mary of the Purification Catholic Church
15850 Marystown Road (County Road 15)
Architect and builder unknown
1882
National Register of Historic Places

Meadowlands (St. Louis County)
Church of St. Joseph
7897 Elmer Road (County Road 199)
Congregation-built
1913
National Register of Historic Places

Mendota (Dakota County)
Church of St. Peter
1405 Sibley Memorial Highway
Congregation-built
1853
National Register of Historic Places (Mendota Historic District)

Miesville (Dakota County)
St. Joseph's Catholic Church
23955 Nicolai Avenue (County Road 91)
Parkinson and Dockendorff, La Crosse, Wisconsin, architects
1912

Millersburg (Rice County)
Christdala Evangelical Swedish Lutheran Church
From Interstate Highway 35, west on County Road 1 approximately 3 miles
Local labor
1878
National Register of Historic Places

Minneapolis
Andrew-Riverside Presbyterian Church
729 Fourth Street Southeast
Warren H. Hayes, Minneapolis, architect
1890–91

Calvary Baptist Church
2608 Blaisdell Avenue South
Warren H. Hayes, Minneapolis, architect (chapel)
Harry W. Jones, Minneapolis, architect (church)
1889 and 1900–1902

Cathedral Church of St. Mark
519 Oak Grove Street
Hewitt and Brown, Minneapolis, architects
1912

Central Lutheran Church
333 South Twelfth Street
Sund and Dunham, Minneapolis, architects
1926

Church of St. Stephen
2211 Clinton Avenue South
Frederick G. Corser, Minneapolis, architect
1889–91
National Register of Historic Places

Church of Scientology
1011–13 Nicollet Mall
Septimus J. Bowler, Minneapolis, architect
1914
McEnary and Krafft, Minneapolis, architects (storefront)
1948

First Baptist Church
South Tenth Street and Harmon Place
Long and Kees, Minneapolis, architects
1888

First Church of Christ Scientist
614–620 East Fifteenth Street
Septimus J. Bowler, Minneapolis, architect
1897
National Register of Historic Places

First Congregational Church
Eighth Avenue and Fifth Street Southeast
Warren H. Hayes, Minneapolis, architect
1888
National Register of Historic Places

First Covenant Church (originally Svenska Missions Tabernaklet)
810 South Seventh Street
Warren H. Hayes, Minneapolis, architect
1886

First Presbyterian Church
1901 Portland Avenue
Warren H. Hayes, Minneapolis, architect
1887

Gethsemane Episcopal Church
905 Fourth Avenue South
Edward Stebbins, Minneapolis, architect
1884
National Register of Historic Places

Grace University Lutheran Church (originally Grace Evangelical Lutheran Church)
324 Harvard Street Southeast
Chapman and Magney, Minneapolis, architects
1904
National Register of Historic Places

Holy Rosary Catholic Church
2201 East Twenty-fourth Street
Edward Stebbins, Minneapolis, architect
1887

Hope Lutheran Church
5740 Cedar Avenue South
Ralph Rapson, Minneapolis, architect
1968

Korean Seventh-Day Adventist Church (originally St. Timothy's Parish)
21 Clarence Avenue Southeast
Long, Lamoreaux, and Long, Minneapolis, architects
1911

Mayflower Community Church (now Enga Funeral Home)
5500 Stevens Avenue South
Bard and Vanderbilt, Minneapolis, architects
1935–36

Norwegian Lutheran Memorial Church Mindekirken
East Franklin Avenue and Tenth Avenue South
Sund and Dunham, Minneapolis, architects
1929

Our Lady of Lourdes Church (originally First Universalist Church)
1 Lourdes Place
Architect and builder unknown
1857, 1881, 1914

St. Charles Borromeo Catholic Church
2739 Stinson Boulevard Northeast
Maguolo and Quick, St. Louis, architects
1958

St. John's Byzantine Catholic Church (originally St. John's Greek Catholic Church)
2201 Northeast Third Street
Cordella and Olson, Minneapolis, architects
1926

St. Mary's Greek Orthodox Church
3450 Irving Avenue South
Thorshov and Cerny, Minneapolis, architects
1956–57

St. Olaf Catholic Church
215 South Eighth Street
Thorshov and Cerny, Minneapolis, architects
1952–53

St. Panteleimon Russian Orthodox Church (originally Prospect Park Lutheran Church)
2210 Franklin Avenue Southeast
Architect and builder unknown
1913

St. Peter's Lutheran Church
5421 France Avenue South
Ralph Rapson, Minneapolis, architect
1957

Scottish Rite Temple
Dupont Avenue South and Franklin Avenue West
Warren H. Hayes, Minneapolis, architect
1894
Harry W. Jones, Minneapolis, architect (addition and alterations)
1906
Bertrand and Chamberlin, Minnapolis, architects (addition and alterations)
1916, 1919
National Register of Historic Places

Second Church of Christ Scientist
4–10 East Twenty-fourth Street
Solon Beman, Chicago, architect
1912–14

Straitgate Church (originally Park Avenue Presbyterian Church)
638 East Franklin Avenue
Charles Sedgwick, Minneapolis, architect
1888–89

Temple Israel
2312 Emerson Avenue South
Liebenberg and Kaplan, Minneapolis, architects
1927

University Episcopal Center/Lutheran Campus Ministry (originally St. Timothy Parish, Holy Trinity Church)
317 Seventeenth Avenue Southeast
Ellerbe and Company, St. Paul, architects
1957

University Lutheran Church of Hope (originally Hope Lutheran Church)
601 Thirteenth Avenue Southeast
Sund and Dunham, Minneapolis, architects
1925

Westminster Presbyterian Church
1201 Nicollet Mall
Warren H. Hayes and Charles Sedgwick, Minneapolis, architects
1896–99
National Register of Historic Places

Money Creek (Houston County)
Money Creek United Methodist Church
18085 Summer Drive. Minnesota Highway 76 to County Road 26; east two blocks, one block north
Architect and builder unknown
1909

Montgomery (St. Peter County)
Holy Redeemer Catholic Church
206 West Vine Avenue
O'Meara and Hills, St. Paul, architects
1924

Moorhead
Church United for the Homeless (originally Swedish Lutheran Bethesda Church)
203 Sixth Street South
Milton Earl Beebe, Fargo, architect (?)
1905

Episcopal Church of St. John the Divine
120 South Eighth Street
Cass Gilbert, St. Paul, architect
1898–99
National Register of Historic Places

Trinity Lutheran Church
210 Seventh Street South
Sovik, Mathre, and Madsen, Northfield, architects
1952

Morton (Renville County; the church is in Redwood County)
St. Cornelia's Episcopal Mission Church
From Minnesota Highway 19, south on County Road 2 to the Lower Sioux Community
Architect and builder unknown
1889–91
National Register of Historic Places

New Ulm
Cathedral of the Holy Trinity
605 North State Street
Adolf C. Ochs, Springfield, Minnesota, architect and builder (?)
1890

Norwood
Church of the Ascension
323 North Reform Street
Buechner and Orth, St. Paul, architects
1905

Norwood United Methodist Church
224 West Hill Street
James Slocum Jr., Norwood, architect and builder
1876
National Register of Historic Places

Oklee (Red Lake County)
Clearwater Evangelical Lutheran Church
From Oklee, 9 miles east, north on County Road 10 (Equality Township)
Aslak and Oscar Nesland, builders
1912
National Register of Historic Places

Olivia
St. Aloysius Catholic Church
300 Tenth Street South
O'Meara and Hills, St. Paul, architects
1925

Opole (Stearns County)
Our Lady of Mt. Carmel
42942 125th Avenue. East of Holdingford on County Road 17
Architect and builder unknown
1929

Oronoco (Olmsted County)
Oronoco Presbyterian Church
Minnesota Avenue South and Third Street Southwest
Architect and builder unknown
1871–72

Ortonville
First English Lutheran Church
Third Street Southeast and Jackson Avenue
Thorwald Thorson, Forest City, Iowa, architect
1939

Ottawa (Le Sueur County)
Ottawa Methodist Episcopal Church
Liberty and Whittier Streets
Architect and builder unknown
1859
National Register of Historic Places

Trinity Chapel (Episcopal)
Sumner and Exchange Streets
Architect and builder unknown
1861
National Register of Historic Places

Owatonna
Trinity Lutheran Church
609 Lincoln Avenue
LeRoy Gaarder, Albert Lea, architect
1958

Pelican Rapids
Faith Evangelical Lutheran Church
423 South Broadway
Architect and builder unknown
1886

Pilot Mound (Fillmore County)
Pilot Mound Church
Between Chatfield and Rushford on Minnesota Highway 30
Architect and builder unknown
1907

Pipestone
First Presbyterian Church
301 Second Avenue Southeast
Architect and builder unknown
1890

Red Wing
Christ Church Episcopal
321 West Avenue
Henry Dudley, New York, architect
1869–71

First Lutheran Church (originally Swedish Evangelical Lutheran Church)
615 Fifth Street West
Pastor-designed (?)
1895

First United Methodist Church
403 East Avenue
Alban and Fisher, St. Paul, architects
1908

Renville
United Methodist Church
123 Main Street North
Architect and builder unknown
1885–1906

Richmond (Stearns County)
Saints Peter and Paul Catholic Church
110 Central Avenue North
Architect and builder unknown
1884–85

Rochester
Our Lady of Lourdes Chapel, Sisters of St. Francis
1001 Fourteenth Street Northwest
Maguolo and Quick, St. Louis, architects
1953

St. John's Catholic Church
11 Fourth Avenue Southwest
Edward F. Wirtz, New Ulm, architect
1956

Rushford
Emmanuel Episcopal Church
217 West Jessie Avenue
Architect and builder unknown
1899

St. Joseph's Catholic Church
103 North Mill Street
Architect and builder unknown
Date unknown

Sacred Heart (Renville County)
First English Lutheran Church
421 Fourth Avenue
Architect and builder unknown
ca. 1900

St. Anna (Stearns County)
Church of the Immaculate Conception
37186 County Road 9
Architect and builder unknown
1902
National Register of Historic Places

St. Augusta (Stearns County)
Church of St. Mary, Help of Christians
24588 County Road 7
Architect and builder unknown
1873
National Register of Historic Places

St. Cloud
Holy Guardian Angels Catholic Church
Third Street and Sixth Avenue North
William Schickel, architect (location unknown)
1883

St. Mary's Cathedral
25 Eighth Avenue South
Leo W. Schaefer, St. Cloud, architect
1922–31

St. James
Calvary Episcopal Church
Third Avenue South and Armstrong Boulevard
Architect and builder unknown
ca. 1883

St. James Catholic Church
623 Fourth Street South
Charles A. Hausler, St. Paul, architect
1933

St. Kilian (Nobles County)
Church of St. Kilian
From Minnesota Highway 91, east 3 miles on County Road 18
Architect and builder unknown
1900
National Register of Historic Places

St. Paul
Central Presbyterian Church
500 Cedar Street
Warren H. Hayes, Minneapolis, architect
1889
National Register of Historic Places

Dayton Avenue Presbyterian Church
217 Mackubin Street
Gilbert and Taylor, St. Paul, architects
1885–86
National Register of Historic Places (Woodland Park Historic District)

House of Hope Presbyterian Church
797 Summit Avenue
Cram, Goodhue, and Ferguson, Boston, architects
1912
National Register of Historic Places (Historic Hill Historic District)

Lutheran Church of the Redeemer
285 North Dale Street
Architect unknown
ca. 1910

Muskego Church, Luther Theological Seminary
2375 Como Avenue West
Architect and builder unknown
1845
National Register of Historic Places

Our Lady of Victory Chapel, College of St. Catherine
2004 Randolph Avenue
Henry Sullwold, St. Paul, architect
1924

Pilgrim Baptist Church
732 West Central Avenue
William L. Alban and V. C. Martin, St. Paul, architects
1928
National Register of Historic Places

St. Casimir Catholic Church
937 East Jessamine Avenue
Victor Cordella, Minneapolis, architect
1904
National Register of Historic Places

St. John the Evangelist Church
Kent Street and Portland Avenue
Cass Gilbert, St. Paul, architect
1902

St. Luke's Catholic Church
1079 Summit Avenue
Comes, Perry, McMullen, Pittsburgh, Pennsylvania, architects
1924
National Register of Historic Places (Historic Hill Historic District)

St. Mary's Roman Catholic Church
261 East Eighth Street
O'Meara and Hills, Minneapolis, architects
1921

St. Paul Seminary Chapel
2260 Summit Avenue
Clarence H. Johnston, St. Paul, architect
1901
National Register of Historic Places (St. Paul Seminary Historic District)

St. Paul's on the Hill Episcopalian Church
1524 Summit Avenue
Emmanuel L. Masqueray, St. Paul, architect
1912
National Register of Historic Places (West Summit Avenue Historic District)

University of St. Thomas Chapel
2115 Summit Avenue
Emmanuel L. Masqueray, St. Paul, architect
1916

Virginia Street (Swedenborgian) Church
170 Virginia Street
Cass Gilbert, St. Paul, architect
1886
National Register of Historic Places (Historic Hill Historic District)

Zion German Evangelical Lutheran Church
780 North Cortland Place
Augustus Gauger, St. Paul, architect
1888

St. Peter
Christ Chapel, Gustavus Adolphus College
Setter, Leach, and Lindstrom, Minneapolis, architects
1961

St. Stephen (Stearns County)
Church of St. Stephen
103 Central Avenue South
John Jager, Minneapolis, architect
1903
National Register of Historic Places

Sauk Centre
First United Church of Christ (originally First Congregational Church)
624 South Fifth Street
Architect and builder unknown
ca. 1905

Sawyer (Carlton County)
Saints Mary and Joseph Catholic Church
1225 Mission Road
Moses Posey, Sawyer, builder
1884
National Register of Historic Places

Shelly (Norman County)
Zion Lutheran Church
1 mile east of Shelly on County Road 3
Tonder Olson, Shelly, builder
1883
National Register of Historic Places

Sherburn
St. Luke's Catholic Church
303 South Lake Street
J. B. Nelson, Mankato, builder
1920

Sleepy Eye
St. John's Evangelical Lutheran Church
221 Walnut Street Southeast
Architect and builder unknown
1902

United Church of Christ (originally Union Congregational Church)
Second Avenue Southwest and Walnut Street
Architect and builder unknown
1902

Spring Valley
Spring Valley Methodist Episcopal Church (now home to the Methodist Church Museum, Spring Valley
Historical Society)
221 West Courtland Street
Architect and builder unknown
1876
National Register of Historic Places

Springvale (Isanti County)
Swedish Mission Church of South Maple Ridge
North of Minnesota Highway 95 on County Road 1 (Maple Ridge Township)
Congregation-built
1897
National Register of Historic Places

Stacy
St. John's Lutheran Church
31095 Genesis Avenue
Hammel, Green, and Abrahamson, Minneapolis, architects
1980

Sterling Center (Blue Earth County)
Sterling Congregational Church
From Minnesota Highway 30, north on County Road 1, then west on County Road 151
(Sterling Township)
Congregation-built
1867
National Register of Historic Places

Stillwater
Ascension Episcopal Church
214 Third Street North
George and Fremont Orff, Minneapolis, architects
1888

Stockton (Winona County)
Grace Lutheran Church (originally Trinity Episcopal Church)
East Main Street and Broadway
Architect and builder unknown
1859
National Register of Historic Places

Taylors Falls (Chisago County)
First Evangelical Lutheran Church
561 Chestnut Street
Alfred L. Garlough, St. Paul, architect
1903

Trondjem (Rice County)
Trondjem Norwegian Lutheran Church
7525 Garfield Avenue. East from Lonsdale on Minnesota Highway 19; right on Garfield Avenue
Architect and builder unknown
1899
National Register of Historic Places

Union Hill (Le Sueur County)
St. John the Evangelist Catholic Church
20687 Hub Drive. From New Prague, west on Minnesota Highway 19, south on Hub Drive (County Road 31)
Architect and builder unknown
1883

Victoria (Carver County)
Lake Auburn Moravian Church
7460 Victoria Drive. From Minnesota Highway 5, north on Victoria Drive (County Road 11)
Architect and builder unknown
1878
National Register of Historic Places

Virginia
Church of St. John the Baptist (now joined with Holy Spirit Catholic Church)
319 South Third Avenue
Architect and builder unknown
1924
National Register of Historic Places

St. Paul's Episcopal Church
231 Third Street South
Cass Gilbert, St. Paul, architect
1895

Wabasha
St. Felix Catholic Church
117 Third Street West
Architect and builder unknown
1893

Waconia
Trinity Lutheran Church
601 Second Street East
William A. Schaefer and Associates, St. Paul, architects
1969

Wadena
St. Helen's Episcopal Church
First Street and Dayton Avenue Southwest
Nathaniel McConachie, Perham, architect
1895

United Methodist Church (originally First Methodist Church)
23 Dayton Avenue Southeast
C. Howard Parsons, Minneapolis, architect
1911

Waseca
Church of the Sacred Heart
Third Street Northwest and West Elm Avenue
John M. Doherty, Rochester, architect
1899

Waterville
St. Andrew's Episcopal Church
210 Lake Street West
Carpenter-built
1870–74

West Albany (Wabasha County)
St. Patrick's Catholic Church
Between Zumbro Falls and Wabasha on Minnesota Highway 60
Architect and builder unknown
ca. 1875

West Concord (Dodge County)
First Baptist Church
225 Arnold Street
F. E. Wright, West Concord, builder
1903

White Bear Lake
Church of St. Mary of the Lake
4741 Bald Eagle Avenue
Sund and Dunham, Minneapolis, architects
1925–26
National Register of Historic Places

Willmar
First Church of Christ Scientist
328 West Fifth Street
John Skoolheim, Willmar, builder
1910

St. Luke's Episcopal Church
422 Sixth Street Southwest
Architect and builders unknown
1872, 1882, 1893

Wilno (Lincoln County)
St. John Cantius Catholic Church
North of Ivanhoe on County Road 5
Hermann Kretz, St. Paul, architect
1901

Winona
Central Lutheran Church
259 West Wabasha Street
Boyum, Schubert, and Sorensen, La Crosse, Wisconsin, architects
1953

Living Light Church (originally German Methodist Episcopal Church)
402 Main Street
Charles Maybury and Son, Winona, architects
1900

St. John Nepomucene Catholic Church
558 East Broadway
Charles Maybury and Son, Winona, architects
1886

St. Mary of the Angels Collegiate Church, College of St. Teresa
700 Terrace Heights
Clarence H. Johnston, St. Paul, architect
1924–26

Architect Biographies

Bruce Abrahamson (b. 1925)

Bruce A. Abrahamson attended public schools in Minneapolis and entered the U.S. Navy after graduation from high school, serving two years during World War II. After the war, he entered the University of Minnesota's School of Architecture and graduated with distinction in 1949. He entered the Harvard Graduate School of Design under a scholarship in 1950 and received his master's degree the following year. He was awarded the prestigious Rotch Traveling Scholarship and spent a year in Europe following graduation, returning to join the firm of Skidmore Owings and Merrill in Chicago. In 1953 Abrahamson was contacted by Curtis Green, whom he had known while working as a student at Thorshov and Cerny, and asked to join the fledgling partnership of Hammel and Green in Minneapolis. Abrahamson accepted and became a member of the firm early in 1954. He remained active in HGA for the rest of his career and retired in 1995.

Carl Bard (1886–?)

Carl John Bard was born in New Carlisle, Indiana. Nothing is known of his education or early employment until he appeared in Minneapolis in 1920, where he worked initially as a draftsman in the architectural firm of Bell and Kinports. From 1921 to 1931, Bard was an architect on the staff of the Builders' Exchange. In 1929 he formed a partnership with Joseph V. Vanderbilt that lasted until 1948.

Bard's place and date of death are unknown.

Edward P. Bassford (1837–1912)

Edward Payson Bassford was born in Calais, Maine, where he attended the local schools and worked as a carpenter before going to Boston to study architecture at the school of Charles Painter. He then served in the Civil War in the Forty-fourth Massachusetts Infantry and returned to Maine, where he set up an architectural practice in Portland with Thomas J. Sparrow. In 1866 he and his wife moved to St. Paul and opened a practice that became one of the most successful in the city in the nineteenth century. Bassford's office also was a training ground for young architects who later became successful in their own right: Cass Gilbert, Clarence H. Johnston, Augustus F. Gauger, Edward J. Donohue and Silas Jacobsen.

BERTRAM BASSUK (1918–1996)
Bertram Bassuk was educated at New York University (NYU), where he received his B.A. in 1938. He subsequently attended Brooklyn College (1939) and then served in the Army Air Force during World War II. Upon his return from the war, he entered NYU's School of Architecture and received a B.Arch. degree in 1947. That same year, Bassuk attended the École des Beaux-Arts in Fontainebleau, France, where he was awarded a certificate. He traveled throughout Western Europe and then returned to New York, where he worked for a series of firms, including Antonin Raymond and L. L. Rado (1947–49), Sam J. Glaberson (1949–50), and Fritz Nathan (1950–52). In 1952 Bassuk set up his own practice, concentrating on the design of housing developments in the New York and New Jersey area and synagogues. He was made a Fellow of the American Institute of Architects in 1986 for his religious architectural work.

PIETRO BELLUSCHI (1899–1994)
Pietro Belluschi was born in Ancona, Italy. He received his architectural and engineering training at the University of Rome (1919–22) and Cornell University (1924). After a stint as a housing inspector in Rome, Belluschi moved to the United States in 1923 and worked for the Bunker Hill and Sullivan Mining Company in Kellogg, Idaho, as an electrical helper for a year. He then joined the firm of A. E. Doyle and Associates in Portland, Oregon, and rose from draftsman to chief draftsman and associate in the years from 1925 to 1942. He opened his own practice in Portland in 1943 and in 1951 was appointed dean of the School of Architecture and Planning at the Massachusetts Institute of Technology. In 1965 he resigned this position to return to private practice, with offices in Boston and Portland.

Belluschi designed numerous churches, educational buildings, and office buildings throughout the United States. His First United Methodist Church in Duluth (designed with Melander and Fugelso, Duluth) is his only commission in Minnesota.

FREDERICK BENTZ (B. 1922)
Frederick Bentz was born in McGregor, Iowa. He was educated at the University of Minnesota, where he received a bachelor's degree in architecture with distinction. He also attended the Eastman School of Music at the University of Rochester (New York) and served in the U.S. Army during World War II.

Bentz was employed in the office of The Cerny Associates, Minneapolis, where he became senior vice president. He and fellow Cerny employees Milo Thompson and Robert Rietow formed a partnership in 1971 as Bentz/Thompson/Rietow that has become one of the most successful firms in Minnesota. Bentz retired from practice in 1993.

George Bergmann (1845–1910)

George Bergmann was born in Germany in 1845. His life, including education and training, up to his arrival in St. Paul remains unknown. He worked as a draftsman in the office of Augustus F. Gauger, a prominent St. Paul architect, and in 1884 formed a partnership with John F. Fischer. In 1898 he set up a partnership with A. E. Hussey in St. Cloud that he maintained for five years. He retired in 1903 and moved with his family to his farm at Fairchild, Wisconsin.

Beginning in the mid-1880s, Bergmann began designing churches for parishes in the heavily Catholic communities in central Minnesota. Among his designs are St. Martin's Catholic Church, St. Martin; St. Agnes Catholic Church, Roscoe; St. Michael's Church, Spring Hill; St. Michael's Catholic Church, Buckman; and the Church of St. Mary, Melrose.

Milton Bergstedt (1907–1998)

Milton Victor Bergstedt attended public schools in his native St. Paul. He graduated from the University of Minnesota's School of Architecture in 1931 and attended the Harvard Graduate School of Design in 1932–33. He worked for the state architect of Illinois and for the firm of Talmadge and Watson of Chicago before returning to Minnesota, where he was employed successively by Mather and Fleischbein, Edwin Lundie, Clarence H. Johnston, and Ellerbe Architects. In 1941 Bergstedt left Ellerbe and joined William Ingemann in St. Paul. When Ingemann entered the Army Air Force during World War II, Bergstedt stayed behind to run the office. After the war, the firm became Ingemann and Bergstedt and was joined in 1948 by W. Brooks Cavin, another graduate of Harvard who had been practicing in Washington, D.C., and who had won the national competition to design the Veterans' Service Building near the state capitol. Cavin relocated to Minnesota and associated with Ingemann and Bergstedt to work on the project. In 1951 Bergstedt set up his own firm with James Hirsch as junior partner. After Charles Wahlberg and Clark Wold joined the firm, it was renamed Bergstedt Hirsch Wahlberg and Wold (BHWW) in 1957. The partnership split in 1962, when Hirsch left to form a practice in Hudson, Wisconsin, and for a time it was called Bergstedt Wahlberg and Wold. Wold departed in 1968, and the name changed again to Bergstedt Wahlberg and Bergquist with the addition of Lloyd Bergquist. When Fritz Rohkohl was named partner and officer, his name was added to the other three. Today BWBR is one of the most successful firms in Minnesota. Bergstedt retired in 1986.

Christopher Boehme (1865–1916)

Christopher Adam Boehme was the son of a German-born father who settled in St. Anthony in the 1850s and became a builder, contractor, and hardware merchant. Boehme was educated at the University of Minnesota, where he took the special course in architecture, the only training possible in the days before the establishment of the Department of Architecture in 1913 (renamed the School of Architecture in 1925). Following his education, he was employed for fourteen years (1882–1896) by the architect Warren B. Dunnell, whose father, Mark, was an early settler of Winona and later a member of the Minnesota legislature. In 1896 Boehme set up his own practice and worked alone until 1903, when he became a partner with Victor Cordella. This partnership was dissolved in 1911, and Boehme returned to private practice.

His religious designs include St. Joseph's Catholic Church at Browerville (1908–9). Among his many nonreligious structures, the one that perhaps stands out above all others is the Swan Turnblad residence, now the American Swedish Institute, at 2600 Park Avenue in Minneapolis (1903–1907).

W. W. BOYINGTON (1818–1898)

William Warren Boyington was born in Southwick, Massachusetts. His early life and education are shrouded in mystery, although he may have obtained training through apprenticeships, which was the normal route for would-be architects up to the 1870s. Boyington is credited with designing the first locomotive cab for the Boston and Albany Railroad (1840) and designed several cotton mills in Massachusetts before 1850. In 1853 he moved to Chicago and opened an office, designing many important structures, including the Chicago Water Tower, which survived the Great Fire of October 1871. After the fire, Boyington became one of the principal rebuilders of the city; in the first year of reconstruction, he claimed to have had commissions totaling $6.5 million. One of his most significant postfire structures was the Board of Trade Building (1881–85), which rested on a "floating foundation" atop the swampy land that underlay much of downtown Chicago. He also introduced improved fireproofing practices in Chicago architecture.

MARCEL BREUER (1902–1981)

Marcel Breuer was educated at the Allami Foreaiskola in his native Pécs, Hungary, from 1912 to 1920 and then received extensive architectural training at the famed Bauhaus in Weimar, Germany. He graduated in 1924 and became a Master of the Bauhaus, first in Weimar and then in Dessau (1924–28). At the same time, Breuer worked as an architect and planner in Dessau (1925–28) and then moved to Berlin in the same capacity. He left in 1931 and went to London, where he eventually entered partnership with F. R. S. Yorke in an architecture and planning firm that lasted about one year (1935–36). In 1936 Breuer came to the United States and joined the faculty of Harvard University's School of Design as an associate professor (1937–46). He also maintained his own firm, Marcel Breuer and Associates, in Cambridge, Massachusetts, from 1937 to 1946, before moving the offices to New York City, where he stayed the rest of his life. He retired from practice in 1976.

EDWIN BROWN (1875–1930)

Edwin Hacker Brown was born in Worcester, Massachusetts. He attended Harvard University and graduated in 1896 with a bachelor of arts degree. He entered Worcester Polytechnic Institute and received a bachelor of science degree. He came to Minneapolis and entered partnership with Edwin H. Hewitt in 1910. During World War I, Brown served in the United States and Europe in the Red Cross. After the war, Hewitt and Brown resumed their partnership. Brown established the Architects Small House Service Bureau, an organization that eventually became national in scope and which provided architect-produced plans for inexpensive houses to help alleviate the postwar housing shortage. Brown died of pneumonia at age fifty-four.

George W. Bullard (1855–1935)

George W. Bullard was educated in architecture at the University of Illinois and returned to his hometown of Springfield to open a practice, which he maintained for more than a decade with his brother, A. S. Bullard. In 1890, he moved to Tacoma, Washington, and spent the rest of his life in that city. He is credited with designing buildings at the University of Illinois (1892) and Washington State University (1899–1900). He also designed the Tacoma Buddhist Temple (1929–31) and several churches in Tacoma.

John L. Bullard (ca. 1831–1895)

John Bullard grew up in Brome County, Quebec, one of ten children. Few details of his life exist, but it is known that he married Susan French and moved to Minnesota in 1855. He settled in Taylors Falls and was in charge of the construction of the First United Methodist Church. He moved to Minneapolis following his retirement and lived there approximately twenty-five years.

Francis Barry Byrne (1883–1967)

Francis Barry Byrne was one of a group of architects associated with the Prairie School style of architecture. Young Barry attended parochial schools in his native Chicago but left his last one, St. Columkille's, at age fourteen to work at Montgomery Ward. From the age of nine his chosen career was architecture—stimulated by an exhibition of Frank Lloyd Wright's work at the Art Institute of Chicago—and he taught himself to draw in his high school years. He left the mercantile world in 1902 and landed an apprenticeship with Wright, who was impressed with the young man's skill. Seven years later he briefly entered the office of Walter Burley Griffin and Marion Mahony, two of the most brilliant architects among the Prairie School group, then left for Seattle to join Andrew Willatzen (1876–1974), whom he'd met in Wright's studio and with whom he'd promised to enter into business. They set up a partnership that resulted in a number of Prairie School houses in the area. The firm dissolved in 1913, and Byrne returned to Chicago to take over Griffin's practice while the latter was in Australia designing the new capitol in Canberra. In 1917 he set up his own office, after Griffin returned, and kept it open until 1930, specializing in church and school design. From 1930 to 1945 he worked in New York City, then returned once again to Chicago after World War II and remained there the rest of his life.

Some of Byrne's most distinguished work is ecclesiastical design. Among his most noteworthy churches are St. Francis Xavier, Kansas City (1947): Church of Christ the King in Cork, Ireland (1929); Church of Christ the King, Tulsa, Oklahoma (1925); Church of St. Patrick, Racine, Wisconsin (1924); Church of Saints Peter and Paul, Pierre, South Dakota (1939); St. Benedict's Abbey Church, Atchison, Kansas (1957); and, of course, Church of St. Columba, St. Paul (1950). Byrne died in Chicago after being struck by an automobile.

James K. Carlson (b. 1924?)

James K. Carlson, architect and engineer, received his training at Iowa State College from 1942 to 1950, interrupted from 1943 to 1946 for military service. He graduated with a B.S. in architectural engineering in 1950 and was employed by Boyum, Schubert, and Sorenson, architects, in La Crosse, Wisconsin, until

1954. He then became an associate architect with Schubert, Sorenson, and Associates in Winona for two years before entering partnership with Edwin Eckert (Eckert and Carlson) in the same city. The partnership was dissolved in 1969, and Carlson was in private practice until 1983, when he formed a partnership with Owen W. Warneke. This ended in 1989, and since that time he has been once again in private practice.

ROBERT CERNY (1908–1985)

Robert Cerny's father was employed in the millwork industry and noticed that his son was, from an early age, interested in architecture. Even before young Cerny graduated from high school in 1926, he was apprenticed in the office of Parkinson and Dockendorff, noted architects in Cerny's hometown of La Crosse (1924–27). He entered the University of Minnesota in 1928 and received his bachelor's degree in architecture in 1932. During his summer vacations, he worked as a student draftsman in the offices of William Ingemann, Jacobson and Jacobson, and A. Moorman, all St. Paul architects. Following his training at Minnesota, Cerny went to Harvard and graduated with his master's of architecture in 1933. He was hired as an architect with the Tennessee Valley Authority (TVA) for a year, then traveled in Europe under a Nelson-Robinson Traveling Fellowship. Returning in 1935, he went back to work for the TVA until 1937, when he moved to Minneapolis and formed the partnership of Jones and Cerny, which existed until 1942. He then left to join Roy Thorshov in what became a prosperous partnership, Thorshov and Cerny, and in 1960 established his own office, Cerny and Associates. Cerny's practice was one of the most successful in Minnesota.

Cerny began teaching architecture at the University of Minnesota in 1937 and continued until his retirement in 1976. He closed his own firm in 1978, which by then had become drastically reduced in size.

HENRY M. CONGDON (1834–1922)

Henry Martyn Congdon was born in Brooklyn, New York. His father, Charles, was greatly interested in architecture and was also a very religious man, being one of the founders of the Ecclesiological Society. Young Henry graduated from Columbia College in 1854 and was apprenticed to the architect John Priest of Newburgh, New York, who happened to be a friend of Charles Congdon's as well as a member of the Ecclesiological Society.

When Priest died in 1859, Congdon and a fellow apprentice, John Littell, opened their own firm in New York City. The partnership was short-lived, and after another brief partnership, Congdon practiced alone for the next forty-five years. In 1907 his son, Herbert Wheaton Congdon, joined his father in a partnership that lasted until Congdon's death.

In his younger years, Congdon was outgoing and served as secretary of the American Institute of Architects for a short time in midcentury. He was elected a Fellow of the institute in 1867. As he grew older, however, he took on some reclusive habits and kept very much to himself, not even attending conventions or meetings.

Congdon continued to practice up until the end. He collapsed and died in New York in his eighty-eighth year, while dressing one morning to go to his office.

CHARLES COOLIDGE (1858–1936)

Charles Allerton Coolidge was born in Boston. He was educated in private schools in preparation for entry into Harvard, where he received the B.A. in 1881. He then studied at the Massachusetts Institute of Technology as a special student in architecture for a year (1881–82), while gaining experience working first in the office of Ware and Van Brunt and then that of H. H. Richardson. Coolidge became a partner in Richardson's successor firm, Shepley, Rutan, and Coolidge, in 1886. From 1892 to 1900, he resided in Chicago, where he operated a practice while remaining a partner in the Boston firm. In 1900 he returned to Boston and, after fourteen years, dissolved Shepley, Rutan, and Coolidge, subsequently forming a partnership called Coolidge and Shattuck (1914–24). After 1924 he became a senior partner in Coolidge, Shepley, Bulfinch, and Abbott in Boston as well as in Coolidge and Hodgson in Chicago, the latter lasting until 1930. During his distinguished career, Coolidge designed Stanford University, new buildings for Harvard Medical School, the Chicago Public Library, buildings at Rockefeller Institute, and medical facilities at Vanderbilt University, Western Reserve University, and the University of Chicago. He was awarded the Chevalier Légion d'Honneur by the government of France in 1900. He married the sister of his partner, George Shepley, in 1889.

VICTOR CORDELLA (1872–1937)

Victor Cordella was born the son of an Italian sculptor in Krakow, Poland. He studied at the Royal Academy of Art in Krakow and at the technological institute in L'viv in Ukraine. After immigrating to the United States in 1893, he apprenticed or worked under a succession of architects in Minneapolis and St. Paul, among them Cass Gilbert, William H. Dennis, Warren Dunnell, and Charles Aldrich. In 1903 he entered partnership with Christopher Boehme for eight years, during which time they produced a number of notable church designs. After the partnership dissolved, each man worked in private practice for the remainder of his career, although near the end of his, Cordella appears to have had a brief partnership with a man named Olson (first name unknown). In the last year or so of his life, Cordella also seems to have suffered from the effects of the Great Depression when he was forced to become a laborer to survive.

RALPH CRAM (1863–1942)

Ralph Adams Cram was born the son of a minister, the Reverend William A. Cram, in Hampton Falls, New Hampshire. He was educated in the schools of Augusta, Maine, Westford, Massachusetts, and Exeter, New Hampshire. Cram received a Litt.D from Princeton University in 1910 and an LL.D from Yale University in 1915. He also attended Williams College and Notre Dame University.

Cram began practicing architecture in 1880 from an office in Boston. His first partnership was with Charles Francis Wentworth (Cram and Wentworth), and he hired Bertram Goodhue as head draftsman for the firm in 1889. Goodhue became a partner in 1891 and remained in the practice until 1914. Cram was supervising architect of Princeton University from 1907 to 1929 and also served as a consulting architect for Bryn Mawr and Wellesley Colleges.

CHARLES DANIELS (1830?–?)

Charles N. Daniels was born in New York about 1830. His exact place of birth is unknown, and nothing is known of his childhood or education. He appears to have been a self-taught carpenter and architect, possibly apprenticing himself to a cabinetmaker early in life. He worked as a cabinetmaker in Minneapolis at an unknown date before moving to Faribault, where he practiced as an architect and contractor. Daniels moved to Fargo, North Dakota, in 1879 and practiced architecture there until 1884, when he moved to Washington State and became an insurance agent. He was a member of the Masonic Order and, through that connection, designed lodges in Fergus Falls, Minnesota, and Casselton and Fargo, North Dakota. It is not known where or when Daniels died, but it was probably in Tacoma, Washington, before 1900.

BERNARD DOCKENDORFF (1878–1952)

Bernard Dockendorff was born to German immigrants in La Crosse, Wisconsin. He attended grade and high schools in La Crosse and, following his schooling, worked for two years in the firm of Stoltze and Schick. Dockendorff then studied at the Technicum in Darmstadt, Germany, in 1897–99. He also became a pupil of Professor Ludwig Becker in Mayence, where he spent four and a half years. He returned to La Crosse and set up his own office for a year before joining Albert Parkinson in partnership in 1905. Dockendorff died in La Crosse on September 23, 1952, only four days after Parkinson's death.

ANTON DOHMEN (1866–1951)

Anton Joseph Dohmen was born in Dusseldorf, Germany. His father, Johann, was a stonemason, originally from Cologne, who moved his family to Krefeld in 1869. Dohmen was trained in architecture and building construction (the latter probably under his father's tutelage) and is said to have worked for twelve years for the architect Peter Schroers in Krefeld. He married in 1886 (his wife's family name was Morf) and had a son and daughter. The family came to the United States in 1892 and settled in Milwaukee, Wisconsin. By 1895 Dohmen had his own practice, which he maintained until his retirement in 1940. He worked in the offices of Jacob Jacobi and Frederick Velguth, both prominent nineteenth-century Milwaukee architects. A brother, Otto, who followed him to America in 1894, was a construction engineer.

EDWARD J. DONOHUE (1869–1915)

Edward Donohue was born in St. Paul and attended the public schools in that city. He received his architectural training as an apprentice in the offices of several St. Paul architects. In 1890, Donohue entered partnership with Edward P. Bassford, one of the city's leading architects, and remained in the firm for five years. After leaving Bassford, Donohue opened a private practice that he maintained for the rest of his life. He became known as a designer of Catholic churches, public buildings, and schools; Humboldt High School in St. Paul was one of his many designs. He married Julia Phelan in 1896; the couple had four children. Donohue died at the age of forty-six after being in ill health for several years.

ADOLPHUS DRUIDING (1839?–1900?)

Adolphus Druiding was born in Hannover, Germany. He studied architecture in Berlin and Munich and immigrated to the United States about 1865. He first appeared in St. Louis in 1867, where he established a private practice that specialized in church architecture, and apparently designed a church that was built there sometime around this period. He also designed St. Joseph's Catholic Church in Jasper, Indiana (1867), and St. John Nepomuk Church in St. Louis for the oldest Czech Catholic parish in North America (1870). Druiding went on to design several more churches in St. Louis, Wisconsin, Indiana, and Illinois through the 1870s and early 1880s. In 1885 he moved to Chicago, where he enjoyed an equally successful career, completing church commissions in Buffalo, Cincinnati, Cleveland, and Chicago, in addition to many small towns and cities throughout the Midwest. He won first prize in a Paris contest for his Chapel of the Immaculate Conception at Mount St. Joseph convent in Cincinnati (built 1892–1901), as well as a gold medal in Munich for his design of St. Hedwig Catholic Church in Chicago (1899). His favorite building material was red brick, which appears in many of his churches.

WARREN B. DUNNELL (1851–1931)

Warren Barnes Dunnell was born in Norway, Maine, to Mark and Sarah Dunnell. In 1863 the family moved to Winona, Minnesota, and two years later to Owatonna. Dunnell attended the University of Minnesota in 1869 and later transferred to the Massachusetts Institute of Technology. He began his career with the supervising architect of the Treasury in Washington, D.C., and then went to Paris to study at the École des Beaux-Arts. Upon his return, he rejoined the federal government and supervised the construction of buildings in Memphis, Tennessee (1878), and Kansas City, Missouri. He had a brief stint in St. Paul in 1876, during which he and short-term partner Samuel J. Brown designed a Methodist Episcopal church for Owatonna.

Dunnell left government service for good in 1880 and returned to St. Paul, where he worked as a draftsman for Abraham Radcliffe, with whom he probably became acquainted in 1876, since they both had rooms in the Ingersoll Building. In 1881 he opened his own office in Minneapolis and established a practice almost exclusively devoted to churches, public buildings, and institutions, including hospitals and schools.

EDWIN O. ECKERT (1926–1990)

Edwin Eckert graduated from Winona Senior High School in June 1942, attended Iowa State College from 1943 to 1944, and served in the U.S. Army Air Force from 1944 to 1946. After the war, he returned to Iowa State College and received his B.S. in architectural engineering in 1949. He was employed in the firm of Boyum, Schubert, and Sorenson in La Crosse, Wisconsin, from 1949 to 1954, when he became an associate architect in Schubert, Sorenson, and Associates in Winona. During this time, he worked with James K. Carlson, with whom he formed a partnership in 1956. After the partnership dissolved in 1969, Eckert became a senior partner in HSR Associates, Inc., architects and engineers, in La Crosse until his retirement in 1989.

GEORGE FEICK JR. (1880–1945)

George Feick Jr. was born in Sandusky, Ohio. His father was a building contractor there, and after Feick graduated from the School of Architecture at Cornell University in 1903, he entered his father's business. From March to December 1906, Feick reunited with his college friend, William G. Purcell, to tour Europe. When they returned, the two men formed an architectural partnership in Minneapolis, and for the next six years, Feick devoted part of his time to the practice in Minneapolis and part to his father's contracting firm in Sandusky. He spent six months in Europe in 1913 and returned to once again enter his father's company, where he spent the rest of his life.

ALPHA HENSEL FINK (1903–1999)

Alpha Hensel Fink was born in Gary, West Virginia. He was educated at Carnegie Institute of Technology in Pittsburgh, where he graduated with his bachelor's degree in architecture in 1926. He entered the office of Sundt and Wenner in Philadelphia in 1926 and became a partner in 1934 (Sundt, Wenner, and Fink). In 1936 the firm became Wenner and Fink, and in 1947 Fink established a private practice that he maintained up to about 1976. He remained a consultant with Lee Warner Architects, Annapolis, Maryland, after his retirement. Fink served as dean of the Department of Architecture at Drexel Institute of Technology in Philadelphia beginning in 1928 for an unspecified term and also served on the Methodist Board of Missions for thirty-five years. He specialized in the design of churches and built hundreds throughout the United States.

ALBERT A. FISHER (1913–2000)

Albert A. Fisher was born in Minneapolis and graduated from the University of Minnesota's School of Architecture with a degree in architectural engineering in 1934. After working for the Insulite Company (1935–1944) and George Washington University (1944–46), he returned to Minneapolis and joined the firm of Hills, Gilbertson, and Hayes. He worked as chief draftsman and then became a partner in 1956, following the death of Hayes. Fisher retired in 1978.

FRANCIS FITZPATRICK (1863–1931)

Francis Willford Fitzpatrick was born in Montreal, Quebec; little is known of his early life, education, or career. He appears to have married Agnes Doutre Lanctot in Quebec and was working in Duluth in 1884. The couple had eight children, one of whom died in infancy. From 1884 to 1887 Fitzpatrick worked as a draftsman for Leroy Buffington in Minneapolis. He then entered the office of the Orff brothers (Fremont and George) in 1888 and, in 1890, was manager of the Minnesota Decorating Company. In that same year, he moved back to Duluth and became a partner of Oliver Traphagen until 1896, when he relocated to Washington, D.C., and was employed as foreman of the Office of the Supervising Architect of the Treasury, 1897–1903. During that time, Fitzpatrick is known to have supervised construction of the Chicago Post Office and possibly the U.S. Government Building in Chicago. He was also a freelance draftsman. In 1903 he set up a private practice that he maintained until about 1918, when he was appointed head of the architectural department of the Bankers Realty Investment Company in Omaha, Nebraska. But he remained in this position only a short time, for by 1920 he was residing in Evanston, Illinois, and was described by a contemporary as a "hearty, red-faced, stoutish man who seemed older than the 56 years" he was by then. Information about the remainder of his life is unknown.

URSA LOUIS FREED (1890–1957)

Ursa Louis Freed was born in Michigan; his family later moved to Huron, South Dakota, where he graduated from high school. He earned his undergraduate degree at Michigan State College in East Lansing and returned to Huron, where he married Mary Elizabeth O'Connor in 1911. The couple moved to Watertown, South Dakota, where Freed went to work for Gray Construction Company. It is known that, in the 1920s, he designed many schools in North and South Dakota, and in the 1930s, like so many architects, was employed as a designer for the Works Progress Administration of the federal government. In 1937, he moved to Aberdeen, South Dakota, and set up his own practice. He remained active into the 1950s, with offices in Fargo, North Dakota, and Watertown, Rapid City, and Aberdeen, South Dakota.

LEROY GAARDER (1891–1982)

LeRoy Gaarder attended public schools in his hometown of Highland, Wisconsin, and in Dodgeville, Wisconsin, and entered St. Olaf College for one year (1912–13). He attended night school at the University of Minnesota from 1913 to 1917, studying architecture while working in the offices of Cecil Chapman (1913), Mather and Boerner (1914), Howard Parsons (1915), and Purcell and Elmslie (1916–17). He also was a student of the viola under the tutelage of Karl Scheuer, concertmaster of the Minneapolis Symphony Orchestra (1916–17). Gaarder moved back to Dodgeville and opened a private practice for one year, then served in the U.S. Army from 1918 to 1919. In 1920 he established a practice in Albert Lea, maintaining it in a studio attached to his house until well into the 1970s. Except for stints in 1934–35 as a consulting architect to the U.S. Treasury on federal buildings and a year (1943–44) as a project planner for the regional office of the Public Buildings Administration in Seattle, Washington, he spent his entire career in Albert Lea.

CASS GILBERT (1859–1934)

One of American's leading architects, Cass Gilbert was born in Zanesville, Ohio. In 1867, his family moved to St. Paul, where Gilbert attended Macalester College. In 1878–79 he attended the Massachusetts Institute of Technology and then went to Europe for another year of study in England and on the Continent. Following this excursion, he returned to the United States and went to work for the distinguished New York firm of McKim, Mead, and White; he soon became a protégé of William Mead's, who is frequently overshadowed by the much more flamboyant Stanford White and the more famed Charles McKim. After two years, Gilbert moved to St. Paul and in December 1882 opened an office as a representative of McKim, Mead, and White. In 1884 he formed a partnership with an old boyhood friend, James Knox Taylor (1857–1929), and the firm of Gilbert and Taylor became one of the most prosperous in the city. The partnership dissolved in 1892, after designing many excellent houses and other buildings, including Dayton Avenue Presbyterian Church (1886–88) and the Endicott Building (1889–90).

Gilbert's national reputation was made by his successful bid for the commission for the Minnesota State Capitol (1895–1905), one of the most beautiful of all the state houses. It directly led to his decision to move to New York City, which he had planned for years, and he maintained an office there for the rest of his life. From that office streamed a number of outstanding buildings, including the Woolworth Building, New York (1910–12); the U.S. Customs House, New York (1899–1907); the University of Minnesota, Minneapolis, General Plan Competition (1908); the Federal Reserve Bank, Minneapolis (1922–24); and the U.S. Supreme Court Building, Washington, D.C. (1928–1934).

Cass Gilbert Jr. took over management of the firm when his father died while touring England.

Victor Gilbertson (b. 1911)

Victor Curtis Gilbertson was born in Velva, North Dakota. He attended high school in Towner, North Dakota, and Luther College, Decorah, Iowa. In 1935 he earned a degree in architecture from the University of Minnesota and the following year attended the Massachusetts Institute of Technology in Cambridge. In the summer of 1935, Gilbertson worked as a draftsman for the North Dakota Highway Department in Minot and then joined O'Meara and Hills in St. Louis, Missouri, as a draftsman (1936–39). He joined James Hills and Mark Hayes in partnership in 1940. He also worked with Shanley, Van Teylingen, and Henningson in Great Falls, Montana (1941), and Mason and Hanger, New York City (1942). Gilbertson retired from practice in 1984.

Bertram Goodhue (1869–1924)

Bertram Grosvenor Goodhue was born in Pomfret, Connecticut. He was educated at Russell's Collegiate and Commercial Institute in New Haven, and trained as an architect for six and a half years in the office of James Renwick, starting at the age of fifteen. Goodhue entered the office of Cram and Wentworth in 1889 as head draftsman and became a partner in November 1891. He remained as a partner with Cram, Goodhue, and Ferguson until 1914, then went into private practice until his death in 1924. Goodhue designed many notable buildings, including several at the San Diego Exposition of 1915; buildings at the United States Military Academy at West Point; and the Nebraska State Capitol, 1920.

Curtis Green (b. 1925)

Curtis Harlan Green attended Edison High School in Minneapolis and the University of Minnesota, from which he graduated in 1946 with a degree in architecture. He worked for about a year in the firm of Magney, Tusler, and Setter and then went on to attend the Massachusetts Institute of Technology, studying under Alvar Aalto and receiving his master's degree in 1948. After graduation, Green accepted employment with the Milwaukee firm of Grassold-Johnson, designing an addition to the public library; he then returned to Minneapolis, where he joined Thorshov and Cerny (1949–51) and Dimond, Haarstick, and Lundgren in St. Paul (1951–53). In 1953 he joined Richard Hammel in partnership, where he remained until his retirement in 1993.

Richard Hammel (1923–1986)

Richard F. Hammel was born in Owatonna, Minnesota, where his family were contractors; his grandfather helped build the National Farmers Bank, designed by Louis Sullivan. Hammel graduated from the School of Architecture at the University of Minnesota in 1944 and, after serving two years in the navy, attended the Harvard Graduate School of Design, where he studied under Walter Gropius and received a master's degree in architecture in 1947. Hammel joined the firm of Richard E. Windisch in Honolulu from 1947 to 1950. He returned to Minnesota to teach part-time in the university's School of Architecture and also worked as assistant consulting architect to the university. In 1951, he became the consulting architect to the St. Paul Public Schools. Hammel and Curtis Green, who was then working in the firm of Dimond, Haarstick, and Lundgren, St. Paul, formed a partnership in 1953. Bruce Abrahamson joined the partnership the following year to form Hammel, Green, and Abrahamson (HGA), one of the largest and most successful firms in Minneapolis. Hammel remained active in the firm until his death.

Mark Hayes (1909–1956)

Mark N. Hayes was born in Williston, North Dakota. He and his parents moved to Minneapolis, where he attended De La Salle High School and the University of Minnesota, from which he earned a degree in architecture in 1932. He worked as a draftsman for the Minneapolis-St. Paul Sanitary District in St. Paul from 1933 to 1937, then joined Patrick O'Meara in partnership in 1937. In 1941, Hayes entered partnership with James Hills and Victor Gilbertson. The firm of Hills, Gilbertson, and Hayes was one of the most successful in Minneapolis.

Warren H. Hayes (1847–1899)

Warren Howard Hayes was born in Prattsburgh, New York, and grew up on a farm operated by his father, George Hayes. The family was reputed to be related to President Rutherford B. Hayes of Ohio. Young Warren attended Watkins Academy and Genessee Wesleyan Seminary, the latter institution in Lima, New York. In 1868 he entered Cornell University, where he studied civil engineering, natural sciences, and modern languages. He graduated with his bachelor's degree in 1871 and opened an architectural practice in Elmira, New York, that same year. Hayes moved to Minneapolis in 1881 (although he maintained a residence in Elmira into 1882) and began a highly successful firm specializing in churches. He also designed a number of commercial buildings, schools, and residences. Hayes adopted the diagonal or Akron plan for church auditoriums in 1882, and many of his churches feature this design (see, e.g., First Presbyterian Church in Mankato). He died at age fifty-two of pernicious anemia after a yearlong illness.

Raymond Hermanson (b. 1916)

Raymond Hermanson was born in Lemmon, South Dakota. He grew up in Staples and St. Cloud, graduating from high school in 1934. Hermanson studied engineering and architecture at St. John's in Collegeville and graduated in 1938. He worked with Nairne Fisher in Minneapolis and Washington, and then was employed with the U.S. Navy, designing docks and other structures for naval bases throughout the world. In 1943 he was commissioned in the Navy Air Corps and studied meteorology at New York University. He was assigned to a weather station in San Francisco and then was sent to the Scripps School of Oceanography for further study. Hermanson returned to St. Cloud after the war and began working as a draftsman in the office of Louis Pinault. In 1949 he formed a partnership with Fred V. Traynor, creating the firm of Traynor and Hermanson, which became one of the most successful practices outside the Twin Cities. They were joined by Gilbert F. Hahn (1922–84) in the late 1960s, and the firm operated as Traynor, Hermanson, and Hahn for several years. In 1983 they merged with the St. Cloud firm of Pauly and Olsen, which became part of Short Elliott Hendrickson (SEH) in the early 1990s. SEH has offices in several cities, including St. Cloud. Hermanson retired from practice in about 1983.

EDWIN H. HEWITT (1874–1939)

Edwin Hawley Hewitt was the son of a distinguished surgeon who practiced in Red Wing. Hewitt attended the public schools and went on to Hobart College for a year before returning to complete his undergraduate work at the University of Minnesota. While at the university, he attended the Minneapolis School of Fine Arts at night and worked in the office of Cass Gilbert during vacations. After graduation from the university, he studied for a year at the Massachusetts Institute of Technology, then entered the office of Shepley, Rutan, and Coolidge in Boston. Hewitt worked there for three and a half years, afterward going to Paris to study for four years at the prestigious École des Beaux-Arts. In 1904 he returned to Minneapolis and set up his own practice. In 1910 he established a partnership with Edwin Brown that was active until the latter's death in 1930. Hewitt resumed private practice, but the firm languished without Brown's keen business sense and the office closed in the early 1930s. Hewitt then became chief architectural supervisor of the Federal Housing Administration for the Minneapolis area (1934–37).

JAMES HILLS (1888–1979)

A native of Binghamton, New York, James Bertram Hills attended Cornell University, from which he received a degree in architectural engineering. He began practicing in St. Paul in 1917 and was a partner in the firms of Patrick O'Meara in that city (O'Meara, Hills, and Krajenski, and Damon, O'Meara, and Hills). After O'Meara's death, Hills organized a partnership in 1940 with Victor Gilbertson and Mark Hayes. The firm was one of the most successful in Minneapolis for many years. After the death of Hayes in 1956, Albert A. Fisher became a full partner and the firm continued as Hills, Gilbertson, and Fisher.

Hills retired only shortly before his death in early 1979.

JAMES HIRSCH (B. 1922)

James Hirsch was born in Medford, Wisconsin, and attended the University of Notre Dame as well as Texas A&M University. He graduated from the University of Minnesota's School of Architecture in 1948 and joined Milton Bergstedt and William Ingemann in partnership in September 1951. Their partnership lasted until 1962, when Hirsch left to set up his own firm in Hudson, Wisconsin. He is retired and living in the state of Washington.

MORRIS HOLMES (1862–1945)

Morris Grant Holmes moved from his hometown of LaPorte, Indiana, to Chicago as a youth and received his architectural training in the office of the prestigious architect Solon S. Beman. He then joined the firm of Patton and Miller, where he became chief draftsman in 1912 and junior partner within a few years afterward. After the death of Normand Patton in 1915, Holmes formed the successor firm of Holmes and Flinn in Chicago, which designed numerous school and college buildings, churches, hospitals, and public libraries.

JOHN JAGER (1871–1959)

A native of Carniola, Austria, John Jager received his architectural and engineering training in the Imperial and Royal Polytechnicum in Vienna from 1892 to 1899. For two and a half years, starting in 1898, he acted as professional assistant in architectural design to Professors Karl Mayreder and Oswald Gruber, during which time—as chief architect for Municipal City Planning in Vienna—he drew up a city plan for Ljubljana, Slovenia, which was part of the Austro-Hungarian Empire. In 1901 Jager was sent to Peking, China, as a captain of engineers in the Imperial and Royal Government Service of Austria. He designed a number of buildings for the military services to occupy in the Chinese capital while they were garrisoning the country following the disastrous Boxer Rebellion.

In 1902 Jager came to the United States to join his father. He settled in Minneapolis later that year and opened an architectural practice. During that time, he drew up a plan for the beautification of the city. The drawing was exhibited at the Louisiana Purchase Exposition in St. Louis in 1904. The following year, he formed a partnership with Carl Stravs that lasted until 1909, when he became a draftsman and planner with the distinguished firm of Hewitt and Brown. After World War I, Jager was sent to Serbia as an inspector for the Minneapolis agricultural unit of the American Red Cross. He returned to rejoin Hewitt and Brown, where he remained until 1933, when the Great Depression, with its severe downturn in building activity, forced him to leave. He assumed the position of supervisor of public works in the Minneapolis City Planning Department. Jager retired in 1943 and spent the rest of his life in self-study of the arts and linguistics, among many other pursuits.

Besides St. Bernard's Catholic Church in St. Paul, Jager designed St. Stephen's in Brockway, Minnesota (1903), and a Catholic church at Rosen, Minnesota (1906).

Clarence H. Johnston (1859–1936)

It is strange that the year 1859 saw the birth of three men who were to leave an indelible and significant mark on Minnesota's religious architecture: Harry W. Jones, Cass Gilbert, and Clarence Howard Johnston.

Johnston was born in Waseca County. He moved with his family at an early age to St. Paul and was educated in the public schools. After completing high school, he received apprenticeship training in the office of Abraham Radcliffe, a prominent St. Paul architect. It was in Radcliffe's office that he met Cass Gilbert and the two became good friends. They both left in 1878 to attend the Massachusetts Institute of Technology, which had the first architecture school in the United States. Johnston left because of financial stringencies before completing one year and returned to St. Paul, where he entered the office of Edward P. Bassford, another of the city's leading architects. In 1880 his old professor at MIT wrote to offer him a position in Herter (Gustave and Christian) Brothers in New York, which he accepted. He worked there for about two years, part of the time on the massive William Vanderbilt mansion that the firm was erecting on Fifth Avenue. Johnston was also among the founders (along with Cass Gilbert) of the New York Sketch Club, the forerunner of the Architectural League of New York.

Johnston moved back to St. Paul in 1882 and opened his own office, which he maintained until his death. In 1885 he formed a highly successful partnership with William Willcox that lasted until 1889. The firm produced many notable buildings in the city, but perhaps the best known are Summit Terrace (1889), residence of F. Scott Fitzgerald, and Shumway Hall at Shattuck School in Faribault (1887). After the dissolution of the partnership, Johnston practiced privately and built his business into one of the most successful in St. Paul until the advent of Ellerbe and Company in the 1920s.

Following his death, his practice was taken over by his son, Clarence H. ("Howie") Johnston Jr. (1888–1959), who continued to operate it for the next twenty-three years.

HARRY W. JONES (1859–1935)

Harry Wild Jones was born near Kalamazoo, Michigan, the son of the Reverend Howard M. and Mary White (Smith) Jones, and grandson of Dr. S. F. Smith, the author of "My Country 'Tis of Thee." Jones was educated at University Grammar School in Providence, Rhode Island, and received his professional training at Brown University (graduated 1880) and the Massachusetts Institute of Technology, from which he received a B.S. degree in 1882. He worked in the office of the famous architect H. H. Richardson in Boston for a year and in 1883 married Bertha J. Tucker, who was a niece of the sewing machine inventor, Elias Howe. The couple honeymooned in Minneapolis, and Jones decided to accept employment in the architectural firm of Plant and Whitney. James Plant (dates unknown) and William Channing Whitney (1851–1945) had a flourishing practice based mainly on the design of large, prestigious houses. After one year, Jones went to Europe and studied and traveled until returning to Minneapolis in 1885. He remained active in his own practice until his retirement in 1918.

EINO JYRING (1906–1992)

Eino "Jerry" Jyring was born in Eveleth and attended public schools in Virginia, Minnesota. After graduating from Virginia High School, he attended the University of Minnesota, where he graduated with honors from the architecture school. He worked successively in Chicago, New York City, and Hibbing, and served with a U.S. government contractor and in the U.S. Navy's Seabees in World War II. When Jyring returned from the service, he established his own architectural practice in Hibbing. He was in partnership with S. P. Jurenes from 1946 until Jurenes's death in 1953, and then was joined in practice by Richard Whiteman in 1955. The firm remains in business today as Architectural Resources, Inc. Jyring was a Fellow of the American Institute of Architects and served as president of the Minnesota Society of Architects. He retired in 1990.

FRANK KACMARCIK (B. 1920)

Frank Kacmarcik was born in St. Paul of Slovak-Polish parentage. After graduating from high school, he attended the Minnesota College of Art and Design to study painting and book design. He entered St. John's Abbey at Collegeville as a novice in the early 1940s and then left to serve in the U.S. Army Medical Corps in Europe as a chaplain's assistant and medical technician. After the war, he studied at the Académie de la Grande Chaumière and the Centre d'Art Sacré in Paris, where he was trained in painting, religious art, and church decoration.

Kacmarcik returned to St. John's in 1950 and became a professor of art. Three years later, he collaborated with Marcel Breuer in the design of the abbey church. In appreciation for his assistance, Breuer designed a house for him in St. Paul, to which he moved in the mid-1950s. Kacmarcik worked as a consultant in church design, printing, and the graphic arts for many years. In 1983 he moved back to St. John's, where he continues to work as an ecclesiastical consultant and designer.

WILLIAM KENYON (1863–1940)

William Marsh Kenyon was born in Hudson Falls, New York. He graduated from Boston Normal School in 1884 and came to Minneapolis in 1893. He worked in private practice until 1913, when he formed a partnership with Maurice F. Maine that lasted until 1929. Kenyon and Maine were appointed architects of the New Carnelia Company to develop the mining town of Ajo, Arizona, in 1914. Kenyon was also the chief architect of the Soo Line Railroad for twenty years, during the 1910s and 1920s, and served on the advisory board for the Greater University (of Minnesota) Campus in 1909. The firm of Kenyon and Maine designed numerous residences, stores, and apartment houses, and is credited with the Northwest Airlines Terminal at Wold Chamberlain Airport and Abbott and Elliott Hospitals in Minneapolis.

HERMANN KRETZ (1860–1931)

Hermann Kretz was born in Essen, Germany, where his father, John, was a merchant. At the age of nineteen, Kretz went to work for his uncle as an architect, after completing his education at the University of Essen and the Technical School at Holzminden. In about 1880 he immigrated to the United States and worked in New York City, Chicago, Winnipeg, and various other western cities before settling in St. Paul in 1886. Kretz became wealthy not only from his highly successful architectural practice but also from real estate investments, including the Commerce Building in downtown St. Paul, which he designed and built in 1912.

CHARLES R. LAMB (1860–1942)

Charles Rollinson Lamb was born in New York City and spent his entire life there, as an architect and interior designer. He left school at age sixteen to join his father in the firm of J. and R. Lamb Studios, which specialized in design of interiors for ecclesiastical structures and the design and manufacture of stained glass and mosaics. Later, Lamb took over management of the company, working with his wife, Ellie Condie Lamb, and a brother, Frederick. He also practiced architecture, but is known to have had only two of his designs built: his own house at Cresskill, New Jersey, and a temporary memorial arch commemorating Admiral Dewey's successes in the Spanish-American War, built in New York in 1899. Lamb also was involved in city planning and is credited with promulgating the "City Beautiful," a scheme for making showcases of metropolitan areas through careful and picturesque vistas of boulevards and elegant buildings. He pioneered the concept of setbacks for skyscrapers to permit sunlight to reach gloomy New York streets, and the idea of skyways between buildings. Most of his innovations were ignored, largely because they were too far ahead of their time, and after 1910 Lamb's frustration and discouragement caused him to lapse into a moody silence for much of the rest of his life.

ANANIAS LANGDON (1812–1893)

Ananias Langdon was born in Saratoga County, New York. He practiced architecture in Troy, New York, until 1855, when he relocated to Winona and opened an office in the young community. He was the designer of St. Paul's Episcopal Church in 1873, but little else is known of his life and work. His obituary noted that he used crutches as a result of an accident about 1883 and that his life in Winona was "quiet and uneventful."

Charles Leonard (1815–1874)

Charles S. Leonard was born in Massachusetts in 1815. Nothing is known of his life and career until he emerged in St Paul in the mid-nineteenth century. He was a partner with Monroe and Romaine Sheire in an architecture and contracting company from 1868 to 1872.

Norman Madson

Norman Madson graduated from Waldorf College in Forest City, Iowa, in 1941, earning an associate of arts degree and, later, his bachelor's degree in architecture from Iowa State College. He joined Edward Sovik and Sewell Mathre in partnership in Northfield in 1953 and remained with the firm until 1973, when he became director of the physical plant at St. Olaf College in Northfield. In 1993, he was appointed college architect at St. Olaf.

Maurice F. Maine (1881–1950)

Maurice Francis Maine was born in Rockland, Maine. He came to Minneapolis at about the age of nineteen and was educated at Hamline University in St. Paul and in art schools in the Twin Cities area. As far as is known, Maine practiced in Minneapolis throughout his life and was in partnership with William Kenyon from 1913 to 1929. With Kenyon he designed numerous residences, apartment houses, and stores, and a number of depots, shops, and other structures for the Soo Line Railroad. Church design appeared to be a very small part of his general practice.

Emmanuel L. Masqueray (1861–1917)

Emmanuel Louis Masqueray was born in Dieppe, France. He studied architecture at the École des Beaux-Arts in Paris from 1879 to 1884, receiving several awards for his designs. Masqueray came to the United States in 1887 to work for the firm of Carrere and Hastings in New York City. Five years later, he joined the office of Richard Morris Hunt, where he helped design many notable buildings, including The Breakers for William Vanderbilt in Newport, Rhode Island. In 1897 he left the Hunt office to work for Warren and Wetmore, also in New York City. Four years later Masqueray was appointed chief of design at the Louisiana Purchase Exposition in St. Louis, a position he held for three years. He resigned shortly after the fair opened in 1904 and was asked by Archbishop John Ireland to come to St. Paul to design a new cathedral for the city.

Masqueray arrived in St. Paul in 1905 and remained there until his death. He designed about two dozen parish churches for Catholic and Protestant congregations in the Upper Midwest as well as three more cathedrals, of which two were built in Wichita, Kansas, and Sioux Falls, South Dakota. He also designed a few residences and several parochial schools for the Archdiocese of St. Paul.

Sewell J. Mathre (b. 1922)

Sewell Jerome Mathre was born in Vancouver, British Columbia. His family moved to the United States while he was still a child, and he graduated from high school in Estherville, Iowa. He attended Waldorf College in Forest City, Iowa, for two years, receiving an associate in science degree in 1942. He graduated with a degree in architecture from Iowa State College in 1949 and earned his master's degree from the

Cranbrook Academy of Art, Bloomfield Hills, Michigan, in 1952. He worked for a succession of firms in Wisconsin, Alaska, Iowa, and New York before returning to Minnesota in 1953. He was employed with Gerhard Peterson in St. Paul that year and then joined Edward Sovik in partnership in Northfield (Sovik and Mathre), where he remained for the rest of his career. Mathre retired from practice in 1993.

CHARLES MAYBURY (1830–1917)

Charles Granderson Maybury was born in Solon, New York. His father was a stone cutter who worked on the construction of the Erie Canal. He was also a farmer, and young Maybury worked on the family farm until he was sixteen. He was educated in the local public schools and, for less than a year, in a private school. Following his education, he was apprenticed to a prominent contractor and builder in central New York State for close to five years, following which he became a partner in the company. After three years, the firm dissolved, and Maybury went into business for himself as a draftsman and builder. Two years later (1856) he headed west and arrived in Winona that same year. His first structure was the Sanborn Building, which he designed and built. It was three stories tall and, at the time, the largest building in the fledgling river town. Maybury continued in the architecture and construction business until 1865, when Abraham Radcliffe, who had come to Winona in 1862 from Minneapolis, returned to the Twin Cities and sold his office and its contents to Maybury. Maybury decided to concentrate on architecture and closed his contracting business for good. He designed many of the larger homes and business blocks in Winona, in addition to churches and the Winona County Court House (1888).

JEFFERSON MAYBURY (1858–1928)

Jefferson Nichols Maybury, oldest son of Charles Maybury, began working in his father's office as a young man. After leaving high school, he trained under Edward P. Bassford in St. Paul for one year (1880) and returned to Winona to become his father's partner. C. G. Maybury and Son, as the firm was called, continued until well past the turn of the century. In 1903–4, Maybury was appointed a specifications writer for the Louisiana Purchase Exposition in St. Louis. After the stint in St. Louis, he returned to Winona for a brief time, then departed for Seattle in 1904, where he became architect of the Board of Education.

A. REINHOLD MELANDER (1894–1979)

Albin Reinhold Melander attended Central High School in Duluth and the University of Minnesota, where he received a B.S. in architecture in 1921. His wife, Florence Knox Melander, also graduated from the university with a degree in architecture. He attended the University of Besançon in France briefly before returning to Duluth. Melander worked as a student draftsman in the office of Anthony Puck from 1919 to 1921, F. G. German's firm in 1921, and Kees and Colburn (Minneapolis), also in 1921. He taught architecture at North Dakota State College in Fargo from 1921 to 1923 and then entered partnership in Duluth with Harold St. Clair Starin (1893–1974) in 1924. The partnership lasted until 1930, when Melander started his own practice. In 1957, the firm of Melander, Fugelso, and Associates was formed consisting of Norman K. Fugelso (1911–76), William Moser, Sanford Porter, and Leon E. Simich. Fourteen years later, in 1971, his son Donald Knox Melander entered partnership with his father and the firm changed its name to Melander and Melander.

ERIC MENDELSOHN (1887–1953)

Eric Mendelsohn was born Erich Mendelsohn in Allenstein, East Prussia (now Olsztyn, Poland). He studied economics at the University of Munich in 1907, then took up architecture at the Technische Hochschule in Berlin from 1908 to 1910. He returned to the University of Munich in 1911 for further study. Following his university training, Mendelsohn worked as a theater designer and interior decorator in Munich from 1912 to 1914 and served in the German army in 1917–18. After the war, he practiced architecture in Berlin and in 1933 fled Germany to escape the persecution of Jews then being carried out by the Nazis. From 1933 to 1941 he lived alternately in London and Palestine, being in partnership with Serge Chermayeff in London from 1933 to 1939. Mendelsohn came to the United States in 1941 and settled in New York City. After the war, he moved to San Francisco, where he maintained a practice until his death.

ALBERT PARKINSON (1870–1952)

Albert Parkinson was born in London, England. He was trained in architecture by his father and in the public schools of Scranton, Pennsylvania, to which the family moved at an unknown date. Parkinson formed a partnership in La Crosse, Wisconsin, with Bernard Dockendorff in 1905, which lasted until Parkinson's death on September 19, 1952. (Dockendorff died only four days later.)

The firm specialized in the design of public buildings and churches throughout the Midwest. Their office was a training ground for many young architects, including Otto Merman, a distinguished architect whose partnership with Percy Bentley resulted in a number of outstanding Prairie School buildings in La Crosse.

NORMAND PATTON (1852–1915)

Normand Smith Patton received a B.A. from Amherst College in 1873 and an M.A. from the same college in 1876. In between, he was a student at the Massachusetts Institute of Technology (1874). Patton opened an office in Chicago about 1876 and two years later joined C. E. Randall in partnership (Randall and Patton). In 1885, with Randall's death, the firm became Patton and Fisher (1885–99), then successively Patton, Fisher, and Miller (1899–1901), Patton and Miller (1901–12), and Patton, Holmes, and Flinn (1912–15). He served as architect for the Board of Education in Chicago in 1896–98 and was an original member of the Western Association of Architects. Patton's firm specialized in public buildings, producing numerous schools, college buildings, and libraries in Chicago and elsewhere, including many Carnegie libraries and libraries for Oberlin College, Indiana University, and Augustana College in Rock Island, Illinois, as well as the campus plan for Carleton College. Patton considered the design of Skinner Memorial Chapel at Carleton College to be the most artistic and satisfactory of his career. He died before construction of the chapel was completed.

ANTHONY W. PUCK (1882–1922)

Anthony Puck was born in Christiania, Norway. Little is known of his life and career. He worked in Duluth starting about 1905, after receiving office training in the practice of John J. Wangenstein. Puck had an active, albeit short-lived, career, designing numerous residences, schools, and industrial and institutional structures in Duluth and throughout northern Minnesota. At some point, he was in partnership with Edgar C. Gilivson in Arnold, Minnesota, but it is not known how long this lasted or what buildings the firm designed. He was a member of the Duluth Boat Club and at one time rowed with its crews.

WILLIAM G. PURCELL (1880–1965)

William Gray Purcell grew up in Oak Park, Illinois, as the son of Charles Purcell, a wealthy commodities broker on the Chicago Grain Exchange. Early in his life, he made the decision to live with his grandparents, Dr. and Mrs. William Cunningham Gray, in an environment rich in literary and cultural contacts. Dr. Gray (1830–1901) was a newspaper editor and writer, and in the late 1800s edited the *Interior,* an influential and widely read magazine that concentrated on literature and nature for its topics. Purcell traveled to northern Wisconsin with the Grays and lived a rustic existence at the family's camp at Island Lake during the summers of the 1880s and 1890s. In 1899 he entered Cornell University, from which he graduated four years later with a degree in architecture. He returned to Chicago and met George Grant Elmslie (1871–1952), who got him a job with Louis Sullivan. Purcell worked there for five months, and then moved to the West Coast, where he worked successively for John Galen Howard in San Francisco and Bebb and Mendel in Seattle.

In January 1906, Purcell embarked on a yearlong tour of Europe with his former Cornell classmate George Feick Jr. They returned to the United States and elected to set up an architectual practice in Minneapolis in January 1907. In 1910 they were joined by George Elmslie, and the three remained in partnership until Feick departed to rejoin his father in the contracting business in Sandusky, Ohio, in 1913. Purcell left the firm in 1917 to become director of advertising for the Alexander Brothers in Philadelphia. Two years later, the company went bankrupt, and Purcell moved to Portland, Oregon, to set up the Pacific States Engineering Company. He stayed in business until about 1930, when tuberculosis forced him to close the office to retire to southern California for treatment. He never fully regained his health and remained virtually inactive the rest of his life.

ABRAHAM RADCLIFFE (1827–?)

Abraham Maby Radcliffe was born in New York City. He entered a partnership sometime prior to 1849 with E. A. and R. L. Stevens in Hoboken, New Jersey, then worked successively in Elmira, New York (1849–52), and Fort Wayne, Indiana (1852–57). In 1857 Radcliffe moved to Minneapolis and opened an office. The next year, he opened another in St. Paul. From 1862 to 1865 he practiced architecture in Winona, then sold out to Charles Maybury and returned to the Twin Cities. He closed the Minneapolis office about 1868 and maintained his St. Paul practice for twenty more years. From 1871 to 1875 he was in partnership with Leroy S. Buffington (1847–1931), who became one of Minneapolis's most successful architects in the next decade.

Radcliffe's office, like others of that day, was a training ground for younger men. Prominent St. Paul architect Edward P. Bassford passed through as an apprentice draftsman in 1868–71 as did Cass Gilbert in 1876. A significant Minneapolis architect of the late nineteenth and early twentieth century, Warren Dunnell, was Radcliffe's draftsman as late as 1880.

Radcliffe remained in St. Paul until 1889, when he moved to San Francisco and entered the office of Randell Hunt and Company, engineers and contractors. Radcliffe himself resided across the bay in

Alameda, where he may have opened an office of his own after leaving Randell Hunt about 1891. Nothing is known of his later life.

RALPH RAPSON (B. 1914)

Ralph Rapson was educated at Alma College (1933–35) in Michigan, then at the University of Michigan, where he graduated with a degree in architecture in 1938. He attended the Cranbrook Academy of Art in Bloomfield Hills, Michigan, operated by Eliel and Eero Saarinen, for graduate study in urban and regional planning (1938–40). In 1942, Rapson entered private practice in Chicago while also serving as head of the Department of Architecture at the Institute of Design, under the directorship of László Moholy-Nagy. Four years later he was appointed an associate professor in the School of Architecture at the Massachusetts Institute of Technology, where he met Alvar Aalto, and opened an office in Cambridge, Massachusetts. From 1951 to 1953, Rapson served a "tour of duty" in Europe, designing American embassies in Stockholm, Copenhagen, Athens, The Hague, and Oslo (the last three were projects only), a consulate and apartments in Le Havre, and embassy staff apartments in Neuilly and Boulogne, France. In 1954, he became professor and head of the School of Architecture at the University of Minnesota, where he remained until his retirement in 1984. Rapson has won numerous awards for his designs and served on architectural advisory boards for the U.S. General Services Administration, Metropolitan Planning Commission, and Federal Reserve System, the Universities of Kansas and Manitoba, and the Minneapolis Committee on Urban Environment, and is a Fellow of the American Institute of Architects.

Rapson's designs are distinctive for their clean lines and geometric shapes. His churches include Prince of Peace Lutheran Church for the Deaf, St. Paul (1958); St. Luke's Presbyterian, Minnetonka (1960); St. Thomas Aquinas Church, St. Paul Park (1969); and Hope Lutheran Church, Minneapolis (1970).

JAMES RENWICK (1818–1895)

James Renwick was born in Bloomingdale, New York, where his father (also named James Renwick) was a successful engineer. Young Renwick studied at Columbia College, graduating in 1836, and joined the engineering staff of the Erie Railroad that same year. He later was a member of the engineering staff for the construction of the Croton aqueduct. Renwick became the superintendent for construction of the Croton distributing reservoir located between Fortieth and Forty-second Streets on Fifth Avenue in New York City, the site today of the New York Public Library.

Renwick designed numerous churches in New York, St. Patrick's Cathedral (opened 1879) being perhaps his best known. He also designed the Smithsonian Institution (1846) and the Corcoran Gallery, both in Washington, D.C., and Vassar College at Poughkeepsie, New York (1865). He was known to favor the Gothic and Romanesque styles in his architecture and became one of the most popular and famous architects of his day.

EDUARD VON RIEDEL (1813–1885)

Eduard von Riedel was born in Bayreuth, Germany. He was educated in his hometown and at the Gymnasium in Munich. In 1829 Riedel entered the university in Munich to study architecture, and in 1834 he scored so high in his exams that he was excused from military service and awarded a state stipend to travel to Rome for further study. But Friedrich von Gaertner, the leading Bavarian architect of the day, tapped him to supervise the construction of the Damenstift (Women's Institute) in Munich, which delayed Riedel's travels to Rome until 1839. He stayed in Rome for six months and in 1840 returned to Munich, where he was given simultaneous commissions as decorator of a private residence for the king of Bavaria and supervisor of a residence in Athens for King Otto of Greece designed by Gaertner.

In December 1840, Riedel was commissioned to decorate the entire palace of King Otto, who became so enamored of the young man's talent that he appointed him chief architect of his court. Riedel married Antonie Mohr of Mannheim in 1842, but soon afterward he and his wife were forced to return to Munich because of the disagreeable climate in Athens. In the next several years, he successively held the posts of *Bauconducteur* (building supervisor) and *Hofbauinspektor* (chief inspector of farm buildings), oversaw the design of the Wintergarden Theater, and also served as professor of architecture at the Polytechnical School. Between 1852 and 1857 Riedel drew plans for a church for the Cistercian community at Mehrerau in Bregenz and a great fountain at Schleissheim. He became court architect to King Maxmilian II in 1857 and designed numerous public and private buildings for him, including a national museum, a mint, and a new university. By 1872 he was adviser to the board of directors of the king's farm buildings and planned Neuschwanstein Castle. After 1872 Riedel's health began to decline, but he continued to work on various projects, including restoration of a number of King Ludwig II's buildings, among them the Trierschen Rooms in the royal residence.

George J. Ries (1860–1937)

George Joseph Ries was born in Lohr, Bavaria. He attended public schools in that city as well as the Würzburg Architectural School, where he received his professional training. He served in the First Pioneer Battalion of the First Army Corps of Bavaria and was discharged with the rank of sergeant. Ries immigrated to the United States in 1881 and worked briefly as a coal miner in Pennsylvania. In 1882 he came to St. Paul by way of Le Seuer and Winnipeg and entered the building business as, first, a bricklayer, then a contractor. He married Catherine Gross on May 20, 1883, and the couple had three daughters. His business failed after six years, and Ries and his family relocated to Tacoma, Washington, and Portland, Oregon, from 1889 to 1892. He returned to St. Paul and restarted his contracting business, which this time was successful. By 1900 he was giving more time to architecture while maintaining his building firm.

Ries entered the political arena in 1906, when he was appointed alderman of the newly created Twelfth Ward; two years later, he was elected to the same position. The bosses of the Democratic party in St. Paul were so impressed with his popularity that they persuaded him to run for Ramsey County auditor in the fall of 1910 and he won the election. Ries served as county auditor for the next twenty-six years. He appears to have abandoned the practice of architecture about the same time he began his political career.

Robert Rietow (b. 1937)

Robert Rietow was born in Sheboygan, Wisconsin. He received his B.Arch. from the University of Minnesota in 1959 and then worked in the office of the Cerny Associates in Minneapolis from 1960 to 1964. He was with Miller, Whitehead, Dunwiddie, Inc., from 1964 to 1967, also in Minneapolis, and in 1967 he rejoined The Cerny Associates as associate and project architect, where he remained until 1971. At that time, he became, along with Frederick Bentz and Milo Thompson, a founding principal in the firm of Bentz/Thompson/Rietow, where he serves as principal in charge of finance in addition to being in charge of many major design projects.

ANDREW ROTH (1856–1920)

Andrew Roth was born in La Crosse, Wisconsin. His education and training are not known, but he began working as a carpenter and appears to have been self-trained in architecture. In 1893 he was advertising himself as an architect in La Crosse. He entered partnership with Hugo Schick in 1901. After Schick's death about 1910, Roth remained in practice until he died at age sixty-three.

CHARLES RUTAN (1851–1914)

Born in Newark, New Jersey, Charles Hercules Rutan was educated in that city's schools until 1867, when he entered the office of Grambrill and Richardson in New York. He was employed as a draftsman in the firm from 1869 to 1878, then worked as a draftsman for H. H. Richardson, in his famous Brookline, Massachusetts, practice from 1878 to 1886. After Richardson's death in 1886, Rutan became a partner in the successor firm, Shepley, Rutan, and Coolidge, and was the firm's engineer.

EERO SAARINEN (1910–1961)

Eero Saarinen was born in Kirkkonummi, Finland, the son of famed architect Eliel Saarinen and the sculptor-weaver Louise (Loja) Gesellius.

The family moved to the United States in 1923, and Eero was naturalized in 1940. He was educated in the public schools of Michigan and studied sculpture at the Académie de la Grand Chaumière Paris in 1929–30. He returned to the United States and attended Yale University, where he studied architecture and graduated with his B.F.A. degree in 1934. He then traveled in Europe on a fellowship and returned in 1936 to enter his father's architectural practice in Ann Arbor, Michigan. Eero practiced there until 1942, when he joined the Office of Strategic Services of the U.S. Army. He became a partner in his father's firm (Saarinen-Swanson-Saarinen); the name of the practice was changed to Saarinen, Saarinen, and Associates in 1947 and remained that until his father's death in 1950. Eero was a principal in the successor firm, Eero Saarinen and Associates, in Birmingham, Michigan, until his own death.

ELIEL SAARINEN (1873–1950)

Gottlieb Eliel Saarinen was born in Rantasalmi, Finland. He was educated in the Klassillinenlyseo secondary school in Viborg from 1883 to 1889, then at the Realyceum secondary school, Tammerfors, 1889–93. He studied painting at the University of Helsinki while concurrently studying architecture at the Polytekniska Institutet in Helsinki, from 1893 to 1897, and received his diploma in architecture in the latter year. Eliel was a partner with Herman Gesellius and Armos Lindgren in the firm Gesellius-Lindgren-Saarinen in Helsinki (1905–7), and then maintained his own office from 1907 to 1923. He immigrated to the United States in 1923 and set up a private practice first in Evanston, Illinois (1923–24), and then in Ann Arbor,

Michigan (1924–37). In 1937 his son Eero entered the firm, and a partnership was formed four years later that included J. Robert Swanson (Saarinen-Swanson-Saarinen). In 1947 Swanson dropped out and the firm became known as Saarinen, Saarinen, and Associates. Eliel was appointed a visiting professor of architecture at the University of Michigan in 1924 and sucessively director (1925–32), president (1932–50), and director of the Graduate Department of Architecture and City Planning (1948–50) of the institution he created, the Cranbrook Academy of Art in Bloomfield Hills, Michigan.

ROBERT Y. SANDBERG (B. 1922)
Robert Y. Sandberg was educated in the public schools of Rice Lake, Wisconsin, and attended the University of Minnesota's School of Engineering from 1940 to 1942. In 1943 he enlisted in the Army Air Corps and served until 1946. He returned to the University of Minnesota and studied for one year. In 1947 he signed a professional football contract with the Chicago Rockets of the American Football League, but did not make the team. He signed with Winnipeg of the Canadian Football League that same year and completed his architectural degree at the University of Manitoba in 1949. From 1949 to 1951, he practiced architecture in Winnipeg and played professional football as well. In 1951, Sandberg moved to Hibbing and opened his own practice, which he maintained until 1990. He continues to practice at Lake Vermillion following the closure of his Hibbing office.

MONROE SHEIRE (1834–1887)
Monroe Sheire (pronounced "Sheer") was born in Lexington, New York, the son of George Sheire, a building contractor. Young Sheire was self-educated, studying architecture in Detroit (probably as an apprentice in various offices), and then joined his father in the building business. In 1860, Sheire moved to St. Paul and two years later became a partner with Charles Leonard in an architecture and construction company. In 1866 the two men were joined by Monroe's younger brother Romaine. The firm is notable for building not only St. Joseph's Catholic Church (St. Joseph) but also the Alexander Ramsey house in St. Paul (1868–72) and the First Congregational Church in Faribault (1867). Sheire also acted as local supervising architect as well as contractor of the First Baptist Church in St. Paul (1875), designed by W. W. Boyington of Chicago. He was known for his preference for building structures that were a mix of the Italianate and Second Empire styles.

When Charles Leonard died in 1874, the firm was renamed Monroe Sheire and Brother.

GEORGE SHEPLEY (1860–1903)
George Foster Shepley was born in St. Louis. He graduated from Washington University in that city in 1880 and studied at the Massachusetts Institute of Technology until 1882. He worked in the office of Ware and Van Brunt for a short time, then entered the firm of H. H. Richardson. He married Richardson's daughter, Julia, in 1886, shortly after Richardson died. Shepley was a senior partner in the successor firm, Shepley, Rutan, and Coolidge for much of his life.

GLYNNE SHIFFLET (1907–1971)

Glynne William Shifflet was born in Winfred, South Dakota. He was educated in the public schools of Aberdeen and graduated from the University of Minnesota School of Architecture in 1929. He attended the École des Beaux-Arts at Fontainebleau, France, for two months in 1930 and returned to the United States to work as a designer and draftsman for Cass Gilbert in New York and then Cyril Pesek in Minneapolis. In 1931 Pesek and Shifflet formed a partnership that lasted until 1942, when Pesek joined Minnesota Mining and Manufacturing Company as an executive officer. Shortly after World War II, Kenneth A. W. Backstrom entered the firm as a partner, followed in the next several years by Marlin Hutchison and Arthur Dickey. The firm was known as Shifflet, Backstrom, Hutchison, and Dickey during the 1950s and part of the 1960s.

EDWARD SOVIK JR. (B. 1918)

Edward Sovik was born in Honan Province of China to missionary parents. He and his identical twin brother, Arne, and an older sister were educated in the cooperative mission boarding school in the province until warfare forced the school to move to Kiangsi Province in southern China. After the family's return to the United States, the three children enrolled at St. Olaf College, where Sovik and his brother graduated in 1939. Sovik studied art at St. Olaf and decided to pursue an interest in painting by entering the Art Students League in New York City. He left after one year and enrolled in Luther Theological Seminary in St. Paul, with the intention of becoming a missionary in China. When World War II broke out, Sovik enlisted in the Marine Corps and became a pilot. At the end of the war, he entered Yale University's School of Architecture.

It was during his years at Yale that Sovik became interested in church design but felt that, while architecture was moving into new stylistic forms, religion was, as he later said, "entrenched in the past." "By the time I was ready to start working myself," Sovik recalled, "I had decided that any church buildings I did would have to be contemporary in style." He graduated from Yale with his architecture degree in 1949. He returned to Northfield and opened an office while, at the same time, teaching art at St. Olaf. Gerhard Peterson (1907–94) opened the St. Paul office of the firm. Eventually, Peterson left to form a partnership with E. Richard Cone in 1950, and Sovik went on to enter partnership with Sewell J. Mathre and Norman Madson beginning in 1953. The firm exists today as SMSQ Architects (Sovik, Mathre, Sathrum, and Quanbeck). Ed Sovik has retired from active practice but maintains a consulting role with the company.

GEORGE STAUDUHAR (1863–1928)

George Stauduhar was educated in the public schools of Mahomet, Illinois, and attended the University of Illinois Academy (1885–86) and the College of Engineering of the same university, from which he graduated in 1888. He opened an architectural office in Rock Island, Illinois, in 1890 and maintained it for his entire career. During World War I, Stauduhar served in the U.S. Housing Corporation and helped design and erect many government-financed homes in the tricity area (Rock Island-Moline-Davenport). He specialized in hospitals, churches, schools—especially for the Catholic Church, of which he was a devout member—and residences, designing many such structures throughout the Midwest. He also is credited with the design of the *J.S., St. Paul,* and *Capitol* river steamers, operated on the Mississippi by the Streckfus

Line in the early 1900s. While in North Dakota on business, Stauduhar died in Valley City in a recently completed hospital of his own design.

MILO THOMPSON (B. 1935)

A native Minneapolitan, Milo Thompson was educated at the University of Minnesota, from which he received his B.A. in 1957 and his B.Arch. in 1962. He attended Harvard University for his graduate education and was awarded the M.A. in 1963. In 1965, he received the Rome Prize, which enabled him to pursue two years of study at the American Academy in Rome. Thompson returned to Minneapolis and became a draftsman in the office of the Cerny Associates. He then worked in the office of Carl Koch, Boston, and with Brown, Dallas Associates in Rome. He came back to Minneapolis to assume the position of vice president and chief designer for The Cerny Associates before forming a partnership with Frederick Bentz and Robert Rietow in 1971. Thompson is credited with the design of two of the earliest Minneapolis skyway bridges, which won an AIA Honor Award in 1969. He is now retired from a professorship at the College of Architecture at the University of Minnesota, where he taught for more than thirty years, and has returned to his practice at Bentz/Thompson/Rietow.

THORWALD THORSON (1879–1962)

Thorwald Thorson's family came to the United States from Norway when he was two years old and settled near Forest City, Iowa. Thorson attended the State University of Iowa and the University of Wisconsin and obtained draftsman's training through the International Correspondence Schools. He worked as a teacher in a country school and also taught science and mathematics at Waldorf College in Forest City between 1903 and 1914, where there is a building named after him. He also worked for architects in St. Paul, but it is not known when or by whom he was employed there. In 1914, Thorson opened his own practice in Forest City, where he remained the rest of his life. In 1937, his son, Oswald, joined him in the firm and became a partner in 1945.

OLIVER TRAPHAGEN (1854–1932)

Oliver Green Traphagen was born in Tarrytown, New York. He moved with his family to St. Paul about 1870 and became an apprentice to architect George Wirth. Traphagen relocated to Duluth in 1882 and worked as a carpenter and architect during the 1880s. In 1890 he became a partner of Francis Fitzpatrick. This very successful partnership lasted until 1896, when Fitzpatrick moved to Washington, D.C. Traphagen continued to practice in Duluth for two more years and then moved to Honolulu because of the ill health of one of his daughters. He designed the Moana Beach Club (1901), the first tourist hotel on Waikiki Beach. Today it is the Sheraton Moana Hotel. He maintained a practice there until 1907, after which he relocated to Alameda, California, where he worked until retiring in 1925.

FRED V. TRAYNOR (1911–1996)

Fred Vincent Traynor was born at Devils Lake, North Dakota. He graduated from high school there and attended the University of North Dakota in Grand Forks for two years. He then entered the University of Illinois, Champaign, where he received his B.S. in architecture in 1935. Traynor moved to St. Cloud,

Minnesota, and was employed in the firm of Nairne W. Fisher from 1935 to 1938 and concurrently in the offices of Pesek and Shifflet, Minneapolis, 1938 to about 1942, and Frank W. Jackson, St. Cloud, from 1938 to 1942. He served in the U.S. Navy during World War II after which, in 1946, he returned to his employment with Frank W. Jackson. In 1949, Traynor formed a very successful partnership with Raymond T. Hermanson (Traynor and Hermanson). Traynor retired from practice in 1986.

JOSEPH V. VANDERBILT (1878–1966)
Joseph Victor Vanderbilt attended grade schools in his native New York City and Rochester, New York, and received his high school preparatory education at Englewood Military Academy. He also attended the Society of Beaux Arts Architects in New York for four years. During that time, he was a student in the ateliers of Emmanuel L. Masqueray and Claude Bragdon.

After his architectural training, Vanderbilt worked successively for C. H. Haswell, civil and structural engineer, New York (1895–97); E. L. Young, architect, New York (1897–99); the Buffalo, Rochester, and Pacific Railroad (1899–1902); Breeze and Ferguson, architects, Norfolk, Virginia (1902–5); and the supervising architect of the Treasury, Washington, D.C. (1905–10). In 1910 he moved to Minneapolis and became head of the design staff in the office of Hewitt and Brown (1910–24) before entering a brief partnership with Carl Gage. In 1929 Vanderbilt and Carl J. Bard formed a partnership that they maintained for nearly twenty years. When it ended in 1948, Vanderbilt operated a private practice until his retirement in 1962.

JOHN H. WHEELER (1871–1958)
John H. Wheeler was born in St. Paul. His father, James Wheeler, was born in Waterford, Ireland, and emigrated first to California and then St. Paul, where he established a contracting business with his brother, Thomas. Young John was educated in the public schools of St. Paul and then attended the College of St. Thomas for two years. After leaving college, he spent fourteen years in various architects' offices, including seven years in the office of Clarence H. Johnston. In 1901–2 Wheeler was in charge of the Building Inspection Department of St. Paul and, in 1902, opened a private practice that he maintained for the rest of his life. He specialized in designing buildings for the Catholic Church—schools, rectories, convents, churches, and chapels. His mother, Joanna Howard, was a cousin of Archbishop John Ireland's, and Ireland was a frequent visitor at the Wheeler house.

LORENZO B. WHEELER (?–1899)
Lorenzo Wheeler was born in or near Danbury, Connecticut. He began practicing as an architect in New York City, part of the time in partnership with Hugh Lamb. Wheeler spent most of his career in the South, with offices in such cities as Atlanta and Memphis, where he designed residences, office buildings, courthouses, libraries, and other structures. He moved to St. Louis about 1890 and practiced there until failing health forced him to return to Connecticut.

RICHARD WHITEMAN (B. 1925)
A native of Mankato, Richard Whiteman was educated in the public schools of Austin and received his architectural training at the University of Minnesota, from which he graduated in 1945. He went on

to earn a master's degree in architecture at Harvard in 1948. Whiteman worked briefly for Ellerbe and Company in St. Paul in 1946 and for William Riseman Associates and Bogner and Richman in Cambridge, Massachusetts (1947). He returned to Minneapolis and entered the office of Thorshov and Cerny in 1948. In 1955 Whiteman entered partnership with Eino Jyring in Hibbing, where he remained for the next three and a half decades. In the small town, he believed he could develop a more personal kind of professional life and a closer relationship with clients. Whiteman is retired from the firm of Jyring and Whiteman, which today is known as Architectural Resources, Inc.

WILLIAM H. WILLCOX (1832–1929)

William H. Willcox was born and grew up in Brooklyn, New York. He was trained in various architects' offices, which was the traditional means of receiving an architectural education in the days before formal schools were established later in the century. He practiced architecture in New York from 1853 to 1860, and during the Civil War drew maps for the Union Army. After the war, he moved to Chicago, where he worked briefly for Dankmar Adler (1871), then maintained his own practice from 1872 to 1879, including a partnership in 1875–77 (Willcox and Miller). Willcox moved to Nebraska to design the state capitol (1879–81) and to St. Paul, where he practiced from 1882 to 1891. From 1886 to 1890, Willcox was a partner of Clarence H. Johnston's, and their firm produced many fine buildings in St. Paul during this four-year period.

In 1891, Willcox moved to Seattle and joined William E. Boone in the firm of Boone and Willcox (1891–93), then practiced alone for the next two years. He relocated successively to Los Angeles (1895–98) and San Francisco (1900–ca. 1906), then left architecture to work as a surveyor in the latter city from about 1907 to 1912. Being at that time eighty years old, Willcox may have retired. His whereabouts are unknown until about 1925, when he moved into the Veterans' Home in Yountville, California.

ALAN K. LATHROP is curator of the Northwest Architectural Archives at the University of Minnesota Libraries in Minneapolis.

BOB FIRTH is owner of Firth Photobank in Carver, Minnesota. He has published a book of photographs, *Landscape of Ghosts,* that includes text by Bill Holm.